Discourses of Ideology and Identity

CW01019823

In this monograph, Chris Featherman adopts a discourse analytical approach to explore the ways in which social movement ideologies and identities are discursively constructed in new and old media. In the context of his argument, Featherman also considers current debates surrounding the role that technologies play in democracy-building and global activist networks. He engages these critical issues through a case study of the 2009 Iranian presidential election protests, looking at both U.S. legacy media coverage of the protests as well as activists' use of social media. Through qualitative analysis of a corpus of activists' Twitter tweets and Flickr uploads, Featherman argues that activists' social media discourses and protesters' symbolic and tactical borrowing of global English contribute to micronarratives of globalization while also calling into question master narratives about Iran commonly found in mainstream Western media accounts. This volume makes a timely contribution to discussions regarding the relationship between cyberrhetoric and democracy, and provides new directions for researchers engaging with the influence of new media on globalized vernaculars of English.

Chris Featherman is an applied linguist and lecturer in English at Northeastern University, USA.

Routledge Critical Studies in Discourse

Edited by Michelle M. Lazar, *National University of Singapore*

Discourses of Ideology and Identity

Social Media and the Iranian Election Protests

Chris Featherman

Routledge
Taylor & Francis Group

LONDON AND NEW YORK

First published 2015 by Routledge

2 Park Square, Milton Park, Abingdon, Oxfordshire OX14 4RN
711 Third Avenue, New York, NY 10017

Routledge is an imprint of the Taylor & Francis Group, an informa business

First issued in paperback 2018

Library of Congress Cataloging-in-Publication Data

Featherman, Chris, 1972–
    Discourses of ideology and identity : social media and the Iranian election
protests / Chris Featherman.
        pages cm. — (Routledge Critical Studies in Discourse)
    Includes bibliographical references and index.
    1. Discourse analysis—Political ascpects.   2. Social media—
Political aspects—Iran.   3. Iran—History—Protests, 2011—Press
coverage.   I. Title.
    P302.77.F43 2015
    302.23'10955090511—dc23
    2014043120

ISBN: 978-1-138-82558-1 (hbk)
ISBN: 978-1-138-54876-3 (pbk)

Typeset in Sabon
by Apex CoVantage, LLC

To Marija and Lukas

Contents

Figures

Tables

Acknowledgments

I wish to express my sincere appreciation to the Department of English, University of Washington, for their generous support during the research of this book. In particular, I would like to thank Professor Anis Bawarshi for his professional guidance, Professor M. Suhanthie Motha for her kind encouragement, Professor Sandra Silberstein for her steady support, and Professor Gail Stygall for challenging and inspiring me. I am deeply grateful to the photographers who kindly allowed me to use their work in this book and to the anonymous reviewers whose insightful feedback on drafts proved invaluable during the revision process. Thank you as well to Margo Irvin, Associate Editor at Routledge, and Routledge Critical Studies in Discourse Series Editor Michelle Lazar for supporting this work, and to Andrew Weckenmann, also at Routledge, for his patient support and guidance.

1 Opening
Protesting the Results

In the days immediately following the June 12, 2009 Iranian presidential election, in which the incumbent Mahmoud Ahmadinejad won by a controversial landslide victory over the reformist candidate Mir-Hossein Mousavi, protests erupted in Tehran over alleged vote-rigging and election irregularities.[1] Although initially peaceful, these demonstrations quickly turned violent as clashes broke out between police and protesters, leading to numerous arrests and casualties. With the protests intensifying, the headlines on reports coming out of Tehran from major U.S. or global news outlets might have read: *Tehran Erupts in Protest* or *Shades of '79 as Demonstrators Challenge Contested Election Results*. Accompanying those reports would have been global press agency images of amassing demonstrators clad in green and their clashes in the streets with police and Basij paramilitary forces. Others might have captured the bloodied faces of protesters, some of them young women in headscarves, perhaps a few burning Basiji trucks. Global media outlets' televised news broadcasts and online reports on the Iranian protests might have featured satellite video framed by standup reports from on-the-scene reporters soundtracked with protesters' chants and backdropped crowds amassing in Tehran's Azadi [Freedom] Square.

But in the early stages of the 2009 Iranian presidential election protests, which would come to captivate a global audience and arguably presage the Arab Spring of 2011, those headlines, images, and videos did not readily appear. Following a tense election run-up, the Iranian government banned foreign media, and when the protests broke out, they instituted a communication blockade to prevent news of the protests from being disseminated outside the country. But Iranian activists using web-based social media eluded the government censors, and some of the first reports of the crisis to reach a global audience were *tweets*, or posts, such as the one shown in Figure 1.1, to the microblogging service Twitter.

With a cultural status rivaling that of the social networking service Facebook and its ubiquitous embedding in *legacy* online news media, Twitter is now a popularly well-known form of social media.[2] A microblogging service, Twitter allows users to write and share with followers posts of 140 characters or less. Because of its brevity, Twitter is especially suited to use on

persiankiwi
@persiankiwi

Follow

we must go - dont know when we can get internet - they take 1 of us, they will torture and get names - now we must move fast - #Iranelection

← Reply   ⇄ Retweet   ★ Favorite   ••• More

13	**58**	
RETWEETS	FAVORITES	

8:34 AM - 24 Jun 09

Figure 1.1   Iranian activist's tweet from the 2009 protests.

mobile devices, such as smartphones, whose availability and popularity, at least for the global elite, have paralleled Twitter's spectacular growth.[3] Since being launched for public use, Twitter has grown from approximately 1,000 active accounts in 2006 to more than 255,000,000 as of June 2014.[4] Prior to 2009, however, Twitter, in all its brevity, was widely seen as little more than a regularly updated commentary on users' everyday lives, with some early critics calling it 'fatuous' and 'banal' while dismissing its value as an application (Arceneaux & Schmitz Weiss, 2010). Even as Twitter gained more popularity (primarily through its adoption by young entertainment celebrities and professional athletes), many, including the mainstream legacy press, continued to view it skeptically. As with the advent of text messaging, or Short Message Service (SMS), some critics even suggested that Twitter's constraints would negatively influence the trajectory of language change and, like other forms of social media, prove harmful to young people's communicative practices (Thurlow, 2006).

By the time of the 2009 Iranian presidential election protests, however, Twitter had not only grown exponentially; it had also begun to shed some of these negative cultural perceptions, surpassing what Grewal (2008) has called the *threshold of visibility*, or the point when a network grows large enough to appeal to what had been non-users. As numerous mainstream journalists began to recognize the advantages of microblogging's instantaneous updates through mobile phones, the adoption and use of Twitter by legacy media reporters helped reshape news gathering and distribution. Twitter also started playing a notable role in political elections, including the

2008 U.S. presidential contest, in which, on election night, before appearing on national television, Barack Obama famously announced victory on Twitter to the hundreds of thousands of followers he had acquired during his campaign.[5] And arguably presaging its use by Iranian activists during the June 2009 crisis, Twitter had become a critical tool for communication and organization during political protests, including the civil unrest that gripped Moldova in April 2009 (Miller, 2010; Morozov, 2011).

When news, then, of the Iranian election crisis broke, reports that activists were using Twitter and other forms of social media became part of the news frame. Seizing this kairotic moment in full, prominent blogger Andrew Sullivan (2009), then writing on June 13 for *The Atlantic*, quickly dubbed the movement 'The Twitter Revolution,' citing the microblogging service as "a critical tool for organizing resistance" (n.p.). Although most mainstream news reports rejected Sullivan's epithet as cliché, they did extend the election news frame to accommodate the social media micronarrative and consider its possible relevance within the context of the election crisis. A series of reports in legacy media outlets in the United States, including the *Washington Post* and the *New York Times*, examined the role of web-based new media in both the election campaigns and the protests that followed. In his book *The Net Delusion: The Dark Side of the Internet*, Evgeny Morozov (2011) has countered Sullivan's—and many others'—moment of jubilant cyber-utopianism, along with the somewhat more tepid conjecture in the initial legacy media reports, with a strong dose of skepticism about the potentially liberatory and democracy-promoting capabilities of social media which, coincidentally, happen to originate in the U.S., arguing:

> the irrational exuberance that marked the Western interpretation of what was happening in Iran suggests that the green-clad youngsters tweeting in the name of freedom nicely fit into preexisting mental schema that left little room for nuanced interpretation, let alone skepticism about the actual role that the internet played at the time. (p. 5)

For Morozov, these interpretations reflected both a triumphalism and sense of Western superiority that has existed since the fall of communism in 1989. Viewed from perhaps an even wider perspective, we might also see how they index the ways in which globalization, power, knowledge, and ideology are caught up in what Mittelman (2004) has called *a vortex of struggle*. In that struggle, I argue, we can see the contingent links between knowledge and political conditions—particularly, in this case, the discourses of democracy and cyber-rhetoric together with those of modernity and tradition that have shaped Western perspectives of Iran and other Islamic countries (Rajaee, 2007). At the nexus of these discourses are, among other notions, ideology, identity, and the ways in which social actors can generate both communication power and counterpower, particularly in relation to language and technology.

Twitter was not the only social media service that activists and social movement participants used to coordinate and document collective actions. Photo- and video-sharing services, such as Flickr and YouTube, were also used to disseminate, respectively, images and video clips, often taken with mobile phone cameras and shared through mobile applications. Networks of activists and followers could then share these images—frequently using hyperlinks embedded in tweets and SMSs—to circulate images such as those in Figures 1.2 and 1.3. Doing so not only helped elude government censorship and spread news of the crisis beyond Iran's borders, but it arguably also helped expand the social movement across new *nodes*, or connection points in a network, which can create new possibilities for collective action.

Discursive practices such as these show the important role of mobile technologies in facilitating the circulation of news and information. They also highlight the ubiquitous, linguistic, and increasingly mobile and visual character of the Internet and information and communication technologies (ICTs) in contemporary society, although predominantly for the global elite (Crack, 2008; Norris, 2001). As part of the mobile turn in communication, such practices have also helped shape the everyday production of culture (Caron & Caronia, 2007). With language infused in this complex and mobile fabric of relations (Urry, 2010), Internet-based mobile communications, particularly social media, have helped further liberate users from many of the temporal and spatial constraints that govern their lives (Giddens, 1991). Across global networks, transcultural flows of images and

Figure 1.2 Mass demonstration in Azadi Square, June 15, 2009.

Figure 1.3 Cellphone video capture uploaded to YouTube.

information cross borders nearly instantaneously, bringing distant places in contact and helping form *sociomental* bonds and *translocal* loyalties across borders (Chayko, 2002). As a result, it is argued that social relations become *disembedded*, or lifted out, from their contexts and restructured across spans of time-space, producing a *rescaling* of social activity that can work to enact forms of identity in discourse (Benwell & Stokoe, 2006; Castells, 1997; Fairclough, 2006; Giddens, 1990). The resulting *deterritorialization* can decouple community from place, removing the primacy of locality in sociocultural meaning and allowing, through collective imagination, social life to be a site for multiple, coexisting worlds (Albrow, 1997; Appadurai, 1996). As a dialectical phenomenon, however, this interlacing of social relations at a distance with local contexts also allows for the competing interpenetration of contexts (Robertson, 1995), novel forms of localization and global identification (Pennycook, 2007), and the mobility of sociolinguistic resources of indexical distinction across scale levels (Blommaert, 2010).

Yet, despite this capacity to restructure social links and events and reformulate possible meanings, global technologies should not be viewed through the lenses of technological determinism at the expense of other processes (Chadwick, 2006; Hopper, 2007). As sociologist Manuel Castells (2009) has explained, "network technology and networking organization are only means to enact the trends inscribed in social structure" (p. 24). To examine, then, the effect of instantaneous communicability over space on language practices, we should draw our attention not strictly to networks and ICTs, but to the novel and diverse spaces which have opened up within global networks (Harvey, 1989). Across these sets of interconnected nodes, in which information, more than capital or labor, is the vital source of value, *identifications* become social actors' primary source of meaning (Castells, 1996, 2000). And in a network society, communication is a source of both power and *counterpower* (Castells, 2009). In the view that power is not absolute but negotiated, the struggle for power today is ultimately the battle to control minds, the struggle over the way people think (Castells, 2010). With respect to the media, this means, as has been widely argued through the critical studies of legacy news media discourse, that both national and global media outlets have a hegemonic power to confirm ideologies. But when used tactically, ICTs and social media can grant social actors a form of counterpower, a capacity to challenge dominant ideologies and resist institutional control over the flow of information (Castells, 2009; Renzi, 2008). And it is in the context of these dynamic processes that I explore, in this project, the way that ideologies and identities can be discursively constructed, in both 'old' and 'new' media and during times of crises such as the 2009 Iranian election protests.

CONTEXTS: GLOBALIZATION AND NEW MEDIA AS FRAMEWORKS FOR SOCIOLINGUISTIC RESEARCH

The complex, multifarious, and intrinsic connections between language and the processes of globalization have been well established in recent sociological and sociolinguistic research (Block & Cameron, 2002; Blommaert, 2010; Giddens, 1990; Tomlinson, 1999). So, too, has been the analysis of legacy news media discourse, including its roles in the construction of ideologies (Fowler, 1979, 1991), the establishing of sociopolitical agendas (Fairclough, 1995), the production of cultural identifications (Hall, 1996), the geopolitics of representations (Mody, 2010), and the global cultural flows disseminated through ICTs (Appadurai, 1996; Castells, 2000). Also well established is the fundamental role that ICTs have played in the shift toward a network society that, according to Castells (1996), "represents a qualitative change in the human experience" (p. 477). With language at the core of human experience, social researchers have widely considered discourse in relation to a society of open networks. Until recently, however, this was frequently done at macro- and institutional levels, including the role of ICTs in social movements and online political identifications (Castells, 2000, 2007; Crack, 2008). But as Hopper (2007) and others have claimed, attending only to macrolevel contexts is insufficient to understand how these processes shape culture and identities. Featherstone (1995), for instance, has argued that in order to understand the effects of globalization's cultural dimensions, we must pay critical attention not only to institutional discursive practices, but also to the informal spaces that exist between modes of organization and the interstices that marginalized communities often inhabit and communicate within and across. This *interstitial* perspective, as Bhabha (2004) has claimed, can be particularly useful when examining identity formations. For this reason, to better activists' identifications during the 2009 Iranian protests, I have looked at their use of social media as part of a lattice of transnational public spheres and overlapping social movement frames.

As the basis of a sociolinguistic research framework, globalization theories can also help account for the relationships between networks of global interconnectedness across various scales as well as the roles of English, a current global *lingua franca*, and ICTs in establishing those connections (Blommaert, 2010; Castells, 2009; Pennycook, 2007). Drawing from these theories is an established body of linguistic research on the more specific relationships between language and the Internet. In outlining the conditions that help make English a global language, Crystal (2001, 2003) has described the relationship between language change and spread, including that of English and the Internet, while Atton (2004) has attended to the everyday practices that construct the Internet and its relations to the world. In researching the evolution of web-based genres, Bauman (1999) has shown how new online writing environments demand novel literacies from readers, which, in turn, affect how writers engage in social practices. Boardman (2005) has examined the language of websites through media and communication frameworks to better understand the technological and cultural factors impacting web-based discourse.

Research has shown, however, that this relationship is multidirectional. As Rowe and Wyss (2009) have contended, the relatively recent proliferation of new media has precipitated a rising interest in studying the effects of *technological mediation* on language and on language change. They have noted in particular that media, as catalysts for social action, offer rich opportunities for observing synchronic and diachronic language change, but that research frameworks and coverage in the literature tend to be outstripped by the rapid emergence, innovation, and adaption of new social media forms. Yet, through linguistic research on email and instant messaging, Baron (2008) has shown that users often transfer established discursive practices and communicative repertoires to novel communicative environments. Thurlow (2006) and Thurlow and Bell (2009) have studied the *metadiscursive* constructions of new media discourse in legacy media as part of the so-called *technologization* of communication, while Manovich (2002, 2009) has widened the spectrum of new media analysis to include visual and media cultures, questioning, in the process, what the shift from media to social media means for the relationship between web use and language. Similarly, Brooke (2009) has argued that critical attention should not only be paid to content or textual analysis, but to the interfaces where such conversations occur, while Hassan and Thomas (2006) have shown that critical political and social issues, such as the political consequences of new communication technologies and the changing experience of time and space, can be engaged through the examination of new media due to their complex relationships with contemporary culture.

With the rise of new media has been a growing established body of research on the discourse of such new media forms as weblogs, wikis, and text messages (Davis, 2005, 2009; Lampa, 2004; Myers, 2010; Thurlow, 2006). In particular, Gurak and Antonijevic (2008) have shown how blogs can serve as a lens to observe how users' discursive practices transform the traditional cultural norms that mediate between the public and the private spheres. Similarly, the widening use of social media such as Facebook in political campaigns and social movements has also attracted linguists' attention. Lim (2012), for instance, has examined how activists used Facebook and other social media during the 2011 Tahrir Square uprising in Egypt to expand their social networks, globalize their resources, and negotiate among competing groups through issue framing and the dissemination of symbolic resources. And Tufekci and Wilson (2012) have shown that during the same social movement, online activism through Facebook, Twitter, and other social media services can lead to increased offline participation in social movements.

Regarding Twitter in particular, Marwick and Boyd (2010) have studied how Twitter users navigate 'imagined audiences' and the collapsing of multiple layers of context in face-to-face conversation to single contexts in social media interaction. Arceneaux and Schmitz Weiss (2010) have examined legacy media coverage of Twitter to measure the current social construction of technology. Using Bakhtinian theories and Twitter data in a dual autoethnography, Gillen and Merchant (2013) have examined the dialogic and sociolinguistic aspects of new media linguistic practice, while Zappavigna (2011), using Systemic Functional Linguistics, has examined linguistic structure and meaning in a large corpus of tweets. Using data from the 2007 Nigerian electoral cycle, Ifukor (2010) has analyzed the linguistic construction of tweets to show that access to social media can empower citizens to participate in a democracy, while Morales, Losada, and Benito (2012), using Twitter data from an online Venezuelan political protest during December 2010, have mapped the structure and dynamics of online political networks. Larsson and Moe (2012) have examined the effectiveness of Twitter use during political campaigns in Sweden and, in a large-scale quantitative analysis, Bruns and Stieglitz (2012) have studied activity patterns in Twitter across a variety of communicative events, such as natural disasters, political elections, and televised events, while the large-scale quantitative analysis by Elson, Yeung, and Roshan (2012) examined

Twitter usage in Iran after the 2009 presidential elections to measure mood and public opinion.

This spate of research on social media has helped establish a foundation for examining emergent new media discourse practices. But much of this research—especially with the increasing popularity of Big Data—has been. As a result, there remains a relative lack of microlevel, qualitative sociolinguistic research on new media discursive practices. This is particularly the case regarding the ways activists create tactical identifications within social movements and imagined links to networked, transnational public spheres (Appadurai, 1996; Myers, 2010; Rowe & Wyss, 2009). Moreover, as Blommaert (2010) has argued, research on language in globalized processes, such as web-based discourse, often adheres to classic sociolinguistic distinctions and biases, including a focus on static variation or stratified language contact, rather than on an approach framed in terms of transnational flows, networks, and social movements. As a case study, Iranian activists' uses of social media during the 2009 presidential elections is, I argue, a compelling opportunity to address this need. For the study of the discourses of ideology and identity, this case also seems particularly relevant given the long-standing nexus between social movements, ideologies, and self-identifications, in particular the notion that during social and political conflicts, activists often use and manipulate language to create novel social identities and express new ideas (Gillan, Pickerill, & Webster, 2008; Poulson, 2005). In addition, the qualitative linguistic research I have done here using a critical discourse analysis (CDA) approach also stands to complement the quantitative and network mapping research studies discussed above. In doing so, I intend that this work enriches our current understandings of how and why activists used social media as they did to address a global audience while also critically questioning, without necessarily refuting, the claims by Morozov and others regarding the effectiveness and significance, or lack thereof, of activists' social media use during the protests. By offering a response to those claims that considers the potential sociocognitive effects of that use, I also aim to address the ways that critical discourse analysis approaches can further be applied and contribute to the study of new media language while also considering how new media discourse shapes the global uses of English as well as our understanding of them.

In stating these objectives, however, it is important to note that I do not intend in any way to view the 2009 Iranian presidential election crisis and the protests that broke out around it as a convenient case study. Doing so, in regard to activists' use of social media, might be misunderstood as an attempt to justify arguments for the liberatory power of technology or, for that matter, my research approach, CDA. Furthermore, as a researcher situated in the West, I do not intend to use theoretical and analytical lenses or the telescopic gaze of the Internet to explain what has happened in the East. Rather, as Bourdieu (1990) argued, the subjectivity of the researcher cannot be avoided. And nor do I think it should not be denied, particularly in view of what Blommaert (2005) has rightly claimed is the imbalance within CDA-based research of so-called First World researchers training their analyses on Third World topics and problems. Furthermore, as Iranian media scholar Gholam Khiabany (2010) has argued, precisely what makes Iran interesting—and thus a suitable and valuable focus of this type of scholarly attention—is that the impact and experience of modernity in Iran makes it not "an exotic or marginalized case but a fascinating example relevant for international communication" (p. 16). Therefore, my intention in this work has been to avoid whenever possible the distorting view afforded by the Internet's vantage on distant occurrences and social practices by paying attention to local contexts and the viewpoints of both Western and Iranian scholars. Furthermore, my presentation of historical contexts is admittedly in no way exhaustive, but for the purposes of this project it is not, I argue, meant to be. Rather, I have accounted for sociocultural and historical contexts as I have in order to examine, embedded in their contexts, the discursive practices that are the focus of this research. And in selecting this case study I have tried to address the present insufficient attention by the West to non-Western discursive practices in new and social media while also adding to present understandings of the way English is used vernacularly around the globe.

With these aims and considerations in mind, I have addressed in this project three clusters of research objectives. First, regarding the discursive construction of ideology, I have sought to determine how the discursive constructions of both the activists and U.S. legacy media, in their documentation and reportage of the post-election protest, intertextually draw on dominant narratives and images of Iran in the U.S. public imagination (Semati, 2008). Relatedly, I have considered how the *polychronic* interaction (Caron & Caronia, 2007) afforded by mobile social media such as Twitter has helped shape online political discourse and microblogging as a field of social action (Gillan, Pickerill, & Webster, 2008). Second, in regard to discourse and identity, I have examined the ways in which Iranian protesters, together with members of the Iranian diaspora and global activists acting in solidarity with them, used social media to locate themselves—geographically, politically, and culturally—and perform their identities online. In conjunction, I have sought to determine how these identifications might also have been shaped by mobile technologies and global vernaculars of English (Caron & Caronia; Pennycook, 2007) as well as the ways in which their identifications compared with U.S. legacy media outlets' discursive constructions of both the protesters and their use of social media. Third, regarding theory and methods, I have argued for a sociocognitive approach to critical discourse analysis while considering whether mobilities and social movement theories could help address its limitations as a research framework, specifically in regard to context and whether network theory helps overcome issues of scale and complexity facing web-based linguistic research, particularly when qualitatively analyzing texts (Brooke, 2009; Zimbra, Chen, & Abbasi, 2010).

In working toward these objectives, I have argued that activists' discursive practices in their use of social media during the 2009 Iranian presidential election protests add to the micronarratives of vernacular globalization while also calling into question master narratives about Iran as constructed in U.S. legacy news media (Semati, 2008). I base this central argument on the notion that both legacy and new media, as part of the *ideoscape* in Appadurai's (1996) five dimensions of cultural flows, allow for possible scripts of social practice and thereby a plurality of social worlds. With the imagination viewed as collective, protesters' discursive practices, though ultimately reflexive, that is, addressing an unknown audience of strangers, nevertheless can positively contribute to the formation of transnational imaginaries and imagined communities (Anderson, 2006; Appadurai). The resulting process of networked identifications can expand social actors' sense of solidarity and thereby encourage further participation, in either ongoing or future social movements (Tufekci & Wilson, 2012). This possibility does not directly rebut the claim by Morozov and others that the statistically small number of Twitter accounts and percentage of mobile phone users in Iran, as well as the ultimate failure of the social movement itself, prove that Twitter and other social media played no significant role in the 2009 protests.[6] However, it does address the weakness of Morozov's arguably teleological focus on end conditions as well as his failure to consider the effect of participation on the construction of new subjectivities or the enabling of political agency at a sociocognitive level. Moreover, I argue that as a form of symbolic exchange (Lash, 2002), protesters' micronarratives and mobile discursive practices in English challenge the insufficient treatment of English as a mediating standard by Grewal (2008) and others in analyses of global networks while also questioning established paradigms regarding the use, politics, and teaching of global Englishes.

PROJECT OVERVIEW

To make these arguments, I begin by opening, in this chapter, the theoretical, sociocultural, and rhetorical space for my project, then establish, in Chapter 2, the macrolevel contexts of my research. As Wodak and Meyer (2009) have argued, the consideration of the broader historical and sociopolitical contexts in which the discursive practices analyzed are embedded is integral to critical discourse analysis. As part of the *principle of triangulation*, analyzing background information, along with considering various data sources and multiple analytical perspectives, not only helps make research more robust, but also works to address some of the potential limitations of CDA-driven research approaches.[7] This contextual analysis includes a closer look at the events of the protests themselves as well as the crucial sociopolitical and cultural developments in Iran leading up to the 2009 elections. In this chapter I also further establish the theoretical contexts, including definitions of discourse, power, and counterpower in a network society, an overview of key theories on language and globalization, my stance on English as a global language, and my overall methodological approach.[8]

In Chapter 3, I examine the discursive construction of ideology and protesters' identities in U.S. legacy media coverage of the Iranian election crisis. Working with a corpus of news articles collected from six U.S. newspapers, I qualitatively examine a selection of articles and compare the results with a quantitative electronic analysis of the entire corpus as well as other publicly available datasets. I locate these analyses in a discussion of specific theoretical and sociocultural contexts directly related to both the events and the reportage of them in U.S. legacy news media. These contexts include both current and historical U.S.-Iranian relations as well as an overview of key theories of legacy and new media discourse and the rationale for the sociocognitive approach I have taken in analyzing these texts (van Dijk, 1998, 2009). Based on my analyses, I argue that U.S. legacy media, through their communicative and discursive practices, help frame protesters' identities within a perspective that is ideologically biased toward their hegemonic institutional interests in the government–media nexus (Entman, 2004; Fairclough, 1995, 2001; Johnson-Cartee, 2005). These analyses also serve as a point of comparison with the protesters' ideological stance-taking and identifications shown by the analyses and arguments taken up in subsequent chapters.

Chapter 4 examines the intertextual and interdiscursive practices of activists both inside and outside Iran across rhizomatic networks in a reticulated, transnational public sphere (Hauser, 1999; Juris, 2008). This includes qualitative analyses of *retweets*, the forwarding of hyperlinks in protesters' Twitter tweets, and the semiotics of protesters' placards as seen in photos uploaded to and shared through Flickr. I situate these analyses in a theoretical argument that links Bakhtin's (1986) notions of *intertextuality* and *dialogism* to Bourdieu's (1991) concept of *habitus*. Supporting this discussion is a look at relevant sociocultural contexts as a means of locating the protests in a cycle of Iranian social movements and thereby comparing the discursive practices of protesters in 2009 with those of the Islamist revolutionaries of 1979 (Poulson, 2005). In addition, because I specifically analyze protesters' discourse in English, this examination allows me to engage arguments regarding English as a global language, in particular the notion of English as a resource in a global commons that users, as active and empowered agents, can borrow, adopt, adapt, and remix through various creative tactics and repertoires according to their communicative needs and rhetorical situations (Canagarajah, 1999; de Certeau, 1984; Pennycook, 2007).

In Chapter 5 I extend and develop the arguments of the preceding two chapters through a further analysis of protesters' Twitter tweets and Flickr photograph uploads together with an analysis of a video poem uploaded to

YouTube by activists. The focus of these analyses is an attempt to understand the various identifications that protesters made through their discursive practices in new media across networks for a global audience. By comparing these identifications with those constructed by U.S. legacy media outlets, I develop arguments made in Chapter 3 regarding nation-state ideologies in legacy media frameworks and the potential of transnational imaginaries and public spheres extended through new media (Appadurai, 1996; Renzi, 2008). I also broaden my arguments regarding English as a borrowed language by situating my claims in both a brief overview of theories on language and identity and a specific discussion of modernity in Iran and the role that new media play in shaping protesters' identifications. I justify these qualitative analyses of protesters' discursive practices in new media through an approach built on established media discourse analytics while, it is my intention, addressing methodological concerns regarding the analysis of Internet-based linguistic artifacts (Androutsopoulos & Beißwenger, 2008; Brooke, 2009; Zimbra, Chen, & Abbasi, 2010). My project concludes, in Chapter 6, with a reengagement of my arguments and conclusions in relation to the theoretical, sociocultural, and rhetorical space established in Chapter 1. I also consider the various trajectories of my findings, including possible directions for future research on new media language and global Englishes.

DÉJA VU ALL OVER AGAIN: CONCLUSIONS

One of my first political memories is of the 1979 Iranian Revolution. More than three decades later, I can still recall the evening news reports of those flickering, grainy images showing massive crowds, supposedly the largest ever amassed, demonstrating in Tehran's Azadi Square.[9] I was awed by how the crowd swelled and flowed, bewildered by their banners in an unfamiliar, squiggled script and the placards of a gray-bearded man in a black turban. The protesters' raucous, undecipherable chants sounded to me like the squawks over a police officer's walkie-talkie, their refrains resembling the call-and-response of Sunday mass. These sounds and images, projected into my young life by the light of a black-and-white television, startled and amazed me. *Where was this place, Iran, I wondered, and if it was so far away, why was it being talked about on the news, in my house, in a small rural town? What could a place with such crowds, who seemed so angry, be like? Why had all these people gathered in this place, and what did they want?*

In a sense, although mostly a less naïve one, these were some of the same questions the world, or at least the West, was also asking about this revolution. As Kurzman (2004) and others have argued, both the scale of the Islamic Revolution and its success shocked many Western leaders. This included then-President Carter, who, before the Shah Mohammad Reza fled

Iran in January 1979, had promised, on the advice of his national security adviser Zbigniew Brzezinski, to support militarily the U.S.-backed Shah to prevent his overthrow (Keddie, 2003). Indeed, it was the fact of U.S. support, along with the Shah's substantial military force and powerful secret police, SAVAK, that led many to believe that a successful Islamic Revolution in Iran was unthinkable (Kurzman). But what for many had been unimaginable became a reality. On February 1, 1979, a few weeks before I turned seven, Ayatollah Khomeini, that black-turbaned, bearded man whose drawn, severe face I kept seeing on television, returned from exile. His seemingly stoic and feeble wave from the top step of an aircraft stairway inspired another massive crowd, thus successfully completing, in many ways, this cycle of protest and the revolution. Seven months later, a group of Iranian Islamist students and militants took over the American embassy in Tehran, capturing 52 Americans and holding them hostage. As the hostage crisis grew, Iran appeared daily on the news, and this place that had once seemed so foreign to me started to seem familiar—in a highly mediated sense, of course. And without my knowing it, notions of what this place Iran might be, as distorted by television news and ideology, had begun to reshape the boundaries of my world.

In June 2009, when the Iranian presidential election protests broke out, it was hard not to hear, in the media reports of anti-Ahmadinejad protesters' shouting "Death to the Dictator!" echoes of the cries that Islamist revolutionaries had hurled at the Shah. Images of crowds rallying in the streets of Tehran resembled those of an overflowing Azadi Square. As the global news networks began to pick up protesters' accounts, images, and video captures, I began to wonder, *Were the protests strong enough to bring down the hardline Ahmadinejad government? Did the support for the more moderate candidate Mousavi signal, a generation after the Islamic Revolution, a shift toward moderation and secularism? How would the U.S., fiercely at odds with Iran over its nuclear program, respond to this situation?* Mostly, though, I wanted to know how the Iranians themselves were identifying with this struggle, and what significance, if any, there was in their use of social media and English to communicate these events with a global audience. As the news frame developed in the U.S., the Iranian protesters' use of social media, particularly Twitter, became nearly as newsworthy as what was happening in the streets of Tehran. Voices such as Frank Rich's in the *New York Times* quickly pointed out the latent American triumphalism, if not cynicism, of the digital evangelists celebrating a "Twitter Revolution" when people were being beaten and killed for what they believed was a just cause. Taking a similar tone, Malcolm Gladwell (2010), writing in *The New Yorker,* argued that compared with the ways in which protesters risked their lives in order to have their votes counted and voices heard, the least important aspect of the 2009 Iranian protest was the use of Twitter.

As an individual, I agree. And by choosing this protest as the case study for my research, I have by no means intended to exploit events in which innumerable lives were affected in order to make an academic argument, not cyber-utopian, cyber-skeptical, or anywhere in between. But as an applied linguist, I disagree with Rich and Gladwell that protesters' use of social media was insignificant, for the exigency of the crisis created opportunities for discursive practices and collective engagement in this relatively new social field of actions. As Blommaert (2005) and others have argued, we must pay attention to such novel spaces if we are to see and try to understand discursive change. That such practices occurred in a non-Western setting also resounds Blommaert's contention that discourse analysts should pay more attention to discursive practices in contexts outside the global north. Moreover, these practices demonstrate the mobility of linguistic and sociolinguistic resources across transcultural flows within the processes of globalization. As such, they allow us to see the creative and ever-changing ways in which social actors innovate existing communicative repertoires across various scale levels, from the global to the local (Blommaert, 2010). Thus, for those interested in examining the ways in which language is destabilized by globalization and why certain repertoires and communicative resources move more successfully than others in globalized contexts, these discursive practices should be important to us (Blommaert, 2010).

Furthermore, it is important for me to say that although in conducting my analyses I have drawn on approaches to critical discourse analysis, my perspective on CDA's emancipatory possibilities, particularly in regard to this project, are somewhat restrained. By this I mean, as explained above, I thoroughly embrace the critical aspect of my approach, namely, that only a critical approach to language analysis is possible. With this project, however, I do not take that approach to directly support any particular position on current U.S.-Iranian relations, which, at the time of writing, are marked by the strains caused by Iran's development of its nuclear program and the U.S.-led embargo against Iran to discourage it. Rather, my goal is to help reveal how dominant constructions of typically marginalized identities and ideologies come about in U.S. legacy media and to understand how counterdiscourses work to challenge those constructions. So, if my approach bears an intrinsic and unavoidable politics, its advocacy, as I intend it, lives in trying to better understand discourses and subjectivities (and, in this research, the way that English is bound to both)—research, in other words, that is part of a larger, ongoing project to promote global understanding (Maingueneau, 2006). And in that sense, my aim here, as in all my work, is unreservedly emancipatory and hopeful.

NOTES

1. Spellings of Iranian names sometimes vary due to differing transliterations from Persian. For the purposes of consistency and clarity, the single spelling *Mousavi* will be used throughout even when it differs from the original secondary source.

2. By *legacy media* I refer to traditional means of communication, such as newspapers, television, and radio, which existed before the rise of the Internet and Internet-based *new media*. I prefer this term to others in the literature, such as *traditional* or *old media*, which, in my view, connote a dichotomy that fails to capture the crucial ways those media have transformed since the advent of new media. For consistency, I have used *legacy media* even when, in the literature, non-preferred terms have been used.

3. By *global elite* I mean here, and elsewhere, those social agents, regardless of their country of residence, with the socioeconomic resources to maintain a status above the social divide between rich and poor. I also use this term to link it to what Norris (2001) and others have referred to as the digital divide that tends to largely correspond with socioeconomic divisions. I prefer this term to past constructions of such divides, such as first- and third-world or industrialized or non-industrialized nations, due to their connotations of hierarchy and negation and their rooting in a sociological perspective based on the primacy of the nation-state. Such perspectives arguably fail to capture the complexities with which the flows of resources and deterritorialization connected with and intrinsic in the processes of globalization have largely obviated distinctions based on nation-states (Albrow, 1997).

4. Source: www.statista.com/statistics/272014/global-social-networks-ranked-by-number-of-users/. Retrieved August 2, 2014.

5. It has been said that then–President-elect Obama's historic tweet prompted, in part, the Library of Congress to acquire, in 2010, Twitter's sizable archives, which not only further raised Twitter's cultural status, but also suggested users' tweets were a rich source of social and linguistic research.

6. The actual number of Twitter users tweeting from Iran during the protests is unclear. Twitter features allow users to identify their location in their account profile, but activists living outside Iran reset their user location to Iran during the protests as signs of solidarity and to help thwart the government's efforts to identify and locate social movement leaders through their Twitter accounts. This will be discussed in further detail—regarding identifications—in Chapter 5.

7. Well established as a principle of sociological research, *triangulation* as I refer to it, here and throughout, is Wodak's version of the "quasi-kaleidoscopic move toward the research object [that] enables the grasp of many different facets of the object under investigation" (2009, p. 33).

8. This discussion will outline my overall methodological approach and my rationale for choosing it. For the sake of clarity and cohesion, I preface, in subsequent chapters, my results with a brief discussion of the methods used specifically for those particular analyses.

9. According to Kurzman (2004), these anti-Shah demonstrations on December 10 and 11, 1978 were the largest protests in history. Reportedly, 6–9 million people, or approximately 10% of the total Iranian population, participated, a far greater percentage than the 1% that participated in the French and Russian Revolutions.

REFERENCES

Albrow, M. (1997). *The global age*. Stanford, CA: Stanford University Press.

Anderson, B. (2006). *Imagined communities: Reflections on the origins and spread of nationalism* (3rd ed.). London: Verso.

Androutsopoulos, J., & Beißwenger, M. (2008). Introduction: Data and methods in computer-mediated discourse analysis. *Language@Internet, 5*, article 9.

Appadurai, A. (1996). *Modernity at large: Cultural dimensions of globalization.* Minneapolis: University of Minnesota Press.

Arceneaux, N., & Schmitz Weiss, A. (2010). Seems stupid until you try it: Press coverage of Twitter, 2006–9. *New Media & Society, 12*(8), 1262–1279.

Atton, C. (2004). *An alternative Internet.* Edinburgh: Edinburgh University Press.

Bakhtin, M. M. (1986). *Speech genres and other late essays* (V. W. McGee, Trans.; C. Emerson and M. Holquist, Eds.). Austin: University of Texas Press.

Baron, N. S. (2008). *Always on: Language in an online and mobile world.* Oxford: Oxford University Press.

Bauman, M. L. (1999). The evolution of Internet genres. *Computers and Composition, 16,* 269–282.

Benwell, B., & Stokoe, E. (2006). *Discourse and identity.* Edinburgh: Edinburgh University Press.

Bhabha, H. K. (2004). *The location of culture.* London: Routledge.

Block, D., & Cameron, D. (Eds.). (2002). *Globalization and language teaching.* London: Routledge.

Blommaert, J. (2005). *Discourse.* Cambridge: Cambridge University Press.

Blommaert, J. (2010). *The sociolinguistics of globalization.* Cambridge: Cambridge University Press.

Boardman, M. (2005). *The language of websites.* London: Routledge.

Bourdieu, P. (1990). *The logic of practice.* Stanford, CA: Stanford University Press.

Bourdieu, P. (1991). *Language and symbolic power* (J. B. Thompson, Trans.). Cambridge, MA: Harvard University Press.

Brooke, C. G. (2009). *Lingua fracta: Toward a rhetoric of new media.* Cresskill, NJ: Hampton Press.

Bruns, A., & Stieglitz, S. (2012). Quantitative approaches to comparing communication patterns on Twitter. *Journal of Technology in Human Services, 30*(3/4), 160–185.

Canagarajah, A. S. (1999). *Resisting linguistic imperialism in English teaching.* Oxford: Oxford University Press.

Caron, A., & Caronia, L. (2007). *Moving cultures: Mobile communication and everyday life.* Montreal & Kingston: McGill-Queen's University Press.

Castells, M. (1996). *The information age: Economy, society, and culture. The rise of the network society, vol. 1.* Malden, MA: Blackwell.

Castells, M. (1997). *The power of identity. The information age: Economy, society and culture, vol. 2.* Malden, MA: Blackwell.

Castells, M. (2000). *End of millennium* (2nd ed.). *The information age: Economy, society and culture, vol. 3.* Malden, MA: Blackwell.

Castells, M., Fernandez-Ardevol, M., Qui, J., & Sey, A. (2007). *Mobile communication and society: A global perspective.* Cambridge, MA: MIT Press.

Castells, M. (2009). *Communication power.* New York: Oxford University Press.

Castells, M. (2010). Communication, power, and counterpower in the network society. Seattle: University of Washington. (Lecture).

Chadwick, A. (2006). *Internet politics: States, citizens, and new communication technologies.* New York: Oxford University Press.

Chayko, M. (2002). *Connecting: How we form social bonds and communities in the Internet age.* Albany: State University of New York Press.

Crack, A. (2008). *Global communication and transnational public spheres.* New York: Palgrave.

Crystal, D. (2001). *Language and the Internet.* Cambridge: Cambridge University Press.

Crystal, D. (2003). *English as a global language.* Cambridge: Cambridge University Press.

Davis, R. (2005). *Politics online: Blogs, chatrooms, and discussion groups in American democracy.* New York: Routledge.

Davis, R. (2009). *Typing politics: The role of blogs in American politics.* Oxford: Oxford University Press.

de Certeau, M. (1984). *The practice of everyday life.* Berkeley: University of California Press.

Elson, S. B., Yeung, D., Roshan, P., Bohandy, S. R., & Nader, A. (2012). *Using social media to gauge Iranian public opinion and mood after the 2009 election.* Santa Monica, CA: RAND Corp.

Entman, R. (2004). *Projections of power: Framing news, public opinion, and U.S. foreign policy.* Chicago: University of Chicago Press.

Fairclough, N. (1995). *Media discourse.* London: Edward Arnold.

Fairclough, N. (2001). *Language and power* (2nd ed.). Essex: Pearson Education Ltd.

Fairclough, N. (2006). *Language and globalization.* New York: Routledge.

Featherstone, M. (1995). *Undoing culture: Globalization, postmodernism, and identity.* Thousand Oaks, CA: SAGE Publications.

Fowler, R. (1979). *Language and control.* London: Routledge & Kegan Paul.

Fowler, R. (1991). *Language in the news: Discourse and ideology in the press.* London: Routledge.

Giddens, A. (1990). *The consequences of modernity.* Stanford, CA: Stanford University Press.

Giddens, A. (1991). *Modernity and self-identity: Self and society in the late modern age.* Stanford, CA: Stanford University Press.

Gillan, K., Pickerill, J., & Webster, F. (2008). *Anti-war activism: New media and protest in the information age.* New York: Palgrave Macmillan.

Gillen, J., & Merchant, G. (2013). Contact calls: Twitter as a dialogic social and linguistic practice. *Language Sciences, 35,* 47–58.

Gladwell, M. (2010, October 4). Small change: Why the revolution will not be tweeted. *The New Yorker.* Retrieved November 16, 2014 from www.newyorker.com/magazine/2010/10/04/small-change-3

Grewal, D. S. (2008). *Network power: The social dynamics of globalization.* New Haven, CT: Yale University Press.

Gurak, L., & Antonijevic, S. (2008). The psychology of blogging: You, me, and everyone between. *American Behavioral Scientist, 52*(1), 60–68.

Hall, S. (1996). The question of cultural identity. In S. Hall, D. Held, D. Hubert, & K. Thompson (Eds.), *Modernity: An introduction to modern societies* (pp. 595–634). Cambridge: Polity Press.

Harvey, D. (1989). *The condition of postmodernity.* Oxford: Blackwell.

Hassan, R., & Thomas, J. (Eds.). (2006). *The new media theory reader.* New York: Open University Press.

Hopper, P. (2007). *Understanding cultural globalization.* Cambridge: Polity.

Hauser, G. (1999). *Vernacular voices: The rhetorics of publics and public spheres.* Columbia: University of South Carolina Press.

Ifukor, P. (2010). "Elections" or "selections"? Blogging and twittering the Nigerian 2007 general elections. *Bulletin of Science, Technology & Society, 30*(6), 398–414.

Johnson-Cartee, K. (2005). *News narratives and news framing: Constructing political reality.* Lanham, MD: Rowman & Littlefield.

Juris, J. (2008). *Networking futures: The movements against corporate globalization.* Durham, NC: Duke University Press.

Keddie, N. (2003). *Modern Iran: Roots and results of revolution.* New Haven/London: Yale UP.

Khiabany, G. (2010). *Iranian media: The paradox of modernity.* New York: Routledge.

Kurzman, C. (2004). *The unthinkable revolution in Iran*. Cambridge, MA: Harvard University Press.

Lampa, G. (2004). Imagining the blogosphere: An introduction to the imagined community of instant publishing. In L. J. Gurak, S. Antonijevic, L. Johnson, C. Ratliff, & J. Reyman (Eds.), *Into the blogosphere: Rhetoric, community, and culture of weblogs*. Retrieved December 12, 2010 from http://blog.lib.umn.edu/blogo sphere/imagining_the_blogosphere.html

Larsson, A., & Moe, H. (2012). Studying political microblogging: Twitter users in the 2010 Swedish election campaign. *New Media & Society, 14*(5), 729–747.

Lash, S. (2002). *The critique of information*. London: SAGE.

Lim, M. (2012). Clicks, cabs, and coffee houses: Social media and oppositional movements in Egypt, 2004–2011. *Journal of Communication, 62*, 231–248.

Maingueneau, D. (2006). Is discourse analysis critical? *Critical Discourse Studies, 3*(2), 229–235.

Manovich, L. (2002). *The language of new media*. Cambridge, MA: MIT Press.

Manovich, L. (2009). The practice of everyday (media) life: From mass consumption to mass cultural production? *Critical Inquiry, 35*, 313–331.

Marwick, A., & Boyd, D. (2010). I tweet honestly, I tweet passionately: Twitter users, context collapse, and the imagined audience. *New Media & Society, 20*(10), 1–20.

Miller, C. (2010, October 30). Why Twitter's C.E.O demoted himself. *New York Times*. Retrieved November 16, 2014 from www.nytimes.com/2010/10/31/technology/31ev.html?pagewanted=all&_r=0

Mittelman, J. (2004). *Wither globalization: The vortex of knowledge and ideology*. New York: Routledge.

Mody, B. (2010). *The geopolitics of representation in foreign news: Explaining Darfur*. Lanham, MD: Lexington Books.

Morales, A.J., Losada, J.C., & Benito, R.M. (2012). Users structure and behavior on an online social network during a political protest. *Physica A, 391*(21), 5244–5253.

Morozov, E. (2011). *The net delusion: The dark side of Internet freedom*. New York: Public Affairs.

Myers, G. (2010). *The discourse of blogs and wikis*. New York: Continuum.

Norris, P. (2001). *Digital divide: Civic engagement, information poverty, and the Internet worldwide*. Cambridge: Cambridge University Press.

Pennycook, A. (2007). *Global Englishes and transcultural flows*. London: Routledge.

Poulson, S. (2005). *Social movements in twentieth-century Iran: Culture, ideology, and mobilizing frameworks*. Lanham, MD: Lexington Books.

Rajaee, F. (2007). *Islamism and modernism: The changing discourse in Iran*. Austin: University of Texas Press.

Renzi, A. (2008). The space of tactical media. In M. Boler (Ed.), *Digital media and democracy: Tactics in hard times* (pp. 71–100). Cambridge, MA: MIT Press.

Robertson, R. (1995). Glocalization: Time-space and homogeneity-heterogenity. In M. Featherstone, S. Lash, & R. Robertson (Eds.), *Global modernities* (pp. 25–44). London: SAGE.

Rowe, C., & Wyss, E. L. (2009). *Language and new media: Linguistic, cultural, and technological evolutions*. Cresskill, NJ: Hampton Press.

Semati, M. (Ed.). (2008). *Media, culture and society in Iran: Living with globalization and the Islamic state*. New York: Routledge.

Sullivan, A. (2009, June 13). The revolution will be twittered. *The Atlantic*. Retrieved November 16, 2014 from www.theatlantic.com/daily-dish/archive/2009/06/the-revolution-will-be-twittered/200478/

Thurlow, C. (2006). From statistical panic to moral panic: The metadiscursive construction and popular exaggeration of new media language in the print media. *Journal of Computer-Mediated Communication, 11*, 667–701.

Thurlow, C., & Bell, K. (2009). Against technologization: Young people's new media discourse as creative cultural practice. *Journal of Computer-Mediated Communication, 14,* 1038–1049.

Tomlinson, J. (1999). *Globalization and culture.* Chicago: University of Chicago Press.

Tufekci, Z., & Wilson, C. (2012). Social media and the decision to participate in political protest: Observations from Tahrir Square. *Journal Of Communication, 62*(2), 363–379.

Urry, J. (2010). Mobile sociology. *British Journal of Sociology, 61,* 347–366.

van Dijk, T. (1998). *Ideology: A multidisciplinary approach.* Thousand Oaks, CA: SAGE.

van Dijk, T. (2009). Critical discourse studies: A sociocognitive approach. In R. Wodak & M. Meyer (Eds.), *Methods of critical discourse analysis* (2nd ed., pp. 62–86). London: SAGE.

Wodak, R., & Meyer, M. (2009). *Methods of critical discourse analysis* (2nd ed.). London: SAGE.

Zappavigna, M. (2011). Ambient affiliation: A linguistic perspective on Twitter. *New Media & Society, 13*(5), 788–806.

Zimbra, D., Chen, H., & Abbasi, A. (2010). A cyber-archeology approach to social movement research: A framework and case study. *Journal of Computer-Mediated Communication, 16,* 48–70.

2 "Down with Potatoes!"
Theory, Methods, Contexts

The atmosphere in Iran during the run-up to the 2009 presidential election had been growing increasingly tense. Of the nearly 500 candidates who had filed their candidacy for Iran's presidency, the 4 approved by the Guardian Council spent the week preceding the election fiercely campaigning and engaged in live televised debates, which, according to Iranian media reports, were watched by upward of 50 million viewers (Addis, 2009).[1] Emerging from these heated debates were 2 leading candidates, the incumbent Mahmoud Ahmadinejad and the reformist candidate Mir-Hossein Mousavi. While Ahmadinejad had maintained a strong lead over his opponents throughout much of the campaign, the former prime minister and Minister of Foreign Affairs Mousavi began to show strong gains during the election run-up. In the final days before the June 12, 2009 vote, masses of Mousavi supporters rallied in the streets of Tehran. According to some reports, there were indications that the rural and urban poor, long a significant source of support for Ahmadinejad, were shifting away from the incumbent toward the reformist candidate. As a result, on election eve, many observers were predicting a close race and speculating that the high voter turnout forecast by the massive debate viewership could tip the result in Mousavi's favor (Addis).

As predicted, and unlike the 2005 election that had brought Ahmadinejad to power, voter turnout on election day in 2009 was extremely high. Eighty-five percent of the voting population cast 39 million total votes, an unprecedented showing that prompted the Iranian Interior Ministry to keep voting centers open in order to accommodate long lines of those still waiting to cast their ballot (Addis, 2009). Despite this record turnout, the election results were announced less than three hours after the polls had closed, with the Interior Ministry declaring that the incumbent Ahmadinejad had captured 62% of the vote. Given the predictions of a much closer contest, this landslide was viewed skeptically both inside and outside the country. Critics, including Mousavi, challenged the legitimacy of the improbable fast ballot counting while others questioned the high levels of electoral support Ahmadinejad had received in the dense urban centers and from communities known to back Mousavi (Howard, 2010). After the public endorsement of the election result by the Iranian supreme leader, Ayatollah Ali Khamenei, Mousavi officially contested the results, lodging an appeal with the Iranian Guardian Council against the alleged voting fraud.

Meanwhile, in the streets of Tehran, Mousavi's supporters, joined by other civil society groups and political activists, rallied to protest the alleged election irregularities and, they charged, inconclusive results. Although initially peaceful, the protests quickly grew bloody. Tensions surged as activists, defying government bans on public protest, marched in increasingly larger numbers and, with police and paramilitary forces amassing, shouted anti-government slogans and cries of "Death to the Dictator!" that echoed those of the 1979 revolution. Bloody clashes broke out, as on June 13, when protesters attempted to set fire to a Basij compound and, in response, the Basij opened fire on the crowd from the compound roof (Addis, 2009). With similar confrontations on the rise during the week following the election, the violence escalated rapidly, causing numerous casualties in the largest protests Iran had seen since those in 1979 that brought down the Shah Mohammad Reza (el-Nawawy, 2010).

Yet, even as the post-election protests swelled in Tehran and, increasingly, other cities, little news about these dramatic events was known outside of Iran. As before and during the elections, Iranian authorities restricted and repressed reports of the post-election protests in the Iranian media. Additionally, they electronically blockaded foreign news broadcasts, jamming the frequencies of Persian-language satellite broadcasts from the BBC and Voice of America. Nearly all foreign correspondents were expelled, innumerable phone lines were blocked, and so-called enemy governments, such as Great Britain's, were publicly accused of spreading misinformation about both the election results and the ensuing crackdown on demonstrations. Using their power over the state-run information infrastructure, the Iranian authorities were able to control the flow of news about the events transpiring after the highly contested election results, a strategy they had also used in 2005, when Ahmadinejad was voted into power and media blackouts largely suppressed reports of alleged voting irregularities during that election.

Unlike 2005, however, Iranian civil society groups and social movement leaders in 2009 had access to an information infrastructure largely independent of the state. Government-led developments during the early 2000s had helped make Iran a highly wired and networked civil society and one of the most technologically advanced nations of the region. At present, there is one mobile phone for every two people in Iran (though predominantly in urban centers) and some 20 million regular Internet users (Howard, 2010; Kamalipour, 2010). The Persian blogosphere is one of the world's liveliest, with Persian currently the tenth most popular blogging language globally (Howard). It is also a highly diversified one, with the government and Basij paramilitaries blogging actively alongside dissidents and student activists as well as common users (Yaghmaian, 2002). But globalization and the information revolution has also brought flows that central authorities struggled to control (Ansari, 2000). During the 2009 protests, this surge in information and communication technologies (ICTs) in Iranian society weakened the government's centralized, 'old media' censorship strategies by allowing for an alternative flow of information about the dramatic, chaotic events unfolding in the streets of Tehran.

Circumventing both internal media censorship and blockades against foreign journalists, activists readily turned to social media services, such as Twitter, Facebook, and Flickr, to find out what was happening and to coordinate participation. During the peak of the protests, Twitter usage was especially high, with more than 480,000 Iranian Twitter users posting over 2 million tweets between June 7 and June 26. On election day, June 12, Twitter streams peaked at over 200,000 tweets per hour, and Twitter was widely used to coordinate a massive rally on June 15 (Howard, 2010).[2] As protesters' social media usage surged, some began using social media to submit firsthand reports and images from the demonstrations to international news agencies (Kamalipour, 2010). As Howard has documented, during protests in Tehran and Isfahan, Iran's third largest city, there was "a flood of digital content from the Iranian streets: photos, videos, blog posts, tweets, and SMS messages [that] flowed between protesters and out to the international community" (p. 6). Although news of the events was still greatly limited by government media censorship and restrictions, activists' use of this new grassroots information infrastructure allowed them to disseminate news and information, creating a vital alternative information flow for both a local and global audience. Inside Iran, the use of SMS text messaging helped activists reach two important domestic constituencies: rural, conservative voters who had few connections to the urban chaos and the clerical establishment (Howard). Globally, protesters' reports of events began to spread, converging in social media and reports from the international news agencies picking up those stories. The global audience that emerged became largely empathetic to the rapidly coalescing opposition Green Movement of demonstrators, citizens, and activists that the world would come to identify with the post-election crisis. But more than empathy, this reflexive address of an unknown global audience (the diaspora notwithstanding) suggested a transnational field of reference as the potential frame for their beliefs—a process that would help decenter their local struggle (Albrow, 1997; Chadwick, 2006; Mittelman, 2004). As Dabashi (2010) has argued, the ability to communicate more freely across national borders engendered not only further possibilities for Iranians to expand their lifeworlds, but also "a strengthening of their multiple consciousness as a guarantor of resistance to widespread governmentality" (p. 205).

But as this battle for the control of information intensified, the Iranian government coordinated its 'old media' censorship strategy with a new media one, using its control over the state-run information infrastructure to electronically blockade both local and global ICTs. In fact, the government already had a new media strategy in place prior to the election. During the election run-up, the government repeatedly lowered bandwidth and filtered social media sites to foil the opposition. On election day, it darkened text-messaging systems, disrupted mobile phone subscribers' services, and took key opposition websites offline. To rally support for their incumbent candidate, the government disseminated its campaign messages through pro-Ahmadinejad websites, with the president himself maintaining a popular blog. But despite earlier restrictions on Facebook and Twitter usage, the government had not counted on activists using social media to submit content to international news agencies and, as the protests grew, was forced to respond with increased ICT censorship and more aggressive cyberwar strategies. They continued disrupting mobile phone and Internet services and set up their own Twitter and Facebook accounts to spread disinformation. Basij paramilitants collected digital video and photos of demonstrators and, through their own websites, asked Iranians online to help identify the protesters (Dabashi, 2010). The government also built an Internet traffic choke point and an inspection system to slow traffic for content analysis in order to learn opposition tactics and identify social movement leaders (Addis, 2009; Bray, 2009). On June 13, the government even disabled Internet service entirely, leaving Iran off the global grid for some 20 hours.

To counter this strategy, activists and opposition leaders both inside and outside Iran engaged in an array of creative cyberwar tactics. To circumvent electronic blockades, they organized a supply of proxy servers unknown to Iranian officials, including some built from the home computers of activists around the world. Online pro-democracy activists and international tech-savvy digerati, alongside opposition members of the Iranian diaspora, helped create secure communication networks and instructed protesters on how to use online encryption and anonymizers to avoid detection by government surveillance (Howard, 2010). With proxy severs in place, activists coordinated cyber-attacks on the government's information infrastructure, in particular pro-Ahmadinejad websites and state media portals, creating a cyberwar that mirrored the violent clashes on Tehran's streets (Bray, 2009). Moreover, with access to social media restored through proxy servers, they used their networks to inform activists how to avoid online surveillance and protect themselves during demonstrations as well as to warn them of the government's disinformation sites, as in these tweets.[3]

> information on using Tor to remain anonymous: www.torproject.org . . . Tor+Wordpress: http://is.gd/12g1P #Iranelection Jun 15, 2009

> @username: WARNING: www.mirhoseyn.ir/ & www.mirhoseyn.com/ are fake, DONT join. #IranElection Jun 16, 2009

> @username: RT @judyrey Updated fake #Iranelection tweeter list—http://twitspam.org/ Take a look Jun 17, 2009

> how to deal with tear gas: http://bit.ly/KfAGs #Iranelection Jun 16, 2009

They were also able to submit more protesters' eyewitness reports to international news outlets, such as CNN, Al Jazeera, and the BBC. As these new media accounts were incorporated into an increasing number of legacy media reports on the election crisis, not only was increased global attention brought to the unfolding events in Iran, but activists could also circulate these reports across their networks as an additional means of countering the Iranian government's effort to control the flow of information.

> @username MirHossein Mousavi Although several reports say that Mousavi is under house arrest, BBC confirms that Mousavi is NOT under house arrest: http://is.gd/11APp 06/14/2009

> Isfahan University Dormitories were attacked last night. #Iranelection http://javanefarda.com/News.aspx?ID=585

> @username MirHossein Mousavi Mousavi's message from GhalamNews now on http://mousavi1388.wikispaces.com/Ghalamnews.org and http://ghalamnews.tumblr.com/ #IranElection 06/16/2009

Global attention and the intensified battle for the control of information caused social media usage to soar. Prominent activists' Twitter accounts such as @persiankiwi and @Mousavi11318 quickly gained thousands of followers from both inside and outside Iran, while, during the height of the protests, tweets *hashtagged* #IranElection appeared at a rate of 30 per minute.[4] Local activists used Twitter to help injured street protesters find safe hospitals, report raids by intelligence agents, and recruit more international cyber-activists, while, globally, thousands complained in tweets hashtagged #CNNfail about the lack of international news coverage of the post-election crisis. As news spread about the role of new and social media in the growing Green Movement, Google decided to fast-track its Persian-language translator, and Facebook quickly released a beta translation of its content into Persian. Even the U.S. State Department, recognizing social media's potential impact on the post-election crisis, asked Twitter to delay a network upgrade on June 16 to prevent a service shutdown during daylight hours in Tehran. News of demonstrators' reliance on Twitter caused the post-election protests to be dubbed the 'Twitter Revolution,' while the viral spread through Facebook status updates, Flickr photo uploads, and YouTube of cell phone video captures of the death of a young Iranian woman, Neda Agha-Soltan, captured worldwide public and media attention, further highlighting news of the conflict.

Ultimately, however, as history shows, the movement did not succeed. The election results were certified and Ahmadinejad retained the presidency. But the protests did create a split among the ruling councils of mullahs over how to credibly authorize Ahmadinejad into power (Howard, 2010). For that reason, the direct effects of activists' use of social media had on the protests themselves are difficult to measure and thus debatable (Morozov,

2011). But does this mean, as Morozov and others have claimed, that they played no significant part in the battle to control minds and information? Despite intense government media censorship, news of both the election irregularities and the post-election protests did eventually reach a global audience and thereby contributed to a transnational public-sphere understanding of what had happened. Moreover, as I will argue in later chapters, in measuring the effect of protesters' tactical uses of social media, Morozov and others have failed to sufficiently consider two key issues: how the identities and ideologies of activists, both locally in Iran and those participating in solidarity around the globe, were shaped through their engagement and access to a global audience, and how that process might contribute to discursive change and, by extension, promote social transformation (Juris, 2008).

This process, and its relation to the syndrome of processes commonly referred to as globalization, may also shed further light on the ways that power, knowledge, and ideology are contingently related in what Mittelman (2004) has called a "vortex of struggle." According to Blommaert (2010), the nature of this contentious relationship "forces sociolinguistics to unthink classical distinctions and biases and rethink itself as a sociolinguistics of mobile resources, framed in terms of trans-contextual networks, flows, and movements" (p. 1). Such a critical rethinking would include a reflexive awareness of the links between knowledge and political conditions, diachronic sociohistorical analysis, a decentered perspective that considers the margins as well as epicenters, and an accounting for the formations of counterdiscourses (Mittelman). As argued in the previous chapter, the events surrounding the 2009 Iranian presidential election offer an opportunity to attempt this rethinking as a means of engaging globalization in the study of language and understanding further how language is inherent in its processes, in particular, how new media discourses can shape global vernaculars of English. I also hope it adds to, and complicates, persistent binary arguments between cyber-skeptics and -utopians on the relations between technology and democracy.

With these aims in mind, I extend in this chapter my discussion of the 2009 Iranian election crisis with an overview of the crucial sociopolitical and cultural developments in Iran leading up to that election. In particular, I look at the sociopolitical reforms of the Khatami presidency of the 1990s and the corresponding sociocultural changes. The purpose of establishing this macrolevel context is premised on the understanding that the consideration of the broader historical and sociopolitical contexts in which the discursive practices analyzed are embedded is integral to my methodological approach, critical discourse analysis (CDA) (Wodak & Meyer, 2009). I go on to discuss the relevance of these contexts in regard to the social theories I have drawn on in my research as a means of establishing an overall theoretical framework. These theories include considerations of discourse and power (and counterpower) in a network society and the role of language in the processes of globalization, with the understanding that theoretical concepts specific to particular analyses will be presented in the chapters where they occur. In regard to presenting my research methodology, I have taken a similar tack, presenting my rationale for an overall sociocognitive approach to CDA in the examination of both context and a dialogic engagement with the key critical arguments levied against CDA as a method of social research, with the provision that methodological concerns specific to particular analyses will be presented in the relevant chapters following this one. In short, if, in Chapter 1, I sought to open a contextual, theoretical, and rhetorical space for this research, in this chapter I establish more concretely the foundations for the analyses, discussions, and conclusions that follow.

THE SEEDS OF PROTEST: THE KHATAMI REFORMS, THE RISE OF ICTS, AND THE IRANIAN YOUTH POPULATION

Arguably, many of the seeds of the 2009 protests were sewn in the 1997 election that brought Mohammad Khatami to power. A reformist politician and Shia theologian, Khatami had served as Iran's Minister of Culture during the 1980s and 1990s before becoming Iran's fifth president. Winning nearly 70% of the vote, Khatami not only earned a clear mandate, but also captured global attention for his reformist positions and policies (Gheissari & Nasr, 2006). At the heart of his popular support were grassroots movements pushing for the reform of many of the hardline social and political policies instituted after the 1978–79 revolution. Within the government, there was also an internal movement that had begun to question the Islamic Republic's past. As Yaghmaian (2002) has explained:

> Finding the earlier project of the Islamic Republic incompatible with the dominant global politico-economic and cultural/technological imperative, a group from within the state . . . called for abandoning the old order, and embracing a new Islamic state embedded in the rational synthesis of modernity and tradition. (p. 7)

This synthesis included a restructuring of the relationships between religion and state as well as the rationalization of the role of Islam in society, specifically the rejection of the *faghih*, the Iranian supreme leader, as the ultimate ruling authority in favor of relocating power in the hands of elected officials (Azimi, 2008). Khatami had been elected by a wide and diverse coalition of individuals and grassroots movements advocating for democracy and justice, that is, a democratic Islamic state with "a human face—a new Islamic Republic accepted by youth, disempowered women, and citizens tired of two decades of religious monitoring of the most private aspects of their lives" (Yaghmaian, p. 8). With this popular and political support, Khatami began instituting a series of cultural and political reforms aimed at bolstering the role of democracy within an Islamic republic, which included strengthening civil society, restoring the rule of law, broadening individual and cultural freedoms, and developing a more exogenous economy while still retaining the Islamic Republic's commitment to public services and freedom from foreign aid dependency (Keddie, 2003).

After decades of political and cultural insularity under the Islamic Republic, this turning outward saw Khatami reopen diplomatic relations with Western European powers and become the first Iranian president to make top-level diplomatic trips to several foreign capitals. Against the resistance of conservative forces within the Iranian government, Khatami also advanced, through the United Nations and open letters to Western religious and political leaders, his theory of a *dialogue of civilizations* that would counter the *new world order* and *clash of civilizations* theses informing many popular conservative geopolitical theories in the West soon after the end of the Cold War (Gheissari & Nasr, 2006). Within Iran, Khatami's reforms allowed for the rise of a critical press, such as the *Jame'eh* and *Rah-e No* newspapers, which helped create a space, if not a multiplicity of public spheres, where marginalized voices could be heard, long-held cultural taboos challenged, and political authorities publicly questioned (Fraser, 1992; Yaghmaian, 2002). The rise of a critical press helped encourage the dialogue and debate around which the July 1999 student protests began. With calls to end the *velayat-e faghih*, or rule by supreme leader, students marched in what were then some of the largest protests in Tehran since the 1979 revolution. According to Yaghmaian, these were transclass student movements calling not for revolution, but for the principles of democracy and, in particular, individual freedoms and civil rights not tied to class and cultural identities. Indeed, as Gheissari and Nasr have argued, popular ideas in Iran of democracy have shifted from notions of nationalism, progress, and modernity toward individual rights and cultural and intellectual freedoms. And unlike contemporaneous Western anti-globalization movements, in which activists were rallying against the colonization of the lifeworld (Habermas, 1975), "Iranian youth embraced all symbols of massification and commodification, . . . creat[ing] forms and sites of collective action unforeseen by the theorists of new social movements" (Yaghmaian, p. 24).

But Khatami's vision for Islamic-Iranian modernity contained efforts to both reengage the international community and preserve Iranian-Islamic culture and the gains of the 1979 revolution (Tazimi, 2012). As student protesters refashioned "Down with the Dictator!" chants and slogans from 1979—on this occasion aimed not at political powers but the theocratic supreme leader—conservative forces within the Khatami government, together with the Guardian Council, began to attack the free press movement, publicly denouncing the media in speeches, threatening and closing various critical newspapers, and hounding journalists into self-censorship.[5] These actions were arguably a prelude to the rise of the forces that would bring the conservative Ahmadinejad into power in 2005 and institute the communications blockades meant to prevent the world from knowing about the protests that would erupt following the 2009 presidential elections, which would ultimately return him to power.

The Rise of the Iranian Youth Population

If the Khatami-led cultural reforms of the late 1990s helped create a space within the Iranian public sphere for dissent, the spike in the Iranian birth rate which followed the 1979 revolution created the youth population that, 20 years later, would begin occupying those spaces (Dabashi, 2010). After the success of the 1979 revolution, the supreme leader, Ayatollah Khomeini, encouraged Iranians to marry and produce large families to help strengthen the new republic and 'make armies for Islam' (Keddie, 2003). Consequently, the Iranian population has nearly tripled since 1979, and currently two-thirds of all Iranians are under 30 years old. Moreover, with 67% of the Iranian population living in urban areas and an overall high literacy rate, these demographics, according to Semati (2008), favor a trend toward social transformation.

Concurrent with this trend has been the development of the media and ICTs in Iran that began during the Khatami presidency. There are presently more than 36 Persian satellite TV channels, plus numerous others in various languages, and although Iranian law prohibits ownership and sale of satellite dishes, the government typically chooses not to enforce this (Semati, 2008). In conjunction with the high penetration of mobile phone usage mentioned above, this means not only that Iran has become a highly wired civil society, but also that the current populous generation of young Iranians has emerged under the influence of the globally dominant youth culture (Howard, 2010). Although the state, including the Khatami government, has tried to limit Iranian youth's exposure to the flows of global information through state-level media controls, they have largely been unsuccessful (Yaghmaian, 2002). If, in part, efforts to limit access to global cultural flows are meant to preserve local cultural traditions (Hopper, 2007), including many of those instituted during the Islamic Revolution, strict state-level control of ICTs may not be the most effective strategy. As Crack (2008) has shown, ICTs can have an ambiguous role in social transformation. On the one hand, by allowing new opportunities for transnational dialogue, cross-cultural engagement, and grassroots political participation, they can facilitate challenges to the status quo by counterhegemonic forces. For young Iranians, the development of ICTs has meant rapidly increasing access to both global cultural flows and critical information technologies and new media forms, such as microblogs, where, through their everyday cultural practices, they can create and project their identities (de Certeau, 1984; Varzi, 2006). But the rise of social media use in Iran has included not only the sizable youth population but all sectors; reportedly, even the Revolutionary Guard has a social media strategy. And while the Iranian blogosphere has become a dynamic public sphere in which young dissidents debate and engage with global audience, including the vocal Iranian diaspora, particularly in London and Los Angeles (Yaghmaian; Howard), state authorities' online countermeasures to thwart organization and dissent show the double bind of using ICT-based communication for social movements (Morozov, 2011; Robbins & Webster, 2006). That is, if, as Bohman (2004) has argued, ICTs like mobile phones and the Internet can help develop a new sort of distributive public sphere that, as a 'public of publics,' decenters traditional public spheres, they can also facilitate state-level surveillance and reinforce centrist power (Morozov).

Similarly, while the rapid growth of the Iranian youth population has meant an infusing of global flows into local culture, it has also contributed to critical social problems. The Iranian youth population has been very negatively affected by the sharp financial downturn and high rates of unemployment caused by the strong economic sanctions against Iran for developing its nuclear program. The current unemployment rate for Iranians under 30 is approximately 50%, with half living below the poverty line. The lack of work has led to, at one extreme, high levels of brain drain. The International Monetary Fund (IMF) has reported that more than 150,000 highly skilled Iranians annually migrate or study and work abroad in places like Dubai.[6] At another extreme, unemployment and poverty, along with a lack of entertainment and cultural activities for young people, have been attributed as the causes of Iran's having the highest rate of opiate addicts in the world (Varzi, 2006). Moreover, the devastating Iran-Iraq war and Iran's relationship with the West reflected in it, together with the complexities of Iran's current nuclear program and the U.S.-led economic sanctions meant to thwart it, has made this large youthful generation highly ideological.

Eventually, some of this ideologically orientated youth population would withdraw its support for Khatami. While his cultural reforms and outward-looking policies may have helped open both rhetorical and cultural spaces for dissent, not all reforms succeeded. Some were blocked by conservatives, and Khatami himself backed away from others (Keddie, 2003). After allowing police and conservatives to attack student-led protests, Khatami lost support for his reform project, and consequently his promises of liberalization were unfulfilled. And while the large youth population that began to come of age during the Khatami era may have been affected by the concurrent growth of ICTs, it is difficult to evaluate the overall effect of connectivity on Iranian politics (Howard, 2010). Furthermore, while a connected youth population did participate in the 1999 protests, they were predominantly students from urban centers, not the rural poor, a pattern of access and participation that in 2009 and challenges lingering cyber-utopian rhetoric of the Internet as a new form of democratic decentralization (Barber, 1995; Featherstone & Lash, 1999). Instead, offline institutional and social power dynamics tend to be reproduced online, with the struggle to control communication and information extending into cyberspace and constituting much of what Castells (2009) has called the fundamental battle in society, the power to control how others think.

COMMUNICATION POWER: A THEORETICAL RESEARCH FRAMEWORK

The above account of the 2009 Iranian presidential election protests, together with the discussion of the Khatami reforms as a potential source of those protests, is more, I intend, than an examination, at multiple scales, of the context in which the discourse I analyzed is embedded. I believe it also shows— and thereby allows me to discuss from a theoretical standpoint—the ways in which the discursive practices I analyze in this research are constitutive of social relations, with social cognition interfacing between the two (Foucault, 1972; van Dijk, 2009). Or, from another perspective, if the analysis of context is essential to the analysis of the discourse embedded in that context (Wodak & Meyer, 2009), it should also, as an intermediary in a dialogic process, shape and delimit the theoretical framework of the research.

As the conflict between Iranian state forces and protesters shows, central to this theoretical framework must be considerations of power. First, for my analyses, I have adopted Castells' (2009) largely Foucauldian understanding of power, which he sees as:

> the relational capacity that enables a social actor to influence asymmetrically the decisions of other social actor(s) in ways that favor the empowered actor's will, interests, and values. Power is exercised by means of coercion (or the possibility of it) and/or by the construction of meaning on the basis of the discourses through which social actors guide their action. (p. 10)

In the 2009 Iranian election crisis we can observe the ongoing shift from a disciplinary society to social control, with police and paramilitary forces' disciplinary response representing a visible, traditional expression of sovereignty and centrist power in the capacity for violence (Blommaert, 2008; Hardt & Negri, 2000). Moreover, the publicness of this response, if only locally at first, can be seen as a secondary expression of traditional statist forms of power, coercion. That is, the violent repression of protesters was also meant to coerce would-be participants, whether those passively protesting or those considering joining the protests in the future. In this sense, coercion can also be seen as a cognitive action, an expression of force by one group of social agents, in this case institutional, on the minds of others. Certainly, coercion is also discursive when it is multifariously circulated throughout society in the form of rules, policies, agendas, representations, threats, attested knowledges, and so forth. As Foucault (1978) argued, it is through social relations that discourse is dispersed, circulated, and thereby enmeshed with power. With discourse constitutive of social relations, this understanding of discourse, therefore, is not limited to a group of signs or a stretch of text, the *small-d discourse* of 'talk and text' or 'utterances beyond the sentence level,' as it is often defined in discourse analysis (Gee, 2005). It also includes the *big-d discourse* of rules, structures, and practices that produce utterances and texts and systematically form the objects they refer to (Foucault, 1972). With dominant power exercised through institutions, power is therefore constituted by discourses, which are strongly bounded areas of knowledge, a complex of statements by which the world is known and by which relationships are deciphered and subjectivities constructed (Mittelman, 2004). Because these forms of power stretch along networks into the smallest and most private aspects of life, setting the parameters of practice, behavior, and thought (Hardt & Negri), this type of force can be seen, in Foucauldian terms, as a *capillary power* formed in discourse that, diffused multidirectionally across society, decenters power yet nevertheless strengthens, rather than weakens, the center. And crucially, in such forms of systemic power, coercion is no longer its defining characteristic; instead, it is a soft power, one shaped by ideology, and those in control rule not only with force and exploitation, but ideological *hegemony*, or the dominance of ideas and culture in the way people think and feel (Blommaert, 2008; Gramsci, 2003). It is also a networked power, relational and inherent in discourse and in mediating social institutions (Foucault, 1978; Grewal, 2008).

Communication and Counterpower

But notions of networked and ideological systemic power need not exclude the power of individual agency. As the events of the 2009 Iranian presidential election protests show, discursive capillary power can circulate not only from institutional forces, such as government and state-sponsored media, but also from social agents themselves. Consider this protester's tweet: "shooting people in Azadi Sq" (@username.twitter.com).[7] Ostensibly, this information, circulated through Twitter under the #IranElection hashtag, was meant to warn local Twitter-using protesters of danger as well as inform a larger Twitter audience of these events. As such, it could constitute—especially when aggregated with other forms of online and offline coordination—a form of counterpower. On a cognitive level, this information, circulated through mobile new media forms as counterdiscourses, could also serve as a klaxon call to participation, although the correlation between social media usage during protests and active engagement has not been established (Howard, 2010). At the same time, these counterdiscourses might also—and understandably so—discourage participation. In fact, as will be discussed below, while the use of decentralizing, ICT-based networked communications has become integral to the planning and operationalizing of social movements (Juris, 2008), it may also ironically serve the ends of statist or centralized forms of power. Moreover, that this discourse was *informationalized* via its circulation in Twitter risks not only commodification (Lash, 2002), but also, as possible dissuasion, a challenge to the forces of imagined solidarity from networked connectivity, a notion I discuss in more detail in Chapters 4 and 5.

The Struggle to Control Minds

Castells (2009) sees the fundamental struggle and decisive form of power in contemporary networked societies as being over the minds of social agents. Social control over how people think determines the fate of institutions, norms, and values that constitute society, with the centrist control over information seen as essential to sovereignty and a form of network power (Castells; Grewal, 2008). During the protests, as well as in the election run-up, the Iranian government used its control over the state-run information infrastructure to blockade the flow of information, electronically jamming satellite broadcasts, expelling foreign news correspondents, and blocking innumerable phone lines and thereby demonstrating a key form of power in a network society (Castells, 1996). According to Castells, "networks constitute the new morphology of our societies, and the diffusion of networking logic substantially modifies the operation and outcomes in processes of production, experience, power and culture" (p. 469). According to the logics of networks, Castells has argued, the flow of power is replaced by the power of flows, and presence or absence in the network is a significant source of both social control and change.

Network power, then, can also take the form of *counterpower*, or the capacity of social agents to resist dominating forces (Castells, 2010). This capacity, though, can be expressed in various ways. The 2009 Iranian protests, made in defiance of anti-demonstration regulations, as well as the protesters' violent responses to government forces' repression, were *hard* forms of counterpower, or, in Gramsci's (2003) term, a *war of maneuver*. In contrast, the symbolic processes of massing in the streets and circulating symbolic resources of social movements across local and global networks constitute forms of *soft* counterpower. In the information technology paradigm of the network society, we also see non-traditional expressions of communication counterpower (Castells, 2009). During the protests, activists and opposition leaders responded to the Iranian government's communication blockade with cyberwar tactics. They organized a supply of proxy servers, instructed in online encryption and anonymizers, and coordinated cyber-attacks on the government's information infrastructure. They also continued to submit eyewitness reports to international news outlets as a means of drawing further global attention to the crisis unfolding in Iran. Though some have challenged the effect of these countermeasures on the protests (Howard, 2010; Morozov, 2011), activists succeeded in circumventing the communication blockade to the extent that the world did learn of the events transpiring in Tehran in June 2009, against the Iranian government's explicit intentions. Yet, this success may have been Pyrrhic. As discussed above, the Iranian government responded with its own cyber-attacks, and with its control over the information infrastructure, it likely tipped what initially had been a successful tactic by the protesters in its own favor, especially when it used surveillance of mobile new media communications to identify, locate, and arrest activists (Howard). What is more, the attention from Western global media on protesters' use of new media caused the Iranian authorities, who had long supported the state-level development of the Internet as an engine of economic growth and a tool for spreading Islam, to begin to view it as a significant threat. Consequently, in the months following the protests, the Iranian government formed a high-level cybercrime team tasked with finding any false information on Iranian websites, including increased Internet surveillance of Iranians and the Iranian diaspora (Morozov, 2011).

Communication Power in a Globalized Context

The above considerations of capillary network power and an information-centered network society, as well as these examples of counterpower, bear crucial aspects of globalization, or the syndrome of global processes and activities that constitute it (Mittelman, 2004). As Castells (2009) has argued, "our historical context is marked by the contemporary process of globalization and the rise of the network society, both relying on communication networks that process knowledge and thoughts to make and unmake trust, the decisive source of power" (p. 16). While an in-depth discussion of the processes of globalization is beyond the scope of this project, it is important, in establishing my overall theoretical framework, to stake out the critical positions I take within the current, ongoing debates about globalization, particularly as they relate to language and the linguistic analyses that follow.[8]

Sociologist Anthony Giddens, though widely criticized for defending modernity and its universalizing modes of thought and description, as well as for his associations with some of the neoliberal policies of British New Labour governments, has nevertheless offered useful theorizations of globalization for research on how its processes relate with language. As a third-wave, transformationalist theorist of globalization, Giddens envisions globalization as a dynamic, dialectical of global-local relations that ultimately renders the world a juggernaut, "a runaway engine of enormous power which, collectively as human beings, we can drive to some extent but which also threatens to rush out of our control and which could rend itself asunder" (1990, p. 139). This vision stresses the unprecedented nature of current economic, political, and cultural flows and levels of interconnectedness (Hopper, 2007), including the role of ICTs in establishing those links and facilitating those flows (Castells, 1996; Crack, 2008). Two related features central to Giddens' globalization theory, and related to the role of language in the processes of globalization, are his notions of time-space *distantiation* and *disembedding* mechanisms. As part of the manifold, multidirectional global flows of culture and information facilitated by mass media and global communications technologies, language helps overcome distances, or the friction of space, transforming the social perceptions of place and the institutional relationship between time and space (Harvey, 1989; Tomlinson, 1999). As a result, space has been torn away from place, which disembeds, or 'lifts out,' social relations from local contexts or interactions and their restructuring across indefinite spans of time-space. This emptying of time and space replaces the experience of space dominated by relations of presence with those of absence, creating a *phantasmagoric* sense of place in which locales are thoroughly permeated by and shaped in terms of social influences quite distant from them (Tomlinson). Crucially, part of what results from these influences is the *reflexivity* of modern social life, in which social practices, including discourses, are constantly examined and reshaped in the light of incoming information about those very practices (Giddens, 1990). This emphasis on reflexive practices evidences a vision of language as recursive, in which knowledges are constituted as discourses and the symbolic order of language is attributed a central role in social practices reformed within a globe frame (Bourdieu, 1991).

In relation to social structures and processes, language, then, as a social practice exists in a dialectical relation to social structure (Blommaert, 2005). This conceptualization mirrors Giddens' (1984) theory of structuration, a dynamic model of the relationships between structure and agency in which social practice is seen as that which constitutes humans as actors and simultaneously manifests social structures. But because Giddens' dialectical of polarities flattens the dynamics of complex global-local interpenetration, he has understandably been criticized for failing to see the possibility for differentiated locales and plural global cultures in which language contributes to the multiple, contradictory, decentered identities of social agents (Featherstone, 1995). Instead, language, as a social activity and a means of praxis, is at once a mediator and an embodiment of agency.

Furthermore, language, together with global media and communication systems and a world capitalist economy, plays a critical role in the dense network of global interconnections and cultural flows that characterize contemporary social life (Albrow, 1997; Appadurai, 1996). For that reason, it has been primary among the forces of globalization that bring distant occurrences to bear on local events and rescale social activity (Giddens, 1991). In these transformed cultural, social, and economic relations, globalization has arguably weakened or decentralized the nation-state (Robertson, 1995; Scholte, 2005). Together with processes of *cultural deterritorialization* (Tomlinson, 1999), this, in turn, has altered the role of languages in a globalized economy. Whereas once they were seen as coterminous with state boundaries and linked to uniform cultures (Anderson, 2006; Billig, 1995), languages— in particular, English, with its predominant role in global mass consumer culture and its worldliness perpetuated by, among other factors, the global

English language teaching industry (Featherstone, 1995; Pennycook, 1994)—can now be viewed as both globalizing and globalized (Fairclough, 2006). What is more, with numerous sectors of the globalized economy based on multilingual or English-as-a-global-language communication (Crystal, 2003; Graddol, 2007), the traditional opposition between the materiality of economy and commodities and the non-materiality of language, signification, and communication has collapsed, resulting in a transformation of the economic and material impact of language (Gramsci, 2003).

The Role of ICTs

Like language, ICTs have played a significant role in intensifying the processes of global interconnectedness. Not only have they helped intensify time-space compression and facilitate global cultural and economic flows, but they have also, through the Internet, helped create a networked space of publics, a new sort of distributive public sphere that, as a 'public of publics,' decenters traditional public spheres (Bohman, 2004; Habermas, 1991). Furthermore, as a reticulation of public spheres, they can enable the agency of social actors engaged in reflexive, participatory activity (Hauser, 1999; Jenkins, 2006). When these actions remain distinct from the exchanges of public authority, they may constitute what Warner (2002) has called a *counterpublic*. Against the background of the public sphere, counterpublics enable alternative spheres of opinion and exchange that can have a crucial relation to power (Warner). Yet, because these public spheres are embedded both in social practices and in the institutions that maintain and preserve public spaces, they must also be viewed through relations of social power. Insofar as information exchanged in such spaces is controlled as a commodity, online public spheres must be seen as reflecting the institutions in which they are embedded, an issue which will be crucial in evaluating, in Chapters 4 and 5, Iranian protesters' use of social media and U.S. legacy media's treatment of it (Morozov, 2011). As such, the use of ICTs in the public sphere can both support the hegemonic practices of an oligopolistic global media and facilitate challenges to the status quo from counterhegemonic forces by allowing new opportunities for dialogue, cross-cultural engagement, and grassroots political participation (Crack, 2008). As a result of the latter, ICTs have played significant roles in social movements, from the Zapatista and anti-globalization movements of the 1990s (Castells, 1996) to the Egyptian Revolution and so-called Arab Spring uprisings of 2011. By providing a powerful platform for political autonomy that bypasses mass media systems, ICTs, in particular mobile communications, can create new possibilities for democratic deliberation in literate public spheres (Castells, Fernandez-Ardevol, Qui, & Sey, 2007).

That said, when considering the role of ICTs both in social movements as well as in the larger processes of globalization, it is important to avoid the cyber-utopian arguments popularized during the Internet's widespread growth and development (Barber, 1995). While research has shown that ICTs can contribute to greater civic participation, they are only one of various factors (Boler, 2008). Moreover, given their relationship to social institutions, they can also be used to spread disinformation that can limit participation, as can digital divide issues that see offline social differentiation concerns being replicated online (van Dijk, 2005). We should also resist technological deterministic viewpoints on the role of ICTs, either in developing networked public spheres or in the interconnecting processes of globalization. Focusing solely on technology risks neglecting the role of other processes, such as capitalism and modernization (Hopper, 2007), while overemphasizing the impact of technology suggests that technological forms have their own inherent properties, a viewpoint that downplays or negates the role of human agency (Chadwick, 2006).

Nevertheless, communication technologies can be seen as contributing to the formation of cybercommunities in which, through the imagined presences in global cultural flows, connections across and into multiple social spaces are created (Chayko, 2002). Participants operating within these cybercommunities navigate what Chayko (2008) has described as a *sociomental space*, or the mental habitat where, as a cognitive analog to physical space, online (and increasingly mobile) communities gather. These online spaces allow not only for a mental mapping of social worlds, but also for the formation of *sociomental bonds* across distances, great or small, in the time-space compression of global interconnectivity (Harvey, 1989). Though these connections tend to be ephemeral, they can also help form the temporary, loose affiliations typical of social movements (Juris, 2008).

Mobilities

Additionally, the growth of mobilities fostered by rapidly developing and spreading wireless communication technologies has helped further overcome the frictions of distance at multiple scale levels (Urry, 2007). As a complication of theorizations of globalization such as Giddens', a mobilities sociological perspective should be seen as involving not dichotomous but diverse connections involving physical movement constituted through circulating entities (Urry). In this perspective, *presence* can be understood as intermittent, performed, and always interdependent with other processes of connections and communication. As a result, mobile technologies such as cell phones and wireless Internet connections can undermine set references of identity (Caron & Caronia, 2007). Whereas identity had come to be for most social actors in network societies the center around which individual and social meanings were organized and sustained across time and space (Castells, 1997), the *delocalizing* effect of mobilities has caused a further reconstitution of identity according to a new logic of *identifications* (Caron & Caronia). That is, being freed from most of the spatial and temporal constraints that govern our lives has changed both everyday interaction rituals as well as our larger shared cultural codes that, as discursive practices, constitute identity, resulting in a performative process of identifications in which language is central. What is more, this instability in the constitution of subjectivities, complicated by global flows and intensified by mobilities, has impelled the work of the imagination as a source of identity (Appadurai, 1996). Images, scripts, models, and narratives flowing through mass media help mark the imagination as a domain of social practice, and thus of agency negotiated against global fields of possibility (Appadurai). Though these symbolic processes are always connected to a physical configuration (Fornäs, 2002), the imaginary as a social collective can generate both a sense of community (Anderson, 2006) and multiple identifications across various networks, a possibility I explore in greater detail in Chapters 4 and 5.

CRITICAL DISCOURSE ANALYSIS: A CONTESTED RESEARCH APPROACH

Because my project, as explained above, engages topics, phenomena, and theories related not only to language, but to history, politics, communications, and sociology, I have chosen, in critical discourse analysis, a research approach that I believe is appropriately interdisciplinary. As Wodak has claimed, "every theoretical approach in CDA is inherently interdisciplinary because it aims at investigating complex social phenomena which are inherently inter- or transdisciplinary and certainly not to be studied by linguistics alone" (cited in Kendall, 2007, para. 30). Not all CDA researchers, however, agree on how that interdisciplinarity should be viewed. Fairclough (2005), for instance, has advocated for a transdisciplinary understanding of CDA that, unlike interdisciplinary perspectives, considers how one discipline may develop through the appropriation of resources and logics of those with which it has been combined. The suggestion that from this process a new theory could be formed presupposes, as he has claimed elsewhere (see Chouliaraki & Fairclough, 1999), that CDA is both a theory and a method, a position for which he has received considerable criticism (see Henderson, 2005), some of which I will address below. In contrast, van Leeuwen (2005) has proposed an integrationist model of interdisciplinarity for CDA. By integrationist he means not incorporating various theoretical frameworks and methodologies into one discipline, as in the centralist model, or gathering diverse disciplines into a framework as equal partners but without merging them, as in the pluralist model, but integrating disciplines so that they inform each other to address the complexity of problems.[9] Agreeing with van Leeuwen, I find it preferable that in this model the values and identities of the various disciplines combined are not subsumed into one or are merely the sum of their parts, but work together to address complex, interdisciplinary problems while accounting for shortcomings in individual theories and approaches. This is what I have aimed to do by integrating, for instance, social movement and new media theories with those of language, ideology, identity, and complementary approaches to discourse analysis.[10]

Method or Theory?

As the discussion above suggests, understandings of what CDA is and how it should be applied vary within its domains of application, even among some of its leading proponents. Yet, most generally agree that CDA is fundamentally concerned with analyzing structural relationships of dominance, discrimination, power, and control as manifested in language (Wodak & Meyer, 2009). According to Fairclough (2003), CDA research explicitly aims, through the close analysis of texts, to investigate critical social inequality as it is expressed, signaled, constituted, and legitimized by or in discourse. Similarly, van Dijk (2001a) has claimed that "CDA is a type of discourse analytical research that primarily studies the way social power abuse, dominance and inequality are enacted, reproduced and resisted by text and talk in the social and political context" (p. 352). That is, it not only focuses on texts but also requires a theorization and description of both the social processes and structures that give rise to the production of a text, and of the social structures and processes within which individuals or groups as social historical subjects create meanings in their interaction with texts (van Dijk, 2008a). For Benwell and Stokoe (2006), CDA is:

> a Foucauldian-inspired, interdisciplinary branch of linguistics that attempts to explore the ideological workings of language in representing the world. CDA begins from the determinist premise that language is not a neutral or transparent medium that unproblematically reflects an objective reality. (p. 43–44)

Beyond its orientation to Foucauldian theories, CDA also has its roots in Hallidayan functional systemic linguistics, classical rhetoric, text linguistics, sociolinguistics, applied linguistics, and pragmatics (Wodak & Meyer), as well as the critical linguistics of Fowler, Kress, and Hodge that emerged in the 1970s. Having developed from a critical view of formal linguistics' decontexualization of language and the corollary need for a new form of linguistics that would examine the relations between language and society (Hodge, 2012), approaches to CDA assume that language is a social phenomenon in which not only individuals, but also institutions and social groups express specific meanings and values in language in systematic ways.

By *critical*, CDA researchers mean the presupposition about the relationship between discourse, power, dominance, and social inequality as well as the analyst's position in such relationships (van Dijk, 2001b). Often focusing on social problems related to power, dominance, hegemony, ideology, class, gender, race, discrimination, interests, reproduction, institutions, social structure, and social order, CDA researchers try to link the micro- and macrostructures of social institutions and societies. In citing the intersection of discourse and social structure as characterized by dominance, they adopt overt emancipatory positions that are critical of the status quo. In part, this political engagement is rooted in Marxism as a social theory and tradition of critique, although CDA analysts would reject the notion of false consciousness in Marxist approaches to ideology as insufficiently complex (Wetherell, Taylor, & Yates, 2001). Instead they tend to favor more complex social theories of power and ideology that would also take into account, for instance, Foucault's formulations of *power/knowledge* and *orders of discourse*, Gramsci's concept of *hegemony*, and Althusser's notion of *interpellation* as well as Giddens' theory of *structuration* (Blommaert, 2005). By doing so, they distance themselves from the descriptivism of other forms of language and discourse studies and foreground their concerns for the social or ideological construction of reality while advocating intervention in the practices they critically examine as a means of support for those dominated or marginalized by the effects of power.

CDA focuses on *discourse*, rather than language, rejecting the notion in formal linguistics of language as a unitary object of study separated from society and thought (Hodge, 2012) in favor of the view that talk and text are the relevant units of language in communication (Wodak & Meyer, 2009). As CDA has developed as a research approach, this understanding of text has extended beyond written and oral modes to include the semiotic or multimodal forms of contemporary communication and interaction (Kress & van Leeuwen, 2001). Much, although not all, of CDA's approach to discourse stems from a Foucauldian orientation, which views discourse as constitutive of society and culture as well as of power relations, that is, a form of historical social action that does ideological work. Consequently, discourse is seen as a hidden or opaque form of power that CDA researchers aim to make more visible (Blommaert & Bulcean, 2000). Foucault saw discourse not as a group of signs or a stretch of text but as *discursive practices*. By this he meant the processes by which cultural meanings are produced and understood, the actions that construct and reflect social realities and systematically form the objects they speak of. This includes ideologies, power, and identities, which Foucault saw as inscribed in discourses, produced by dominant discourses linked to social relations and practices that constitute subjectivities (Benwell & Stokoe, 2006). Consequently, the discursive constructions of ideologies and identities, particularly in conjunction with the reproduction of social inequalities, is, together with analyses of power, a common focus of CDA-inspired research.

Criticisms of CDA

This common theoretical ground and range of interests have, to a large degree, established CDA as a research tool and mode of inquiry that, since its advent in the late 1980s, has grown in application and popularity (Hodge, 2012). As the field has matured, the research landscape has diversified, accommodating various approaches, including, among others, Reisigil and Wodak's discourse-historical approach, Jäger and Maier's Foucauldian dispositive analysis approach, van Dijk's sociocognitive approach, and Fairclough's dialectical-relational approach. These approaches share common theories, aims, and concerns, but they lack, as critics of CDA have pointed out, a unitary theoretical framework and analytical methodology (Breeze, 2012; Frantz, 2004). As a result, critics contend, despite the specificity of CDA's linguistic focus, its lack of systematic analysis and use of a range of theories of language (relying heavily instead on Hallidayan systemic-function linguistics) limit both the space and scope of analysis as well as its replicability (Blommaert, 2005; Toolan, 1997; Widdowson, 1998). All CDA approaches, though some more than others, employ a wide range of tools and strategies for close analysis of actual, contextualized uses of language that, when supported by sophisticated theorizations of the relationship between social practices and discourse structures, offer rich possibilities to examine an array of factors that exert an influence on texts, including patriarchy, racism, and hegemonic power relations (Lazar, 2005). But the vagueness of particular constructs and eclectic theories present operationalization problems as well as those of mediation, or relating the linguistic and social dimensions of analysis (Breeze; Wodak & Meyer, 2009). Consequently, though certain CDA theorists, such as Fairclough, have attracted more criticism than others, the field as a whole has largely been questioned as a legitimate field of academic inquiry.

In response, some critical discourse analysts, including Fairclough, have tried to systematize analytical approaches, although not always with a clear or substantiated backing for that system (Widdowson, 2000). For Jones (2007), this is problematic for several reasons. First, using grammar-based systemic functional linguistics (SFL) separates discourse from behavior, which, Jones has contended, is where bias, ideology, racism, and other concerns of CDA are located. Second, the inconsistency of communicative behaviors across contexts makes it "impossible to ascribe any general, invariable function value or effects to these acts, contrary to CDA's assumptions" (Jones, p. 359). This variability, like the charges of a lack of analytical rigor in the approach to text analysis, can make CDA hermeneutic and its findings no more than the analysts' interpretations (Toolan, 2007), although this problem, according to Chilton (2005), might be mitigated by further addressing the cognitive aspects of communication, as I have tried to do in this research. In addition, because of CDA's explicit political engagement and advocacy, which contradict principles of scientific objectivity, this interpretative mode, critics have argued, leads to *a priori* findings of questionable reliability and validity while attracting criticisms of bias (Widdowson, 1998; Wodak & Meyer, 2009). As Jones (2007) has also claimed, this critical stance fundamentally skews the analysis of communicative practices. Conversation analysts in particular have stridently rejected the view that an overt political stance should be part of analysis, claiming it produces a 'theoretical imperialism' and 'hegemony of the intellectuals' that may ultimately mean that the analyst is never surprised by the data and thus fails to contribute to describing the world (Schegloff, in Wetherell et al., 2001). Compounding these concerns, critics have claimed, is critical discourse analysts' use of large theoretical frameworks that tend not to fit the data, broad contexts to interpret texts, and vague positions toward what constitutes discourse (Widdowson, 1998). Relatedly, critics have raised questions regarding problems of scale, citing the lack of an explicit model of the various scales at which discursive practices occur, especially one that would capture the processes of social meaning in a complex, multiscalar world (Hodge, 2012). Similarly, Blommaert (2005) has argued that for all its focus on inequality, CDA research has typically been concentrated on objects of analysis from the global north and should have a broader, more latitudinarian approach.

The Sociocognitive Approach as a Way Forward

Certainly, the criticisms levied against CDA have been substantial, though they perhaps reflect no less a disciplinary 'turf war' than that waged by critical linguists against formal linguistics. If sound criticism, then, is meant to sharpen, not destroy, as I believe, I argue that it is wise in going forward with CDA-based research to heed these judgments without entirely capitulating to them. Therefore, in this work, I have used a composite interdisciplinary approach that draws on methods and theories of various CDA frameworks. I intend this not to be a further example of CDA's eclecticism and lack of theoretical rigor, but what I see as a means of addressing the weaknesses of one approach with the strengths of others, which is plausible given the common theoretical and methodological ground they share. That is, as van Dijk (2008b) has claimed, CDA is not a method but a domain of scholarly practice, a cross-discipline distributed all over the humanities and the social sciences, integrating many different methods of research, depending on the aims of the investigation, the nature of the data studied, the interests and the qualifications of the researcher, and other research parameters. I also take the position that CDA scholarship should not follow the approach of any particular researcher and instead be multidisciplinary, integrating the best work of various researchers from different disciplines and research trajectories (van Dijk). This is why I have formed the basis of my research framework on van Dijk's sociocognitive approach and complemented it with the strategies and methods of other leading CDA researchers whose work is relevant to research topic and questions as well as my datasets and their contexts.

The sociocognitive approach considers social cognition as the interface between society and discourse. Not only does this mitigate the general micro and macro concerns of social research, but it also addresses the key theoretical shortcoming of most critical discourse analysis research, the neglect of social cognition (van Dijk, 2009). If the aim of CDA is to relate discourse and society, it is necessary to also analyze the role of social representations in the minds of social actors (van Dijk). Integrating cognitive linguistics with a critical approach to discourse analysis also reinstates the mind into meaning (Hodge, 2012) in a way that might address Jones's (2007) concerns regarding behavior, not language, as the locus of ideology, bias, racism, and so forth. Similarly, as Hart (2012) has argued, cognitive linguistics provides a set of tools, as SFL does for linguistic analysis, for examining psychological strategies of manipulation in discourse that, when supporting CDA, can help make CDA more revealing and its claims better attested. For those reasons, to supplement my linguistic analyses, I have drawn on Chilton's (2004, 2005) cognitive-based approach to studying political discourse and, in particular, Hart's (2008) methods of analyzing metaphor based on conceptual blending theory, as I discuss in detail in Chapter 3.

In addition, while the sociocognitive approach requires a solid structural-functional linguistic basis, I have complemented its techniques and approaches of text analysis with Fairclough's (2001) orientation towards linguistic meaning and identity as social constructions and Foucauldian notions of power as reticulated and relational. As a potential counterweight to the interpretive nature of CDA's findings, I have also drawn on, for the analysis of legacy media discourse, corpus linguistics methodologies. The electronic text analysis of a corpus of news articles in Chapter 3 has arguably allowed me to broaden my empirical base while offering a quantitative perspective that can complement—or balance—the qualitative approach of CDA (Mautner, 2009). While the decontextualized language of corpus data is no substitute for context, it can, as Mautner has contended, still serve as comparative evidence. Furthermore, as March and Taylor (2009) have shown, while combining corpus linguistics with CDA guarantees neither validity nor neutrality, it can offer researchers analytical depth and creative potential, or, as Adolphs (2006) has argued, a quantitative analysis as "a way into a more qualitative, functional analysis" (p. 119). Additionally, when analyzing the visual rhetoric and social semiotics of protesters' Flickr and YouTube uploads, I have drawn on the approach to analyzing multimodal discourse outlined by Kress and van Leeuwen (2001).

Although the sociocognitive approach foregrounds the importance of context, Weiss and Wodak's (2003) triangulatory method offers perhaps a more rigorous way of handing the various contextual layers involved in this research. Following their approach, I have accounted for four levels of context: (1) the microlevel linguistic analyses of the texts, (2) intertextual and interdiscursive relationships, (3) the extralinguistic sociological variables in a specific context, and (4) the broader sociopolitical and historical contexts in which the discursive practices are embedded. As a further move toward integrative interdisciplinarity, I have also supplemented my approach with the social movement research design and cyber-archaeology for text collection methods advocated by Zimbra, Chen, and Abbasi (2010). Their framework has three phases: (1) identification of research focus (social movement of interest, associated virtual communities, and target cyber-artifacts); (2) artifact collection; and (3) analysis from social movement theory perspectives—in my case, the theoretical framework of social movement cycles outlined by Poulson (2005). Yet, because the emphasis of my research is less on the Iranian election protests as a social movement and more as an opportunity to examine discursive practices and global vernaculars in transnational public spheres, I have focused in the third phase on how protesters, as collective actors, used symbolic resources and globalized vernaculars to discursively construct their movement together with their ideologies and identities. Finally, I intend that by focusing on discourse circulating out of both Iran and multiple global contexts, I have worked toward addressing Blommaert's (2005) concern regarding the typical global north insularity of CDA-based research.

The criticisms of CDA discussed above are well considered and important, particularly the claim that results solely based on interpretation are neither replicable nor generalizable. Certainly, in many disciplines, this would make CDA-derived findings little more than a set of conjectures, grounded in and informed by theory, but not scientifically objective. While these postulations might echo or reinforce those made by other researchers, perhaps like claims from the interpretation of history or literary texts, they could also contribute to reification or the stabilizing of attested bodies of knowledge (Laclau & Mouffe, 1985). It would seem, then, that findings of CDA-based research hold little scientific value, that CDA is, at best, a 'soft science.' If so, why should analysts even bother? First, it must be acknowledged, by both proponents and critics of CDA, that observer bias is unavoidable, even in scientific disciplines. That is, arguing against the possibility of true objectivity is, in my view, little more than pandering to notions of philosophical relativism, with any arguments made regarding truth necessarily understood less as judgments and more as the bringing to bear of an informed individual perspective on a particular issue in the public sphere. Moreover, I hold that any attempt at denying subjectivity and reflexivity in research fails to account for the complex relations between discourse and society in which the researcher is inextricably enmeshed (Bourdieu, 1990). Instead, CDA researchers should simply account for their biases in their research, as van Dijk (2001a) has argued:

> Crucial for critical discourse analysts is the explicit awareness of their role in society. Continuing a tradition that rejects the possibility of a 'value-free' science, they argue that science, and especially scholarly discourse, are inherently part of, and influenced by social structure, and produced in social interaction. Instead of denying or ignoring such a relation between scholarship and society, they plead that such relations be studied and accounted for in their own right, and that scholarly practices should be based on such insights. Theory formation, description

and explanation, also in discourse analysis, are sociopolitically 'situated', whether we like it or not. (p. 352)

Second, value-based interpretation is accepted in other disciplines, including cultural and literary studies. What this comparison perhaps, then, suggests is that CDA is not a science but a way of knowing among other ways of knowing, a mode of inquiry which, like other modes of inquiry, suggests an understanding of certain phenomena rather than indisputable facts about the world. Accordingly, the findings of our studies, including this one, might therefore be seen as arguments made in an ongoing conversation about the world and, specifically, the global transformation of society (Maingueneau, 2006). That is, though speculative, the claims of CDA retain their critical 'power' by suggesting the connections between social practices and interests, whether of dominating or dominated groups, as directions for other forms of social research and praxis (Maingueneau). Like the findings of ethnographic studies, they might even be formative of social theories, providing a measure of empirical support (van Leeuwen, 2005), just not theories themselves (Widdowson, 1998). In short, I see CDA's weakness less in its lack of methodological rigor, which can at least be partially addressed, than in the overvaluing of its findings, though that does not negate its value as a research tool, a claim I take up in Chapter 5.

COUNTERPOWER AND COERCION, WINNERS AND LOSERS: CONCLUSIONS

Activists' use of social media during the 2009 Iranian presidential election protests arguably extended their relational capacity—among each other, the Iranian diaspora, and empathetic activists around the globe—and thus became a source of counterpower. Moreover, it challenged the coercive force of the state's non-social relationships, lodged in both the government and the ruling mullahs, and its structural domination backed by violence. In a sense, although the anonymity and profligacy of social media often minimize or obviate social actors' individual identities, the repetition of discursive practices across social media forms can both aggrandize protesters' collective agency and, perhaps ironically, humanize that counterpower. For even when networks become large and seemingly faceless, they remain social, and network connections, whether at the busiest nodes or an outlying, fractal edge, are social connections premised on communication. On the contrary, the relational capacity of an institution, such as a state government, whether viewed in its capillaries or its *dispositifs*, coheres in discourse, through practice across time and space, unhinged from individual actors and collective social imaginaries. Indeed, this somewhat spectral dispersion of power throughout society is what made such power so effective, encompassing, and, one might say, insidious.

Yet, as a potential form of resistance against this perfidy is the possibility of communication power as a form of counterpower. As Castells (2009) has argued, "to challenge existing power relationships, it is necessary to produce alternative discourses that have the potential to overwhelm the disciplinary capacity of the state as a necessary step to neutralizing its use of violence" (p. 16). Certainly, such alternative discourses could circulate in the spaces for rhetorical dissent created, in part, by the Khatami reforms. Communication within these spaces can invigorate a public sphere. Or, when paralleling the rise of online culture and new media, it may animate multiple, reticulated public spheres networked both inside and outside nation-state boundaries, even though it may not directly lead to social action or change (Howard, 2010). As this discourse circulates across *rhizomatic networks*, pulsating at the nodes, vibrating across the transnational imaginary worlds of social agents (Appadurai, 1996; Juris, 2008), it may generate possibilities for new identifications that could influence future actions, a consideration at the heart of the analyses in the following chapters.

To examine the discourse inherent in and constitutive of these complex social relations and possibilities, I have made the argument that CDA offers suitable theoretical and methodological purchase, albeit, as its critics have justly shown, a sometimes precarious one. A sociocognitive approach to CDA that dynamically blends top-down cognitive mental models with the bottom-up understandings of meaning making as social action seems especially pertinent to understanding the role of discourse in shaping the *sociomental spaces* of social movements in which networked identifications might be formed. Whether or not these understandings, or the interpretative findings of CDA research upon which they are founded, can be said to be truly liberatory if they offer little reliability or validity, they can nevertheless be of significant critical value. By pointing out directions for other forms of research in the human and social sciences as part of the larger project of social transformation (Maingueneau, 2006), they help sustain the belief that the social production of meaning is more influential and important than social production of coercion (Castells, 2010). Yet, perhaps a more important consideration of value is that of the protesters' and activists' discursive practices I have examined. According to Blommaert (2010), globalization has created

> new and complex markets for linguistic and communicative resources . . . [that] include winners and losers, and many people nowadays find their linguistic resources to be of very low value in globalized environments. (p. 3)

If so, why, then, were many of the activists and protesters who used social media, at least from a communicative standpoint, 'winners'? That is, were they only successful in communicating across cross-contextual networks by using elite pathways within those global flows? Was it only because those addressing that global audience did so in English, a current global 'network standard' of communication (Grewal, 2008)? Or did their networked identifications resonate with ideological interests that allowed their mobile voices to be readily amplified by mainstream Western legacy media? And if so, does that complicate the potentially liberating process of opening up sociomental spaces in collective imaginaries through this communication? Before taking up these considerations, however, it is important to establish how, within the forces of communication power expressed in the government-media nexus, protesters were created as subjects in the ideological discourse of U.S. news media covering the 2009 election crisis, a subject I take up in the next chapter.

NOTES

1. The Iranian Guardian Council is composed of 12 legal experts who are responsible for interpreting the Iranian constitution, a duty which includes approving presidential candidates and supervising elections (Keddie, 2003).
2. The actual number of Twitter users tweeting from Iran during the protests is unclear. Twitter features allow users to identify their location in their account profile, but numerous activists living outside Iran reset their user location to Iran during the protests as a sign of solidarity and to help thwart the government's efforts to identify and locate social movement leaders through their Twitter accounts.
3. The entire corpus of tweets used in this study listed in Appendix A.
4. In Twitter, a hashtag is a word or phrased prefixed with the symbol # and used, like a keyword, as a bottom-up means of classifying the message in which it appears. In my research, I have limited my data to the #IranElection hashtag, which was one of the most widely used by protesters (and those sympathetic to them) and, at the time of writing, is still active.
5. Although this chant, in Persian, *Marg bar Diktator*, is usually translated in the U.S. media as "Death to the Dictator," some have argued that it should be rendered as "Down with the Dictator." Accordingly, Iranian protesters' chants of *Marg bar Amrika*, which are commonly reported as "Death to America," would be softened to "Down with America." Some argue that the former translation has been preferred by the media for its polarizing effect and the ideologies such an effect might support. Interestingly, support for the latter version has come from reports in response to Ahmadinejad handing out potatoes to opposition protesters, who were rallying against rising food prices during his 2009 campaign and shouting, *Marg bar sibzamini*, or "Death to potatoes." While ironic, this is a less likely translation than "Down with potatoes," although a figurative sense of *death* as in "I'm sick to *death* of these potatoes" is also possible (Mackey, 2009; Tait, 2009).
6. Source: http://news.bbc.co.uk/2/hi/middle_east/6240287.stm. Uploaded January 26, 2013.
7. Here, and in the analyses that follow, I have anonymized Twitter users' account names.
8. As needed, I also discuss relevant theories and aspects of globalization in later chapters as a means to explain my data analyses.
9. For me, the crucial distinction between van Leeuwen's integrationist view and Fairclough's transdisciplinarity is that while the latter propounds that integrated research resources could be fused, rather alchemically, into a new

theory, the former only seeks a weaving of theory that can—and maybe should—be undone once a project has ended.

10. Taking a complementary approach has been commonly done since the development of CDA as a research tool. See, for example, Fowler (1991) on news discourse, Fairclough (2006) on neoliberal discourse, Thurlow (2006) on new media language, and Pennycook (2007) on global English.

REFERENCES

Addis, C. (2009). *Iran's 2009 presidential elections*. Washington, DC: Congressional Research Service.

Adolphs, S. (2006). *Introducing electronic text analysis*. London: Routledge.

Albrow, M. (1997). *The global age*. Stanford, CA: Stanford University Press.

Anderson, B. (2006). *Imagined communities: Reflections on the origins and spread of nationalism* (3rd ed.). London: Verso.

Ansari, A. (2000). *Iran, Islam and democracy: The politics of managing change*. London: Royal Institute of International Affairs.

Appadurai, A. (1996). *Modernity at large: Cultural dimensions of globalization*. Minneapolis: University of Minnesota Press.

Azimi, F. (2008). *The quest for democracy in Iran: A century of struggle against authoritarian rule*. Cambridge, MA: Harvard University Press.

Barber, B. (1995). *Jihad vs. McWorld*. New York: Random House.

Benwell, B., & Stokoe, E. (2006). *Discourse and identity*. Edinburgh: Edinburgh University Press.

Billig, M. (1995). *Banal nationalism*. London: SAGE.

Blommaert, J., & Bulcaen, C. (2000). Critical discourse analysis. *Annual Review of Anthropology, 29,* 447–466.

Blommaert, J. (2005). *Discourse*. Cambridge: Cambridge University Press.

Blommaert, J. (2008). *Notes on power. Working papers in language diversity*. Jyväskylä, Finland: University of Jyväskylä.

Blommaert, J. (2010). *The sociolinguistics of globalization*. Cambridge: Cambridge University Press.

Bohman, J. (2004). Expanding dialogue: The Internet, the public sphere and prospects for transnational democracy. In N. Crossley & J. Roberts (Eds.), *After Habermas: New perspectives on the public sphere* (pp. 131–156). Oxford: Blackwell Publishing.

Boler, M. (Ed.). (2008). *Digital media and democracy: Tactics in hard times*. Cambridge, MA: MIT Press.

Bourdieu, P. (1990). *The logic of practice*. Stanford, CA: Stanford University Press.

Bourdieu, P. (1991). *Language and symbolic power* (J.B. Thompson, Trans.). Cambridge, MA: Harvard University Press.

Bray, H. (2009, June 19). Finding a way around Iranian censorship: Activists utilize Twitter, web tricks to sidestep blocks. *Boston Globe*. Retrieved November 27, 2010 from www.boston.com.

Breeze, R. (2012). Critical discourse analysis and its critics. *Pragmatics, 21*(4), 493–525.

Caron, A., & Caronia, L. (2007). *Moving cultures: Mobile communication and everyday life*. Montreal & Kingston: McGill-Queen's University Press.

Castells, M. (1996). *The information age: Economy, society, and culture. The rise of the network society, vol. 1*. Cambridge, MA: Blackwell.

Castells, M. (1997). *The power of identity. The information age: Economy, society and culture, vol. 2*. Malden, MA: Blackwell.

Castells, M. (2009). *Communication power.* New York: Oxford University Press.

Castells, M. (2010). Communication, power, and counterpower in the network society. Seattle: University of Washington. (Lecture).

Castells, M., Fernandez-Ardevol, M., Qui, J., & Sey, A. (2007). *Mobile communication and society: A global perspective.* Cambridge, MA: MIT Press.

Chadwick, A. (2006). *Internet politics: States, citizens, and new communication technologies.* New York: Oxford University Press.

Chayko, M. (2002). *Connecting: How we form social bonds and communities in the Internet age.* Albany: State University of New York Press.

Chayko, M. (2008). *Portable communities: The social dynamics of online and mobile connections.* Albany: SUNY Press.

Chilton, P. (2004). *Analyzing political discourse: Theory and practice.* London: Routledge.

Chilton, P. (2005). Missing links in mainstream CDA: Modules, blends and the critical instinct. In R. Wodak & P. Chilton (Eds.), *A new agenda in (critical) discourse analysis: Theory, methodology and interdisciplinarity* (pp. 19–52). Philadelphia: John Benjamins.

Chouliarki, L., & Fairclough, N. (1999). *Discourse in late modernity: Rethinking critical discourse analysis.* Edinburgh: Edinburgh University Press.

Crack, A. (2008). *Global communication and transnational public spheres.* New York: Palgrave.

Crystal, D. (2003). *English as a global language.* Cambridge: Cambridge University Press.

Dabashi, H. (2010). *Iran, the Green Movement and the USA: The fox and the paradox.* London: Zed Books.

de Certeau, M. (1984). *The practice of everyday life.* Berkeley: University of California Press.

el-Nawawy, M. (2010). The 2009 Iranian presidential election in the coverage of CNN and Al-Jazeera English websites. In Y. Kamalipour (Ed.), *Media, power, and politics in the digital age: The 2009 presidential election uprising in Iran* (pp. 3–14). Lanham, MD: Rowman & Littlefield.

Fairclough, N. (2001). *Language and power* (2nd ed.). Essex: Pearson Education Ltd.

Fairclough, N. (2003). *Analyzing discourse: Textual analysis for social research.* London: Routledge.

Fairclough, N. (2005). Critical discourse analysis in transdisciplinary research. In R. Wodak & P. Chilton (Eds.), *A new agenda in (critical) discourse analysis: Theory, methodology and interdisciplinarity* (pp. 53–70). Philadelphia: John Benjamins.

Fairclough, N. (2006). *Language and globalization.* New York: Routledge.

Featherstone, M. (1995). *Undoing culture: Globalization, postmodernism, and identity.* Thousand Oaks, CA: SAGE Publications.

Featherstone, M., & Lash, S. (1999). *Spaces of culture: City, nation, world.* London: SAGE.

Fornäs, J. (2002). *Digital borderlands: Cultural studies of identity and interactivity on the Internet.* New York: Peter Lang.

Foucault, M. (1972). *The archaeology of knowledge and the discourse on language.* New York: Pantheon Books. (Original work published in 1971.)

Foucault, M. (1978). *The history of sexuality* (Vol. 1). New York: Vintage.

Fowler, R. (1991). *Language in the news: Discourse and ideology in the press.* London: Routledge.

Frantz, R. (2004). *In defense of critical discourse analysis.* Retrieved February 21, 2009 from www.tc.columbia.edu/tesolalwebjournal/frantz.pdf

Fraser, N. (1992). Rethinking the public sphere: A contribution to the critique of actually existing democracy. In C. Calhoun (Ed.), *Habermas and the public sphere* (pp. 109–142). Cambridge, MA: MIT Press.

Gee, J. P. (2005). *An introduction to discourse analysis: Theory and method.* New York: Routledge.

Gheissari, A., & Nasr, V. (2006). *Democracy in Iran: History and the quest for liberty.* New York: Oxford University Press.

Giddens, A. (1984). *The constitution of society.* Berkeley: University of California Press.

Giddens, A. (1990). *The consequences of modernity.* Stanford, CA: Stanford University Press.

Giddens, A. (1991). *Modernity and self-identity: Self and society in the late modern age.* Stanford, CA: Stanford University Press.

Graddol, D. (2007). *English next.* London: British Council.

Gramsci, A. (2003). *Selections from the prison notebooks of Antonio Gramsci* (Q. Hoare & G. Nowell-Smith, Trans.). New York: International.

Grewal, D. S. (2008). *Network power: The social dynamics of globalization.* New Haven, CT: Yale University Press.

Habermas, J. (1975). *Legitimation crisis* (T. McCarthy, Trans.). Boston: Beacon Press.

Habermas, J. (1991). *The structural transformation of the public sphere: An inquiry into a category of bourgeois society.* Boston: MIT Press.

Hardt, M., & Negri, A. (2000). *Empire.* Cambridge, MA: Harvard University Press.

Hart, C. (2008). Critical discourse analysis and metaphor: Toward a theoretical framework. *Critical Discourse Studies, 5*(2), 91–106.

Hart, C. (2012). Analyzing political discourse. *Critical Discourse Studies, 2*(2), 189–195.

Harvey, D. (1989). *The condition of postmodernity.* Oxford: Blackwell.

Hauser, G. (1999). *Vernacular voices: The rhetorics of publics and public spheres.* Columbia: University of South Carolina Press.

Henderson, R. (2005). A Faircloughian approach to CDA: Principled eclecticism or a method for a theory? *Melbourne Studies in Education, 46*(2), 9–24.

Hodge, B. (2012). Ideology, identity, interaction: Contradictions and challenges for critical discourse analysis. *Critical Approaches to Discourse Analysis Across Disciplines, 5*(2), 1–18.

Hopper, P. (2007). *Understanding cultural globalization.* Cambridge: Polity.

Howard, P. N. (2010). *The digital origins of dictatorship and democracy: Information technology and political Islam.* Oxford: Oxford University Press.

Jenkins, H. (2006). *Convergence culture: Where old and new media collide.* New York: New York University Press.

Jones, P. (2007). Why there is no such thing as "critical discourse analysis." *Language and Communication, 27,* 337–388.

Juris, J. (2008). *Networking futures: The movements against corporate globalization.* Durham, NC: Duke University Press.

Kamalipour, Y. (Ed.). (2010). *Media, power, and politics in the digital age: The 2009 presidential election uprising in Iran.* Lanham, MD: Rowman & Littlefield.

Keddie, N. (2003). *Modern Iran: Roots and results of revolution.* New Haven/London: Yale University Press.

Kendall, G. (2007). What is critical discourse analysis? Ruth Wodak in conversation with Gavin Kendall. *Forum: Qualitative Social Research, 8*(2). Retrieved November 18, 2009 from http://nbn-resolving.de/urn:nbn:de:0114-fqs0702297

Kress, G., & van Leeuwen, T. (2001). *Multimodal discourse: The modes and media of contemporary communication.* London: Arnold.

Laclau, E., & Mouffe, C. (1985). *Hegemony and socialist strategy: Towards a radical democratic politics.* London: Verso.

Lash, S. (2002). *The critique of information.* London: SAGE.

Lazar, M. M. (2005). *Feminist critical discourse analysis: Gender, power, and ideology in discourse.* Basingstoke, UK: Palgrave Macmillan.

Mackey, R. (2009, July 20). *For Iran's opposition, 'Death to Russia' is the new 'Death to America.'* Message posted to: http://thelede.blogs.nytimes.com.

Maingueneau, D. (2006). Is discourse analysis critical? *Critical Discourse Studies, 3*(2), 229–235.

March, A., & Taylor, C. (2009). If on a winter's night two researchers . . . A challenge to assumptions of soundness of interpretation. *Critical Approaches to Discourse Analysis Across Disciplines, 3*(1), 1–20.

Mautner, G. (2009). Checks and balances: How corpus linguistics can contribute to CDA. In R. Wodak & M. Meyers (Eds.), *Methods of critical discourse analysis* (2nd ed.). London: SAGE.

Mittelman, J. (2004). *Wither globalization: The vortex of knowledge and ideology.* New York: Routledge.

Morozov, E. (2011). *The net delusion: The dark side of Internet freedom.* New York: Public Affairs.

Pennycook, A. (1994). *The cultural politics of English as an international language.* London: Longman.

Pennycook, A. (2007). *Global Englishes and transcultural flows.* London: Routledge.

Poulson, S. (2005). *Social movements in twentieth-century Iran: Culture, ideology, and mobilizing frameworks.* Lanham, MD: Lexington Books.

Robbins, K., & Webster, F. (2006). From public sphere to cybernetic state. In. R. Hassan & J. Thomas (Eds.), *The new media theory reader* (pp. 92–100). London: Open University Press.

Robertson, R. (1995). Glocalization: Time-space and homogeneity-heterogenity. In M. Featherstone, S. Lash, & R. Robertson (Eds.), *Global modernities* (pp. 25–44). London: SAGE.

Scholte, J. A. (2005). *Globalization: A critical introduction* (2nd ed.). New York: Palgrave Macmillan.

Semati, M. (Ed.). (2008). *Media, culture and society in Iran: Living with globalization and the Islamic state.* New York: Routledge.

Tait, R. (2009, May 14). Spuds of wrath: Potatoes-for-votes protests blights Iranian election. *The Guardian.* Retrieved March 23, 2013 from www.guardian.co.uk.

Tazimi, G. (2012). *Revolution and reform in Russian and Iran: Modernization and politics in revolutionary states.* New York: I. B. Tauris.

Thurlow, C. (2006). From statistical panic to moral panic: The metadiscursive construction and popular exaggeration of new media language in the print media. *Journal of Computer-Mediated Communication, 11,* 667–701.

Tomlinson, J. (1999). *Globalization and culture.* Chicago: University of Chicago Press.

Toolan, M. (1997). What is critical discourse analysis and why are people saying terrible things about it? *Language and Literature, 6,* 83–103.

Urry, J. (2007). *Mobilities.* Malden, MA: Polity Press.

van Dijk, J. (2005). *The deepening divide: Inequality in the information society.* Thousand Oaks, Calif: SAGE.

van Dijk, T. (2001a). Critical discourse analysis. In D. Schiffrin, D. Tannen, & H. E. Hamilton (Eds.), *The handbook of discourse analysis* (pp. 352–371). Malden, MA: Blackwell.

van Dijk, T. (2001b). Principles of critical discourse analysis. In M. Wetherell, S. Taylor, & S. Yates (Eds.), *Discourse theory and practice* (pp. 300–317). London: SAGE.

van Dijk, T. (2008a). *Discourse and context: A socio-cognitive approach.* Cambridge: Cambridge University Press.

van Dijk, T. A. (2008b). *Discourse and power.* Houndmills, Basingstoke, Hampshire: Palgrave Macmillan.

van Dijk, T. (2009). Critical discourse studies: A sociocognitive approach. In R. Wodak & M. Meyer (Eds.), *Methods of critical discourse analysis* (2nd ed.; pp. 62–86). London: SAGE.

van Leeuwen, T. (2005). Three models of interdisciplinarity. In R. Wodak & P. Chilton (Eds.), *A new agenda in (critical) discourse analysis: Theory, methodology and interdisciplinarity* (pp. 3–18). Philadelphia: John Benjamins.

Varzi, R. (2006). *Warring souls: Youth, media, and martyrdom in post-revolution Iran.* Durham, NC: Duke University Press.

Warner, M. (2002). *Publics and counterpublics.* New York: Zone Books.

Weiss, G., & Wodak, R. (2003). *Critical discourse analysis: Theory and interdisciplinarity.* Houndmills, Basingstoke, Hampshire: Palgrave Macmillan.

Wetherell, M., Taylor, S., & Yates, S. (Eds.). (2001). *Discourse theory and practice.* London: SAGE.

Widdowson, H.G. (1998). The theory and practice of critical discourse analysis. *Applied Linguistics, 19*(1), 136–151.

Widdowson, H.G. (2000). On the limitations of linguistics applied. *Applied Linguistics, 21*(1), 3–25.

Wodak, R., & Meyer, M. (2009). *Methods of critical discourse analysis* (2nd ed.). London: SAGE.

Yaghmaian, B. (2002). *Social change in Iran: An eyewitness account of dissent, defiance, and new movements for rights.* Albany: State University of New York Press.

Zimbra, D., Chen, H., & Abbasi, A. (2010). A cyber-archeology approach to social movement research: A framework and case study. *Journal of Computer-Mediated Communication, 16,* 48–70.

3 Constructing the Protesters' Identities in the U.S. Media

In a June 13, 2009 report on the Iranian election crisis, the *New York Times* pitted the "conflicting claims" of Ahmadinejad supporters calling for order and the ratification of the election results against those of opposition demonstrators charging "election irregularities" (Worth & Fathi, 2009, June 12). The following day, as clashes broke out between protesters and government forces in what called "the most intense protests [in Iran] for a decade," their coverage broadened to include scenes of violence and "turmoil" in graphic language that added expressive force to the established news frame (Johnson-Cartee, 2005; Worth & Fathi, 2009, June 14). This frame was further expanded a few days later, first, with reports of complaints in Twitter feeds regarding CNN's lack of coverage on Iran, then, on the growing use of social networks in the demonstration, though it rejected Sullivan's 'Twitter Revolution' label as a "cliché" (Stelter & Stone, 2009, June 18).[1] Although Twitter had largely inspired negative responses from legacy media before 2009 (Arceneaux-Schmitz Weiss, 2010), the *Times* did not dismiss the microblogging service as a whole. Instead, it identified some of the most popular feeds and hashtags being used in conjunction with the protests. It explained as well what Twitter was and how it worked, an inclusion which suggests how far, at the time, Twitter had penetrated mainstream culture. Other mainstream media sources also began covering the demonstrators' use of social media. This added consonance to the newsworthiness of this subnarrative in the larger news frame, which, in turn, magnified the subtle indexing of the link between the opposition demonstrators and, through their use of U.S.-based social media, the West (Entman, 2004; Johnson-Cartee, 2005). In fact, despite the *New York Times'* perhaps more cautious referencing of the Twitter Revolution as a cliché, this subnarrative in the election crisis news frame expanded in scope, both in legacy and in new media outlets, as the protests continued. Meanwhile, Sullivan continued touting Twitter's value as a critical organizing tool, and activists encouraged Twitter users to set their backgrounds to green as a sign of solidarity with the Green Movement.

But not all mainstream media agreed that 'the revolution would be tweeted,' as Sullivan (2009) had claimed, nor did they all see this coverage as just another angle in a larger news story. For *New Yorker* columnist Malcolm Gladwell (2010, 2011), the use of social media during the Iranian protests and Arab Spring uprisings was the least interesting aspect of these movements, given that Twitter and Facebook use was relatively low in countries where these protests occurred and—above all, Gladwell pointed out—the risks opposition demonstrators undertook in protesting. Saying that television news couldn't "get enough of [the Twitter Revolution] cliché," *New York Times* opinion columnist Frank Rich (2011) took a similar tack, arguing that attention paid to the role of social media in the protests grew out of legacy media's commercial and economic interests as they sought to compete with the rising power and cultural cachet of web-based media—to appear 'in the know' about social media as a means of appealing to the demographic most actively using it then. Even more vocal in challenging the cyber-optimistic evaluations of the role of social media in the protests, Morozov (2011) lambasted the media's Twitter Revolution labels as cyber-utopian, arguing:

> If anything, Iran's Twitter Revolution revealed the intense longing for a world where information technology is the liberator rather than the oppressor, a world where technology could be harvested to spread democracy around the globe rather than entrench existing autocracies. (p. 5)

If the celebratory media clichés declaiming a Twitter Revolution are a further instance of capitalist triumphalism in a globalized information society, they might also reflect what Russell and Echchaibi (2009) have claimed is the West's post–Cold War sense of superiority toward the rest of the world. Morozov's claim for a similarly ideological reading of the 2009 Iranian presidential election protests also indexes the complex historical and political relationship that has existed between the United States and Iran.

With these concerns in mind, I present in this chapter a critical discourse analysis (CDA) of a corpus of U.S. legacy newspaper articles on the key events of the 2009 Iranian elections and the protests that followed. Following the sociocognitive approach to CDA argued for above, I analyze a corpus of news reports, focusing on the discursive constructions of subjectivities and subject positions for the protesters and the defeated reformist candidate and opposition leader Mir-Hossein Mousavi. Through my analyses, which I attempt to triangulate with the contextual analyses presented in Chapter 2 and the selected use of corpus analyses, I intend to show that shifts in the protesters' discursive subject positions arguably index larger ideological constructions in the news discourse. Specifically, I argue that Iranian activists' identities are discursively constructed to positively correlate with hegemonic Western perspectives in ways that suggest particular U.S. responses to the Iranian election crisis. Before presenting these analyses and arguments, I first give a brief historical overview of U.S.-Iranian relations. In doing so, I aim to show how this context could constrain the news discourse and shape readers' uptake according to their ideological perspectives. Afterward, I present the theoretical and methodological arguments for analyzing ideology in discourse.

A CONTENTIOUS COUPLE: AN OVERVIEW OF RECENT U.S.-IRANIAN RELATIONS

The relationship between Iran and the United States significantly intensified after World War I. As the United States began to assert itself further on the global stage, Iran, after it ceased to be a British protectorate in the 1920s, turned to the U.S. for aid and backing, which readily offered in exchange for access to oil (Keddie, 2003). This influence grew during the Second World War, when Allied pressure forced the Shah Reza, the Iranian monarch and political leader and father of Mohammad Reza, to abdicate, after which Iran was divided by the Allies into zones of influence and control. As American troops arrived with war supplies, American officials took charge of key Iranian economic departments, while American oil companies, along with the Soviet Union, began negotiating in Iran for oil concessions. After the war, the U.S. maintained its political and economic interests in Iran, with the Central Intelligence Agency (CIA) participating in the 1953 *coup d'état* that brought about the overthrow of a democratically elected government, converted Shah Mohammad Reza from a constitutional to an absolute monarch, and shifted control of half of Iran's oil production to the hands of the world oil cartel companies (Kurzman, 2004). In Iran, the CIA's involvement in the coup, along with that of the British, was widely known, causing Iranian public opinion toward the U.S. to plummet dramatically while helping to ensure a quarter century of authoritarian rule. With the U.S. heavily influencing the Iranian government and military through advice and support, Shah Mohammad Reza established oil and strategic policies that favored U.S. political and economic interests. American oil companies, controlling up to 40% of consortium sales of Iranian oil, profited heavily, as did manufacturers of sophisticated military equipment, which the Shah began purchasing heavily (Keddie). A well-armed Iran served the U.S.'s regional Cold War interests, fighting communist rebels and helping to maintain stability in the volatile Middle East.

That stability ended when the 1979 Iranian Islamic Revolution toppled Shah Mohammad Reza, America's strongest and most loyal ally in the region at the time. Led by exiled spiritual leader Ayatollah Khomeini, the revolution came as a shock both to the U.S. and the West given the Shah's substantial military resources and well-armed internal security forces, along with his U.S. backing (Kurzman, 2004). Blaming the U.S. for Iran's problems, a student group affiliated with the revolution overran and occupied the U.S. Embassy in Tehran on November 4, 1979, taking 52 Americans hostage and capturing the world's attention by humiliating one of the world's superpowers. The resulting 444-day hostage crisis brought U.S.-Iranian relations to its lowest point. Khomeini, after initially wanting to distance himself from the students' actions, which he had not approved beforehand, ultimately used the student takeover as a political opportunity to advance his political vision for Iran, and the hostage crisis proved a massive humiliation of a global superpower by a so-called Third World nation (Axworthy, 2013; Kurzman).

In the era that followed, U.S.-Iranian relations were largely marked by, on the one hand, the Iran-Contra Affair, in which the U.S. sold arms to Iran and funneled profits to finance the Nicaraguan Contra rebels after Congress had cut off legal funding, and, on the other hand, the devastating Iran–Iraq war, during which the U.S. supported the Iraqis. This intervention created widespread resentment among an Iranian population deeply scarred by the terror and tragedies of a war in which Iran suffered devastating economic losses and upward of one million casualties, some to chemical weapons. Few Iranians survived untouched by a conflict that had made their generation a highly ideological one, with anti-American resentment high for the support given to their opponents. This feeling abated, though only slightly, during the 1990s with the election of the moderate, outward-looking Khatami to the Iranian presidency and the Clinton administration's adoption of a dual-containment policy toward Iraq and Iran that included partial economic sanctions against both countries while fending off Iran's hostility toward the Arab-Israeli peace process. After 9/11, Iran supported the Northern Alliance in Afghanistan in its fight against the Taliban, which indirectly supported U.S. interests, suggesting a possible détente between the two countries. However, when, shortly after, then–President George W. Bush aligned Iran with those countries he dubbed the 'Axis of Evil,' any feeling of trust or respect in Iran toward the U.S. rapidly dissolved into enmity.

At the time of the 2009 election crisis, therefore, U.S.-Iranian relations remained severely strained. In the U.S., this was largely due to the opposition to the incumbent Iranian president Mahmoud Ahmadinejad's hardline stance, his provocative threats toward regional U.S. allies, particularly Israel and economic and military support for Hezbollah, the Islamic militant group and political party, and Iran's continued development of its nuclear program despite massive global economic sanctions. As a result of Iran's refusal to comply with United Nations Security Council resolutions aimed at halting its development of weapons-grade enriched uranium, the somewhat softened discourse of the early stages of the first Obama administration, which sought diplomatic engagement with Iran, became increasingly strident. Obama has called for further crippling economic sanctions and a 'nothing off the table' diplomatic policy that could include military intervention should Iran continue to resist full compliance with UN resolutions. This geopolitical tension, along with U.S. pressure on its allies, including the European Union, to uphold crippling sanctions, has polarized domestic

Iranian views. On the one hand, because of what seems yet another attempt by the West to influence and control Iran, some Iranians have hardened their anti-U.S. stance while supporting their national nuclear program. On the other hand, the largely negative experience of clerical government has produced an attitudinal shift that has seen, in certain sectors, an increasingly favorable opinion of the U.S., with some, fueled by the Iranian diaspora, feeling nostalgic for the cultural freedoms of the Shah Mohammad Reza era (Gheissari & Nasr, 2006). Yet, after struggling against foreign control for more than a century, and having been burned by the U.S. in the past, that upswing in popularity remains tenuous. Meanwhile, in the U.S., persistent media labels of Iran as a theocratic or fundamentalist society or, in Bush-era discourse, a 'rogue nation,' continue to feed hegemonic U.S. and Western narratives about Iran that would appear to serve ideological purposes (Semati, 2008).

DISCOURSE IN MENTAL SPACES: THEORETICAL AND METHODOLOGICAL FRAMEWORKS FOR ANALYZING IDEOLOGY IN MEDIA DISCOURSE

Despite the various critics who claim ours is a post-ideological age, that concepts and considerations of ideology are part of an outdated epistemology, Slavoj Žižek (1994) has argued that ideology nevertheless "seems to pop up precisely when we attempt to avoid it, while it fails to appear where one would clearly expect it to dwell" (pp. 3–4). If so, perhaps the question is not whether ideology still exists, but rather what, in a network society shaped by the cultural logics of transnational flows of capital and information, *ideology* might still mean. In a neutral sense, ideology might be defined as a systematic body of ideas, organized from a particular point of view (Hodge & Kress, 1993), while pejorative connotations, such as those in contemporary discourse, would also index the polarized biases that mark contemporary U.S. political and cultural debate and division. Either way, this definition feels unsatisfactory from a socioconstructivist and cognitive perspective. Though the notions of *system* and *organize* in this definition imply the underpinnings of institutional processes and power, it nevertheless pivots on the concept of *ideas*. But the notion of a *body of ideas*, though vaguely reminiscent of Foucault's theory of capillary power, still conceals ideology's complex relation to institutions and individuals. In contrast, for Žižek, ideology

> can designate anything from a contemplative attitude that misrecognizes its dependency on social reality to an action-oriented set of beliefs, from the indispensable medium in which individuals live out their relations to a social structure to false ideas which legitimate a dominant political power. (pp. 3–4)

Although this definition is itself not without limitations, we can nevertheless see traces of broader considerations of ideology that, when unpacked, offer a useful theoretical purchase for the analysis of the discursive construction of ideology in U.S. legacy media discourse I present later in this chapter.

In his definition, Žižek (1994) points to both institutions and individuals, structure and agency, as the loci of ideology. For Althusser (1972), ideology was in fact the relationship between the two, or, more precisely, the material practices in which that relationship is expressed. His notion of *interpellation*, the process by which an individual is 'hailed' by ideology to be a subject, encompassed what he saw as the two primary functions of ideology: recognition and misrecognition. The process of an individual recognizing himself in society's ideological ideas and beliefs is nothing more than ideology's functioning, that is, a process by which an individual is discursively constituted as a subject by seeing himself as what others say he is. Yet, this process is actually one of misrecognition because, as Žižek has also claimed, it coerces individuals into falsely seeing themselves in relation to a presentation of reality systematically organized by others, namely those in power. For Gramsci (2003), this was an expression of soft power, of an ideological hegemony by which rule was maintained not only by exploitation and force, but through the cultural dominance of ruling-class ideas that worked to control minds and thus behavior. It is in this process that ideology is naturalized, that is, becomes—or seems to, in popular understandings—non-ideological the normal state of affairs that shapes a group's commonplace assumptions about the world (Blommaert, 2008; Fairclough, 2001).

Enmeshed in social relations, language has inevitably been seen as bound up with ideology. As both a form of social practice and a system of categories and rules, language is based on assumptions about the world, which constitute thought, and therefore, given the arguments above, can also be an ideological instrument of control (Hodge & Kress, 1993). Moreover, given both the primacy of language in social action as well as our dependency on commonsense assumptions when using language, ideology can be located at the level of discursive practice (Fairclough, 2001; Voloshinov, 1973). Put another way, if discourse consists of the structures, rules, and practices that produce utterances and is thereby constitutive of social relations, it is also a system of concepts and images, of ideas organized in relation to perspective, a way of understanding texts and thus ideological (Fowler, 1979). This means that if ideology is dispersed in discourse throughout social relations, it is not, as some have argued, hidden and opaque, but manifest and apparent (Hall, 1977). What is required, then, to see what can be readily seen—what is hiding in plain view—is an analysis not of language or text themselves, but the assumptions, as well as the processes that form them, in which ideology is located.[2] From a structuralist perspective, this means that ideological factors, not subjectivity, determine the range and type of subject positions available to a speaker (Pêcheaux, 1982; Wallis, 2007). But post-structuralists have argued that individuals retain the agency to work creatively within those limits or resist and revise them (see Butler, 1990) with the view of language as discursively countering divisions between structure and agency (Talbot, 2007). How, then, to reconcile these two views, theoretically and methodologically?

One way might be to consider that ideologies, as systems of commonly held assumptions, that is, of ideas and beliefs, are neither entirely structural nor individual, epistemological or performative, but are simultaneously social representations and cognitive constructs. Van Dijk (1998) has argued that mental models, as a theoretical construct, can serve as "an interface between socially shared representations and personal practices, that is, a theoretical device that enables us to connect social (semantic) memory with personal (episodic) memory and their respective representations" (p. 79). Built upon concepts of *schemata*, organizations of belief-clusters, and *scripts*, what people know about stereotypical cultural events, mental models consist of both personal beliefs and situated instances of social beliefs and thereby link the personal and social (Chilton, 2004; van Dijk). Moreover, because these mental models consist of both individual and social beliefs, they contribute to the formation of generalized inferences about situations. As evaluative, these inferences can help form, on the personal level, individual opinions, or, on the social level, the attitudes and values that come to constitute the ideologies that social actors and groups formulate and express in discourse. In addition, because these beliefs are formed in the mind as sets of knowledge and opinions shared by a group, ideologies can therefore be viewed as both mental and social, with mental models serving as the starting point of ideological discourse (van Dijk). With cognition, then, as the interface between society and discourse, ideology might also be thought of as the basis of the social representations shared by members of a group, that is, not simply a systematically organized perspective, but the foundation of the abstract social beliefs that actors discursively construct as ideologies. Working from this definition, we can see that such expression could include both the discursive construction of social groups and how different groups can express their ideologies as a means of serving their interests.

For these reasons I argue that the examination of ideology in discourse—and, in particular, how groups are discursively constructed in the news—must examine the ways talk and text contribute, on a cognitive level, to the construction of these mental representations. This stance warrants my adopting a sociocognitive approach to CDA as the basis of my overall methodological approach, as explained in Chapter 2. As I have also argued, the top-down nature of this approach can be balanced with systemic functional linguistics (SFL)–based, bottom-up approaches to CDA, such as those commonly used to study media discourse. But before applying that approach to the critical news discourse analysis that follows, it is important to explain, in both theoretical and methodological terms, the specific foci of a sociocognitive approach to ideology and the ways in which the analysis of news frames and metaphor fit and support that approach as well as how corpus linguistics can complement CDA.

In van Dijk's sociocognitive approach, ideology is produced discursively through the ways that text and talk contribute to the construction of mental models. This could come through the direct expression of ideological discourse or attitudes, as in manifestos or propaganda. It could also occur in the instantiation of ideological beliefs in, on the microlevel, mental models of episodic memory and/or on the macrolevel, event models that represent general ideological attitudes in discourse about concrete events (van Dijk, 1998). This latter form of discursively constructed ideology can be seen in the news media in the way contexts are constrained and situations defined according to conventional categories in both schematic structures and global discourses. Analysis of ideological discourse structure might also focus on the topic or semantic macrostructures that define discursive coherence expressed as commonsense facts in mental models together with rhetoric, style, and meaning, both implicit and explicit.

Metaphor

Long seen as central to linguistic expression, metaphor has been widely discussed in such domains as literary and orality studies, but its treatment in approaches to discourse has been uneven. Those approaches have tended, in part, to draw on the Hallidayan perspective of grammatical metaphors as instances of meanings typically carried out by one language choice being realized by less typical ones (Eggins, 2004). Discourse analysts have also considered metaphors as perceptions that can privilege certain language uses, for instance, referential over non-referential, or vice versa, over others (Johnstone, 2002), while critical approaches, such as those by Koller (2004) and Charteris-Black (2005), have examined metaphor in gender and political discourse. But in the way that perception can be a slippery concept in discourse studies, the analysis of metaphor has been inconsistent if not largely neglected in most approaches to CDA generally due to the lack of a theoretical framework within CDA to accommodate metaphor (Chilton, 2005; Hart, 2008).

In other disciplines, the analysis of metaphor, which is fundamental to human understanding, tends to emanate from a cognitive perspective: that metaphor constructs a mental framework of social knowledge and worldview in which a cognitive link emerges from the mapping of conceptually concrete source domains onto conceptually abstract target domains (Chilton, 2004; Croft & Cruse, 2004; Kövecses, 2010). The resulting transfer of meaning produces entailments that formulate our understanding of the concept and, through the linking of common attributes, novel cognitive connections about a topic or issue (Johnson-Cartee, 2005). In this sense, metaphors both relate to reasoning and operate indexically, signaling ideology implicitly through the transfer of the ontological meanings of subjects, topics, and issues into conceptual frames more consistent with ideological purposes. (In saying that, however, it is important to note that frame representation can affect how metaphors are understood, a point which I will expand on below.) Consequently, metaphors can be considered ideological in that they help define what is taken as reality, and thus should be considered when examining the discursive construction of ideologies.

Yet, most approaches to CDA, rooted in socioconstructivism and developed, in part, as a response to the cognitive psychology of Chomskyan linguistics, tend to shy away from these cognitive considerations. But this may be a weakness of CDA, given that metaphor, like discourse, is concerned with a coherent view of reality (Hart, 2008). To reconcile, then, the bottom-up socioconstructivist underpinnings of CDA with the top-down theories of cognition, Hart has suggested employing concepts developed in cognitive linguistics to understand how metaphor works in discourse. Common approaches to metaphor, such as that of Lakoff and Johnson (1980), have typically centered on *conceptual metaphor theory*, in which source domains are mapped onto target domains, as explained above. But because target domains tend to be abstract, this approach can be conceptually problematic (Hart). Conversely, in approaches to metaphor analysis based on *conceptual blending theory*, linguistic choices are not understood as pointing to specific elements, such as concepts, actions, or processes, but instead open up mental spaces, or "small conceptual packets constructed as we think and talk, for purposes of local understanding and action" (Fauconnier & Turner, 1996, cited in Hart, 2008, p. 95). In metaphorical discourse, two different concepts are brought together into a space, or *blend*, which networks with other spaces, creating new relations of meaning (Hart).[3] As these relations become entrenched diachronically, metaphors become conventionalized much in the way that discourses become stabilized. It is arguably in this sense that the bottom-up socioconstructivist perspective of CDA and the top-down cognitive approach of blended theory can be seen as compatible (Hart). Because both conceptual blending and discourse occur in short-term memory but play out against conceptual forms in long-term memory, they can plausibly both be said to contribute toward the social cognitions that reside in semantic memory. As such, within CDA, in particular within the sociocognitive approach, blended theory can help link the ideological properties of metaphor with those of other discursive formations.

Ideology and News Framing

Developed in communication studies (Goffman, 1974) and drawing on cognitive concepts, the concept of news framing offers a theoretical ancillary that further helps link texts—in particular, news texts, such as those analyzed below—with both the mind and ideology. In the news media, the process of framing refers to highlighting or selecting specific aspects of a news story or linking them in particular ways as a means of promoting a certain understanding or view of that story (Entman, 2004). As Johnson-Cartee (2005) has argued, "by framing social and political issues in specific ways, news organizations declare the underlying causes and likely consequences of a problem and establish criteria for evaluating potential remedies" (p. 26). News frames can either be substantive, which define effects, identify causes, convey judgment, and endorse response, or, most commonly, procedural, in which the legitimacy of social actors is evaluated through representations (Entman). These representational cues and devices are expressed in multimodal news discourse not only in language and visuals, but also through attention to themes, length and frequency of coverage, and types of stories, for example, hard news, features, opinion columns, or blog posts (Mody, 2010). When experienced, they prime or activate schema, our mental interpretive processes networked in clusters and nodes of ideas and beliefs stored in long-term memory (Entman). On the microlevel, this process can affect what individuals know or are aware of, what they believe regarding a certain topic or issue, and how they respond emotionally to it; on the macrolevel, it can work to maintain status quo attitudes, structures, and institutions (Johnson-Cartee, 2005). For these reasons it has been argued that news frames and narratives can also have a normative role that helps legitimate, for instance, the right of groups to exist as public actors and to continuously shape discourse in sociopolitical contexts (Christians et al., 2009). According to Entman, this normative effect, which arguably parallels many of the ideological concepts discussed above, is strongest when frames are repeated within and across news media outlets, and thereby amplified in magnitude.

Ideologies and Identities in News Discourse

That news discourse is a worthwhile object of language study has been well established in approaches to critical language studies, including CDA (Fairclough, 1995; Fowler, 1979, 1991; Talbot, 2007). Along with education and government, media is a key public domain of language use, with media discourse paramount in the construction of identities and circulation of shared meanings across society (Johnson & Ensslin, 2007; Talbot). With the development of communication media enmeshed in the ways modern societies have transformed, studying the media is of central concern to understanding social and cultural change (Thompson, 1995). As in other applications of CDA, the analysis of news discourse, including its articulation of ideology, means examining texts' propositional content, typically through SFL-driven clause analysis, as well as their specific textual properties, including lexical choice, grammar and cohesion, presuppositions, implicatures, metaphors, and aspects of genre structure (Talbot).

But before discussing how best to approach the analysis of news discourse that follows, it is important to consider in more depth my rationale for doing so. In an early study of the cultural functions of the modern media, Hall (1977), working from a neo-Marxist perspective, saw ideologies, like knowledge, as materialized productions embodied in social organizations and spread through language. The media contributed to this process by selecting and privileging certain social knowledge, images, and ideologies to *encode*, in symbolic form, the preferred meanings and interpretations of the dominant social group. These preferred codes, through their selection, transmission, and reproduction, come to seem natural and universal and thereby work to shape our beliefs about the world in the ways discussed above. Moreover, as a systematic tendency, this ideological reproduction through the media can come to classify the world within the discourse of dominant ideologies and thus contribute to reproducing structural domination.

Also informed by neo-Marxism, Fowler (1991) has argued that because news is a social construction of the world in language, it is in the media where we encounter the most common and familiar kinds of discourse that present the social ideologically. Working from Halliday's principle that linguistic form is shaped systematically by social context, representations and categorizations in discourse, such as stereotypes, can be seen as relating systematically and predictably to the context of that discourse and thus indicative as well as constitutive of it. Similarly, Hodge and Kress (1993) saw language as a potential instrument of control and therefore, by extension, with language central to the media, media as linked with the processes of discursively constructing ideologies. In particular, they claimed that the study of grammar, especially syntax, should move beyond the Chomskyan orthodoxy of linguistics as a branch of cognitive psychology to consider further the social uses of language. In doing so, it could help relate language and the mind with language and society and thereby the ways in which discursive processes constitute ideologies. In particular, they saw the critical analysis of language as providing an accessible way of analyzing the system by which individuals are categorized, through language, into the classification system of their society.

Furthermore, media discourses, according to Fairclough (1995), have the power to influence knowledge, beliefs, values, social relations, and social identities. That they do this around implicit assumptions in texts that work to construct social relations and identities in particular ways also renders them ideological. To help make these ideological presuppositions more visible, Fairclough has called for the systematic linguistic analysis of text that, based on Hallidayan SFL, center on clauses, which roughly correspond to propositions, and the local coherence between clauses that can show in elaborations, extensions, and enhancement the nature of social relations and identities. But Fairclough concedes that this analytical approach is limited because it focuses on only a few texts and thus should be combined with a complementary form of analysis, as I have, for the reasons given in Chapter 2, with both corpus linguistics and van Dijk's sociocognitive approach.

Fairclough, however, is critical of van Dijk's approach for the strict focus on representation at the expense of social relations and identities, and so, in the spirit of interdisciplinarity that both Fairclough and van Dijk have advocated, combining the two approaches seems optimal. Furthermore, van Dijk does not call for intertextual analysis, which Fairclough sees as a vital way of moving beyond the limitations of linguistic analysis. Although, Fairclough (1995) has contended, "language analysis can help anchor social and cultural research in a detailed understanding of the nature of media output" (p. 16), it is also important, he goes on to say, that we consider such discursive processes as intertextuality, which provides a view of language users' relations to texts in which they are variously positioned as social subjects (Scollon, 1998; Talbot, 2007).

The concept of *intertextuality*, developed by Julia Kristeva, indicates that all texts are in ongoing dialogue with past and future texts, a process by which textual meanings shape other texts (Kristeva, 2002). Underpinning this concept are Bakhtin's ideas of *dialogism* and *heteroglossia*, according to which there are, because of the social nature of language, multiple voices in a single utterance that, when their everyday associations interact dialogically, shape texts and their meanings while producing new associations. Fairclough has employed Kristeva's theory to illuminate the relational nature of discourse by extending her definition of intertextuality into the formation of discourses (Mills, 2004). This means placing intertextuality within a social context and emphasizing its role as a mechanism of discursive change. According to Fairclough (1992), intertextuality "points to the productivity of texts, to how texts can transform prior texts and restructure existing conventions (genres, discourses) to generate new ones" (p. 103). Fairclough further distinguishes between two types of intertextuality, manifest and constitutive. While the former refers to the ways in which quoted utterances are selected, changed, and contextualized in texts, the latter describes how texts are constituted by heterogeneous elements, such as style, register, generic conventions, and discourse types. According to Fairclough, this distinction is crucial because it helps discourse analysts account for how texts are produced in relation to specific social and discursive practices. For this reason, intertextuality can illuminate how certain discourse types come to dominate discourse along with the strategic effects behind them, which would include ideological assumptions, as demonstrated by Wodak and Meyer (2009), who utilized intertextuality to trace the constitution of anti-Semitic stereotypes in an Austrian presidential campaign. Similarly, Li (2009) has explored how various linguistic features of a text and numerous aspects of its organization are shaped by intertextuality and thereby show how the discourse of conflicts represented in daily newspapers works to establish social relations and construct national identities. Given the relevance of this approach to my analytical aims, I have drawn on it, together with the methods and theories above, in the analysis that follows.

A FLUID CONTINUUM OF IDEOLOGIES:
U.S. LEGACY MEDIA ANALYSIS

As discussed above, because the news is a social construction of the world in language, it can arguably be linked with the discursive construction of ideologies. Accordingly, early news discourse theorists, such as Hodge and Kress (1993), contended that the media could help relate language and the mind with language and society in ways that support dominant social groups in charge of the media. In this belief, Lash (2002) has argued that "the media are weapons of ideology through which the dominant class can enforce a system of beliefs on the subordinate social classes that will reinforce the domination of the dominant classes" (p. 67). That is, with dominant groups in charge of the media, the media could be a potential instrument of control.

But the widespread and profound social transformations that have produced increasingly dense global networks of connectivity and communication have both accelerated news circulation across the globe and decentralized news gathering processes (McNair, 2006). As a result, long-established legacy media hierarchies and strategies have become integrated with, if not undermined by, new media mobilities and tactics (Boler, 2008). For McNair, this has necessitated, in the sociology of news, a shift from a control to a chaos paradigm. Whereas a control paradigm emphasized the maintenance of social asymmetries through the communication of elite hegemonic ideologies to a passive audience, a chaos paradigm, although continuing to acknowledge the elite's desire for control, sees that control as interrupted and challenged by the potential of an active audience's dissent from elite accounts, in part, through participatory forms of new media. Not only has this destabilized existing legacy media hierarchies, but controlling ideological hegemonies of the news have given way to ideological competition in a chaotic news environment defined by plurality and unpredictability (McNair). That is, the media no longer tend to set ideological agendas, but follow them (el-Nawawy, 2010). Admittedly, in a U.S. media environment currently marked by explicit ideological polarities and unabashed efforts in those media outlets to shape discourse, political or otherwise, the notion of a fluid continuum of ideologies may seem counterintuitive, especially when looking at the poles, where, as Saunders (2007) has said, the 'braindead' ideological megaphones are turned up the loudest. But in legacy media outlets such as the *New York Times* and the *Washington Post*, which tend to position themselves as centrists, the fluidity, as I intend to show in my analyses, is, though oblique, more apparent. It is also, therefore, arguably more complex in that, without the clear stance-taking at the outer reaches of the politico-media complex spectrum, the subtle and implicit ideological shifting, especially within the hard news genre, can be harder for readers to process cognitively. In other words, in a chaos paradigm, the center of so-called centrist media outlets is more fluid than fixed, and thus more difficult for readers to identify ideologically. For this reason, when analyzing news discourse, we can no longer justly say the news is wholly manufactured or constructed, but instead is emergent and contingent, with consensus giving way to dissensus and old 20th-century bipolarities yielding to the more fluid ideologies of a globalized network of information and cultural flows (McNair).

To try to account for this shift from control to chaos and support that theory with evidence, I have analyzed a corpus of news articles and reports in U.S. online newspapers on the 2009 Iranian presidential election. My approximately 200,000-word corpus consists of 217 news articles collected through the LexisNexis Academic search tool from six leading U.S. newspapers: the *New York Times*, *USA Today*, the *Washington Post*, the *Wall Street Journal*, the New York *Daily News*, and the *Christian Science Monitor*. With the exception of the last source, all are among the top ten daily newspapers by circulation.[4,5] All the articles were published June 1–30, 2009, a date range chosen to include the final days of the election run-up, the election itself on June 12, and the election certification by the Iranian Supreme Council on June 30.[6] For my linguistic analyses, I have strived for balance by selecting texts from each source in the corpus, though I have inevitably looked at a higher number of *New York Times* and *Washington Post* articles simply because they published a larger number of reports on the topic during that date range. As further linguistic backdrop for both this evidence and as a potential counterweight to the interpretative findings of CDA-based analyses such as mine, I have compared, when applicable, my analyses with results from the electronic text analysis of my entire corpus as well as the Brigham Young University Corpus of Contemporary American English (BYU COCA).[7] In the analyses that follow, I look for evidence of the fluid ideological conjecture discussed above, first, in the shifting discursive positioning of the reformist candidate Mousavi as an opposition leader; then, in the apparent strategies with which protesters' identities were discursively constructed, with an emphasis on the interdiscursive links between the protesters and their use of social media. In analyzing my research corpus around these particular themes and keywords, I aim to complement existing analyses of media discourse about this event, such as the comparative textual analysis of CNN and Al Jazeera English coverage by el-Nawawy (2010), in which, it was concluded, CNN's more biased coverage reflected the historically tense U.S.-Iranian relations.

Fluid Ideologies

In the run-up to the June 12 election, reformist candidate and former prime minister Mir-Hossein Mousavi had emerged as the primary challenger to incumbent president Mahmoud Ahmadinejad. Given Ahmadinejad's open hostility to the West, especially to the U.S. and its regional ally Israel, together with the U.S.'s regional geopolitical aims discussed in Chapter 2, it is perhaps unsurprising that, in ideologically framed news discourse, the hard-line incumbent, as Ahmadinejad is typically labeled, is less preferred to the reformist Mousavi. In the June 12 *New York Times* election run-up report "In Iran, a Real Race, and Talk of a Sea Change," Mousavi is labeled as "pragmatic," an adjective which appears in connection with Mousavi 11 times in the corpus, or as frequently as *theocracy, politician,* and *vote-rigging* (see Table 3.1).

As the BYU COCA corpus data in Figure 3.1 below show (as well as line 1 of the key word in context [KWIC] data in Table 3.1) the adjective *pragmatic* has also been used in the media to describe President Obama, who had, at the time, recently won an historic election. Within the Iranian election news frame, this lexical choice, then, could cue both episodic and semantic memories that might suggest, if not equivalence as change agents, then perhaps a degree of political compatibility.

That is, this label might also be seen as a means of constructing Mousavi as the candidate most likely to be amenable to the policy of diplomatic engagement with Iran proposed by the Obama administration early in Obama's first term. By entailment, this construction could also legitimate a particular U.S. response to the Iranian election crisis. Moreover, if *pragmatic* is understood as evaluative and thus, from a Western perspective that values secular rationality over theocratic traditionalism or, at its extreme, radical dogma, it arguably might also imply that Obama, as a fellow pragmatist, should support Mousavi, first, as a candidate and, later, as the election crisis began and the news frame grew, as an opposition leader (Silverstein, 2003). That is, for readers who share this set of beliefs, this type of description plausibly creates not only Mousavi as a subject, but also subject positions for him and, through interdiscursivity, Obama to occupy.

Table 3.1   Election corpus keyword in context (KWIC) results for *pragmatic*

keyword *pragmatic*		
"Moreover, in an attempt to be	pragmatic	Obama wants to keep
moral course; it is the most	pragmatic	and realistic. / 4./ June
around the world has become a	pragmatic	politician who firmly
from a revolutionary to a	pragmatic	manager," said Masoud
is a third group of more	pragmatic	military and security
back down, establishing the	pragmatic	tone he would set on
evolved over time to a more	pragmatic	view, analysts say./
hard-liners and the more	pragmatic	conservatives. This time
of government, wanted a more	pragmatic	approach to the economy
analysts say. He is more	pragmatic	than Mr. Khatami, and

2010	SPOK	Fox_Beck	A	B	C	, it's one mile from the Capitol back to the Monument. And that **sea of people** goes all the way! That's one mile long!
2009	SPOK	CNN_Cooper	A	B	C	weighing in on Iran; that as the world -- the whole world watches a **sea of people** marching and at least one person
2009	SPOK	CNN_Cooper	A	B	C	weighing in on Iran, that as the world, whole world, watches a **sea of people** marching and at least one person dying
2009	SPOK	CNN_Cooper	A	B	C	President Obama weighing in on Iran. That as the whole world watches. A **sea of people** marching, and at least one
2009	SPOK	Fox_Hannity	A	B	C	. Why would they continue attacking the American people? Why would they diminish the **sea of people** out there this
2009	NEWS	CSMonitor	A	B	C	, and the light crowd intensified. By daylight, they were trapped in a **sea of people**, with even adults and teenagers a
2008	SPOK	CBS_Early	A	B	C	Ms-FERNANDEZ: Slow dancing was fun. Ms-YANIZ: Yeah. RODRIGUEZ: In that **sea of people** that night, there was or
2008	NEWS	Houston	A	B	C	. I stake out a place in a corner of the upper gallery in a **sea of people** and listen to something such as Alopecia (yo
2007	SPOK	CBS_SunMorn	A	B	C	dream when I was younger was I wanted to have -- I just wanted a **sea of people** to sing the words that I was singi
2007	NEWS	Atlanta	A	B	C	for the phone to ring and the tiring search for your soul mate in the **sea of people**. # My parents, grandparents, aun
2006	SPOK	CNN_OnStory	A	B	C	for you to be standing up in the middle of all these people, a **sea of people**, particularly journalists who are meant to
2005	SPOK	NPR_Morning	A	B	C	, the hotel Royal Palm. All the people ran away. XAYKAOTHAO: A **sea of people** were seen running toward the hills i
2005	NEWS	Houston	A	B	C	so he got into her car and headed to the Astrodome. Inside was another **sea of people**. In the cavernous Dome, the

Figure 3.1   BYU COCA KWIC results for Obama collocated with pragmatic n±4.

Cohering with this label were the descriptions in June 4 and June 12 *Washington Post* articles of Mousavi as "a painter and architect" and "an urbane, soft-spoken architect," in which these post-positional appositives create a sense of equivalency between agent and noun phrase (Fairclough, 2003). Cohering with the pragmatist label, this discursive construction of Mousavi as a rational, level-headed candidate, as both a renaming and a definition, sets up an implicit comparison with the widely established discursive constructions of Ahmadinejad as the volatile, hard-line incumbent. A similar strategy can be seen in a June 12 *Christian Science Monitor* article, in which a quotation from an opposition supporter who calls Mousavi a "a correct thinker" is pulled into a subhead. Not only does this label seem to cohere with the *Times'* construction of Mousavi as "pragmatic," but it amplifies the emphasis already given to this reported speech by creating a powerful intertextual reference in which the Mousavi supporter's words are appropriated into the text's macrostructure.

Such constructions, which could be seen as positively correlated with hegemonic Western perspectives, are extended in a June 8 *New York Times* article in which the contentious run-up debates and campaigns are described as a "carnival," a description that is repeated in a post to its news blog a day after the June 12 election.[8] This metaphor suggests that Iranian politics are unruly, loosely regulated, and perhaps irrational. This conceptual blend coheres with other representations of the pre-election events, as in the June 8 *New York Times* article that described the final presidential debates as "raucous" and an evening rally in Tehran as a "screaming, honking bacchanal." From Western perspectives, the IRANIAN POLITICS AS IRRATIONAL metaphor, while arguably deprecating and condescending, could work, through entailment, to implicitly call into question the legitimacy of the election process and, by extension, the notion of democracy in Iran. If so, under the presupposition that legitimately democratic governments are rational, this mapping would suggest that, on the one hand, it is possible that any doubt raised about the democratic practices or legitimacy of an Ahmadinejad government could serve as further justification for a U.S. response.[9] This could include maintaining the lack of formal diplomatic relations with

Iran and its status under George W. Bush as a 'rogue nation' as well as the strong economic sanctions levied against Iran for defying United Nations sanctions regarding its nuclear program. Even more, a discourse of delegitimization, whether explicit or implicit, could become a pretext for military intervention, a consideration that had in fact been raised during the Bush era and was debated during the 2008 U.S. presidential elections. On the other hand, if this metaphor is, as I argue, operating indexically, it could also be questioning, from a different ideological stance, the value and rationality of nation-building as part of American global geopolitical strategy. In fact, this latter interpretation gathers some weight as after the election, in the *New York Times* and other sources in the corpus, the very notion of democracy as compatible with a theocratic Iranian society is questioned, as in the June 18 editorial "Reading Tea Leaves in Tehran" (2009) in the *Christian Science Monitor*:

> This basic tension between an *Islamic dictatorship* and the popular principles of democracy has kept Iran in *political turmoil and economic backwardness* ever since the 1979 revolution. Yet even if the candidate backed by the protesters, Mir Hossein Mousavi, should somehow take power, it is likely the country would shift only slightly toward more tolerance of popular will and openness while the *top clergy would retain ultimate powers* [emphasis added]. (p. 8)

Like the Bush-era labels of Iran as a fundamentalist society or rogue nation in the 'Axis of Evil,' metaphorical descriptions of Iranian politics as 'irrational' could cohere to established U.S./Western ideological discourses of Iran as a theocracy run by 'mad mullahs' (Semati, 2008). Given how conceptual metaphorical blends can both network with news frame representations and shape reasoning (Chilton, 2004), this type of discursive construction, in the fluid ideological context of a chaos news paradigm, might influence the stores of structured cultural knowledge and social beliefs needed to support a variety of political—even military—responses to Iran and the election crisis.

The semantic meaning of Mousavi as a pragmatist in a carnivalesque political atmosphere is extended and deepened when, in the same June 8 *New York Times* article, Mousavi is described as "less confrontational" than his rival. Against the backdrop of the IRANIAN POLITICS AS IRRATIONAL metaphor, the more favorable notion of a rational pragmatist is further established, with the comparative structure working to further contrast the stances of the two leading candidates. While this move is understandable in a news analysis that seeks to present the leading presidential candidates to a foreign audience potentially unfamiliar with them (at least in the case of Mousavi), the negative comparative form collocated with the emotionally charged *confrontational* could index a preferred view of passivity and rationality that would likely suit a Western hegemonic agenda (Chilton, 2004). Considered metaphorically, that is, POLITICS AS CONFLICT, this lexical choice also opens up a space in which Mousavi, as a pragmatist, is networked with nodes of semantic meaning related to Middle East stability and relations between the U.S. and its strongest regional ally, Israel, which is also the target of numerous aggressive verbal threats from the Ahmadinejad regime, as summarized in Table 3.2.

Arguably, these metaphors and the network of discursive entailments that help form them work to link the wider shared representations of social/semantic memory with personal/episodic memory in a way that could shape social beliefs toward a particular ideological perspective. Moreover, a lexical choice like *confrontational* can activate schemata linked to U.S.-Iranian relations, currently centered on the political standoff over the Iranian nuclear program and historically marked by tension and mistrust. As such, indirectly raising the nuclear standoff topic within the election news frame could function ideologically by clustering beliefs about the present with those in readers' episodic memories. If so, this could shape, on individual levels, mental models about the election crisis and larger sociocultural beliefs regarding Iran. What, in turn, would result from these more favorable descriptions of Mousavi in the pre-election reports is the discursive construction of a candidate possibly more amenable to U.S.

Table 3.2   Political metaphors with linked and related terms from the U.S. legacy news corpus

Political metaphor	Examples of discursively linked and related terms
IRANIAN POLITICS AS IRRATIONAL	"Islamic dictatorship" (*Christian Science Monitor*)
	"political turmoil and economic backwardness" (*Christian Science Monitor*)
	"top clergy would retain ultimate powers" (*Christian Science Monitor*)
	"raucous" (*New York Times*)
	"screaming, honking bacchanal" (*New York Times*)
POLITICS AS CONFLICT	"lesser of two evils" (*Daily News*)
	"ease tensions with the West and especially with Israel" (*Daily News*)
	"less confrontational" (*New York Times*)
	Mousavi as a (non-confrontational) "urbane, soft-spoken architect" (*Washington Post*)
	"the only serious alternative for those who oppose the policies of Ahmadinejad" (*Washington Post*)
	"the only guy who can beat Ahmadinejad" (*Washington Post*)

geopolitical aims for the region and thus the candidate the U.S. should support, a suggestion that would underscore the ideological constructions in the media discourse discussed above. Arguably, this could also index the government–media nexus, in which the mesh of interdependence between the media and politics creates cognitive constraints in which traditional geopolitics shape representations of foreign events, and media discourses become a space in which global elites can negotiate political positions (Mody, 2010).

Further evidence of this stance might be seen in the explicit represen-tations in a June 13 New York *Daily News* article in which Mousavi is described as "the lesser of two evils" for the U.S. Supporting this label is the reported speech of an opposition supporter who dubbed Mousavi "our Obama" and the positing of the prevailing conventional political thinking of unidentified "experts" who have said that "a Mousavi victory might ease tensions with the West and especially with Israel." Some might argue, and justly so, that the tabloid-format *Daily News*, whose infotainment factor is noticeably—and, perhaps, purposefully and explicitly—higher than in broadsheets like the *Washington Post* and *New York Times,* is a less reliable source for measuring the seeming opacity of ideological media discourse. Nevertheless, the institutional power of the *Daily News*, through its wide circulation, remains similar to the broadsheets and thus relevant to under-standing how these meanings are constructed and circulated both in dis-course and their fluid ideological context.

Representations of Mousavi, however, began to shift in the days imme-diately following the election, as the contested results brought opposition supporters onto the streets and into conflict with government and para-military forces. In a June 8 *Washington Post* article, Mousavi was described as largely unknown to the Iranian youth population:

> Each night, tens of thousands of youths gather in Tehran's main squares to cheer their support for a man who just a month ago they barely knew by name. Mousavi has emerged as *the only serious alternative for those who oppose the policies of Ahmadinejad*, who has the support a small group of *hard-line clerics* and some influential members of Iran's Revo-lutionary Guard Corps.
>
> "Mousavi will make us free," a girl shouted from a car Saturday night, waving at the masses of young supporters. "I don't really know who he is. But he is *the only one that can beat Ahmadinejad* [emphasis added]." (Erdbrink, 2009, p. A6)

After the June 12 election, however, as the crisis began to develop, Mousavi is discursively positioned as the face of a 'wired' opposition, as can be seen in the evidence summarized in Table 3.3.

In the notion that identities can be discursively constructed according to ideological beliefs through not only descriptions, but also representations of

Table 3.3　Research corpus evidence of discursive links between Mousavi and social media/technology

Source	Date	Example
Washington Post	June 14	Mousavi, who had said on Friday that he won, **posted a statement on his Web site** rejecting the vote tally as rigged.
Christian Science Monitor	June 16	it seems [Ahmadinejad supporters] have underestimated, **not only the crowds, but Mr. Mousavi**
New York Times	June 16	A couple of **Twitter feeds** have become virtual media offices for the supporters of the leading opposition candidate, Mir Hussein Moussavi. . . . Mr. Moussavi's **fan group on Facebook** has swelled to over 50,000 members, a significant increase since election day.
New York Times	June 18a	the opposition candidate Mir Hussein Moussavi was **using his public profile page on Facebook to organize protests** scheduled for Thursday
New York Times	June 18b	. . . dismissive toward Mr. Moussavi, when he has become **a symbol of freedom and democracy in Iran**. . . . Mr. Moussavi, who is rapidly becoming **a political icon in Iran** . . .

actions, roles, and affiliations (van Dijk, 1998), the conjoining of Mousavi with references to the web and social media services originating in the U.S., as seen in the examples in Figure 3.4, could plausibly create a cognitive link between them. In addition, the establishment in the news frame of semantic links among technology, democracy, and the opposition helps further cohere the cluster of meanings and associations of Mousavi's globally oriented, modern identity discussed above. Furthermore, the implicit connections established in the parallel clause structure in the second example could create a local cognitive coherence in readers' mental models between the reformist candidate and the protesters, in particular the urban youth activists who are thought to be an ideological, highly wired generation open to the influence of Western culture and ideas, as discussed in Chapter 2.

While these constructions of Mousavi's identity in the evolving news frame may have reflected the context and political realities of the election aftermath (Johnson-Cartee, 2005), in which opposition supporters rallied more specifically behind Mousavi, and Mousavi himself actively took up the mantle of populist opposition leader, this shift in the media discourse nevertheless can be seen as working to create an identity for Mousavi— wired and popular with the youth—that, as argued above, resonated with characterizations of then newly elected President Obama, whose use of social media during his historical 2008 campaign was widely reported. As Morozov (2011) has argued, the linking of technology with the spread of democracy is not only an example of cyber-utopianism, but also highly problematic because of how it obscures the ways authoritarian regimes, such as Ahmadinejad's, use technologies in repressive ways. Furthermore, this construction of Mousavi's identity helps create a micronarrative within the larger news frame: the rational pragmatist of the political carnival steps forward as an advocate for democracy by resisting the alleged vote-rigging of the authoritarian regime on behalf of the *demos*. By arranging readers' comprehension process in this ideological way (van Dijk, 1998), the identity of Mousavi, the defeated challenger, is reconstructed in the discourse as an opposition leader in a manner that, during a crisis over the legitimacy of Iran's presidential election results, works to legitimate his position according to U.S. hegemonic perspectives.

'Murky Motives': Shifting Subjectivities

As the election crisis developed, however, and the main legacy media election news frame started to grow with the appropriation of other micronarratives, earlier constructions of Mousavi's identity were complicated and, to an extent, problematized. In a June 18 *New York Times* article profiling Mousavi as the challenger around which the opposition had rallied, he is described as:

> an *accidental leader*, a moderate figure anointed at the last minute to represent a popular upwelling against the presidency of Mahmoud Ahmadinejad. He is *far from being a liberal in the Western sense*, and it is not yet clear how far he will be willing to go in defending the broad democratic hopes he has come to embody.
>
> Mr. Moussavi, 67, is *an insider* who has moved toward opposition, and his motives for doing so remain *murky* [emphasis added]. (Worth & Fathi, 2009, June 17).

Similarly, in a June 17 *Washington Post* editorial, Mousavi is defined as "a veteran of the 1979 revolution who promised a restoration to its true principles." While factually accurate, the link to the Islamic Revolution in Iran, by that time well established in the news frame through descriptions of the opposition crowds being regularly described as the largest in Tehran since 1979, works to complicate identifications of Mousavi as a pragmatic leader whom the U.S. might be able to engage diplomatically to defuse the ongoing standoff over Iran's nuclear program. Furthermore, taking the view of van Dijk (1998) that "lexical and grammatical style is one of the most obvious means speakers have to explicitly express or subtly signal their ideological opinions about events, people, and participants" (p. 272), the lexical choices *restoration* and *true principles* arguably index the conservative orthodoxies with which Iran is typically framed in Western news media reports (Semati, 2008). If so, this construction would destabilize earlier ones which distanced Mousavi from the hard-line Ahmadinejad and aligned him more closely with rational Western views. In their place is the construction of a "murky" subjectivity linked, through the past, to the Iranian Revolution and, in the present, to possibly opportunistic, and therefore, cynical motives. Admittedly, this historically contextualized portrayal of Mousavi could be seen as an effort within the media, as the election crisis unfolded, to develop and expand the earlier, less nuanced constructions discussed above. If so, it would allow readers to form a more complex understanding of both Mousavi as a political actor and his role in the evolving news story. Nevertheless, it is also possible that in a chaotic media environment, identities can be readily rendered as abstractions that, through the subtle process of shifting signals I have traced above, are then more easily manipulated according to ideological purposes.

These shifts, summarized below in Figure 3.2, show how the changing, or complicating, labels discussed above work to construct Mousavi in relation to dominant U.S. ideologies. With the +/– of the *y*-axis referring to values and ideals commonly associated with the West, such as pragmatism and democracy, it appears that as the election crisis unfolded, Mousavi was constructed as a leader increasingly less likely to be amenable to diplomatic engagement and nuclear talks. If so, this might help legitimize—or create new arguments for—a certain response by the U.S. to the election crisis. Moreover, as the connecting lines intend to show, these labels create clusters of networked meaning that index a complex set of social beliefs. In some instances, as indicated by the dashed lines, they also cohere across clusters such that the mental representations signaled by these constructions could reflect shifting and various political interests in the media discourse. While, to a certain extent, in a context in which both information about the election aftermath was compromised by the Iranian government's communication blockades and censorship policies, and understandings in the U.S. of local events in Iran is colored by political and historical strains, past and present, between the two countries (Johnson-Cartee, 2005; Mody, 2010), a changing, even contradictory, understanding of Mousavi, as challenger-cum opposition leader, is understandable. Nevertheless, I argue it is hard not to see the bearing of certain interests encoded in these discursive constructions of Mousavi's identity. These could range from the apparent wholesale skepticism of the *Christian Science Monitor* toward any popularly elected Iranian leader or the cautious optimism of the more centrist *New York Times*, a position that for the most part paralleled that of the Obama administration, in contrast to Republicans' generally more triumphalist 'Twitter Revolution' rhetoric. Moreover, this flux might also substantiate McNair's (2006) claims that U.S. legacy media, drawing at least initially on reports coming from Tehran through new media, have become less constitutive of and more responsive to the discursive construction of ideologies. If so, this would not discount legacy media's power to shape ideologies and identities, but it could ask important questions about the reach or effects of that power in a decentered news environment. It might also force us to consider how we analyze both that power and the discourses that work to constitute it.

Discursive Constructions of the Protesters

Like the ideologically shaped representations of Mousavi discussed above, the labeling of protesters in U.S. legacy media also suggests implicit interests favorable to U.S. geopolitical aims. During the immediate election aftermath, early reports of confrontations between opposition demonstrators and government forces emphasized the violence of those clashes. Graphic lexical choices describe scenes of unrest, chaos, bloodshed, repression, and resistance that charge the reports with an affective power that may reflect the tendency of media discourse to increasingly conflate news with entertainment (Fairclough, 1995; Scollon, 1998; Silberstein, 2004). If so, this might, in the case of the early coverage of the opposition, construct readers as sympathetic toward protesters as underdogs being repressed by powerful government and paramilitary forces. This, however, is not to suggest that all U.S. media representations of the protesters in the early stages of the election aftermath carried this particular emotional valance, as seen in the examples presented in Table 3.4.

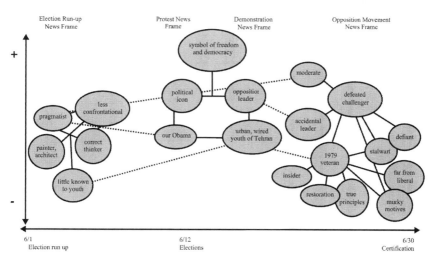

Figure 3.2 Conceptual blending networks of constructions of Mousavi in U.S. legacy media.

Table 3.4 Examples of agentive identity constructions of the protesters in the research corpus

Source	Date	Example
Washington Post	June 14	Supporters of defeated candidate Mir Hossein Mousavi **burned** dumpsters, **threw** stones and **clashed** with police in the worst **rioting** in Tehran in many years
Daily News	June 16	Showing **inspiring courage,** hundreds of thousands **flowed** onto Tehran streets in a **rage** over the preposterous result of Friday's election.
New York Times	June 14	. . . clusters of young men **hurled** rocks at a phalanx of **riot** police officers . . .

Whereas passive clausal constructions in discourse can deprive social actors of agency, active constructions, as in these examples, can grant it. However, these agentive constructions could be understood as either empowered and (though enraged) bravely resistant, as in the second example, or violent, as evidenced in the expressive value of emotive active verbs such as *burn* and *hurl* and the nominative *riot* in the first and third examples. Arguably, constructions of empowered protesters challenging the disputed election results would likely resonate with a U.S. audience, whose civic and political enculturation rests on historical mythos of resistance against oppression in the struggle for democracy. That is, by implicitly indexing readers' mental models and episodic memory in which civil protest, as inherent in the rights to free speech and assembly, is an attribute and positive condition of democracy, such representations could help create an audience sympathetic with the protesters and the opposition movement. If so, it might also index a wider ideological discursive construction of U.S. geopolitical aims and strategies that cohere around theories of spreading democracy and nation-building. But descriptions of protesters' unrest could also establish what Boykoff (2006) has called the *violence frame* that tends to dominate mass media coverage of social movements. According to Boykoff, legacy media's cueing of the violence frame within the larger news narrative of the social movement may clash with the impetus for the demonstrations themselves, in this case the disputed election results. What is more, once a violence frame is established in the discourse, as Boykoff has shown, it can be easily re-evoked, even through entailment when protests are reported as peaceful, that is, non-violent, as was the case with subsequent demonstrations organized by the Iranian opposition movement. How these various potential interpretations might index particular ideologies is not definite.

But regardless of interpretation, these representations suggest the potential for larger unrest, if not revolution, an implicit syllogism made plausible by news frame references to the 1979 revolution that had caught the world by such surprise (Kurzman, 2004).

As coverage of the growing opposition demonstrations expanded over the following days, representations of individual resistance and, at times, violence tended to give way to depictions of mass gatherings, with the lexis *crowd* appearing with greater frequency later in the research corpus 66 times. Cohering to metaphorical mappings common to the descriptions of crowds, the mass gatherings of protesters are repeatedly referred to as a *sea*, as seen in the data from the research corpus sampled in Table 3.5, which also shows examples of non-metaphorical usage of *sea*, as references to the Caspian Sea, which borders Iran to the north.[10]

In the BYU COCA, *sea of people* is an established collocation and metaphorical construction. The highest frequency of overall occurrence (32%) is in the fiction genre, while within the newspaper genre (11% of all tokens) the highest frequency of occurrence is in the lifestyle sections. The frequencies of these occurrences might suggest, on the one hand, that this metaphorical construction has lapsed into cliché; on the other hand, it could point toward a commonplace, or *topos*, for conveying a sense of amassed

Table 3.5 Sample concordances of *sea* from the research news corpus

keyword *sea*	
"Moses on the shores of the	Sea of Reeds, his staff raised
Vali-e Asr Street amid a	sea of green, the opposition's
between the oil-rich Caspian	Sea and the oil-rich Persian Gulf
Sq. will turn into a	sea of green, biggest march in
Street, the march became a	sea of people eight across and
and unrest in the Caspian	Sea city of Rasht and the central
pouring into the tunnel, a	sea of women with sunburned faces
in Roodsar, near the Caspian	Sea./Things like bombs on airplanes
is great". / "There was a	sea of people and the crowd stretched
a nuclear problem. / his is a	sea change. Iran has been denuclearized
and samizdat video showing a	sea of people at least tens of
of people is unbelievable a	SEA OF GREEN. I am returning home
were hundreds of thousands of	Sea of Green chanting 'my brother
followers, who formed a	sea of people that blocked traffic
victory yesterday after a	sea of voters swamped polling stations"

humanity that could readily fit within mental models of a mass demonstration. In either case, however, these occurrences also suggest support for the trends in media toward entertainment and conversational discourse, as discussed above. In the research corpus, this CROWD AS FLUID metaphor mapped by the source domain *sea* creates a blended space in which other fluid-related lexical choices can cohere to the established metaphor, as seen in the examples in Table 3.6.

That the fluid metaphor also appears in the active verbs *flowed* and *flooded*, as well as in the nominalization *outpouring*, could work to establish a more complex network of metaphorical meanings that, through this interdiscursive linking of representations, strengthens and stabilizes its meaning through coherence (Fairclough, 2001). Although this metaphorical construction is common, its operation in media and political discourse may have ideological underpinnings. If we consider, as Kövecses (2010) has argued, that EMOTION IS A FLUID IN A CONTAINER is a typical conceptual metaphor that characterizes feelings, the cluster of meanings mapped by this metaphorical construction, particularly those networked to the CROWD AS FLOOD metaphor, offers the possible interpretation, through implicit entailment relations, of overflowing emotion. While that sense of emotional overflow might, in general, carry a positive or negative valence, that is, be either joyous or enraged, either associative link would connote a lack of control, a sense somewhat at odds with pragmatic rationality. In addition, given the descriptions of the protesters' riotous actions within the established violence frame, this entailment could also plausibly include an imminent violence. In the chaos media paradigm, in which the constructions of ideologies tend to be more fluid than fixed, the CROWD

Table 3.6   Examples of CROWD AS FLUID metaphors in the news research corpus

Source	Date	Example
USA Today	June 15	The parallels between the present **outpouring** and the 1970s uprisings
Washington Post	June 16	the march became a **sea** of people
Daily News	June 16	Showing inspiring courage, hundreds of thousands **flowed** onto Tehran streets
New York Times	June 18	tens of thousands [of protesters] who again **flooded** the streets
New York Times	June 19	Hundreds of thousands of silent protesters **flooded** into the streets. . . . As the streets filled with protesters for yet another day
Washington Post	June 25	a **sea** of green

AS FLOOD metaphor could be viewed by a U.S. audience as cohering with the instability of the IRANIAN POLITICS AS IRRATIONAL metaphor discussed above. It might also readily link to the established comparisons between the election protests and the 1979 revolution, during which the deposing of the U.S.-backed Shah Mohammad Reza and subsequent taking of U.S. hostages was, as discussed above, a political debacle that both risked American lives and weakened foreign views of U.S. power. Within these contexts, this metaphorical construction of the protesters' identities could help shape reasoning and views about the crisis and thus contribute to the formation of ideologies as well as a particular U.S. response (Chilton, 2004). In fact, as reported in a June 19 *USA Today* article, hawkish conservative (and, at the time, recently defeated presidential candidate) Senator John McCain used the news of protests against the regime that had brought this instability to suggest a firmer response from President Obama, saying— in a tweet, no less—"Mass peaceful demonstrations in Iran today, let's support them & stand up for democracy & freedom! President & his Admin should do the same."

Linking the Protesters to Social Media

That McCain, defeated by the famously tweeting Obama only months earlier, would use Twitter to criticize the president for his response to the Iranian election crisis and the social-media 'empowered' opposition protesters is clearly political theater, not irony. Nor does it seem ironic that, as news of the protesters' use of social media increased, the protesters' identities frequently became conjoined with the use of technology. Arguably, for U.S. readers, this identification coheres with the dichotomous constructions discussed above of the conservatism of hard-line Ahmadinejad and his large working-class and rural poor electoral base with the 'urbane' Mousavi and his support among the wired, urban youth. Even before the elections and the subsequent protests, there is evidence of this micronarrative within the overall election news frame, as in the June 9 *Washington Post* article titled "In Iran Election, Tradition Competes With Web," in which Ahmadinejad supporters are presented as traditionalists:

> More than 100,000 backers of President Mahmoud Ahmadinejad *gathered in traditional fashion at a central mosque*, arriving in buses organized by members of *the baseej, Iran's voluntary paramilitary force*. The *crowds were so dense* that Ahmadinejad's vehicle was unable to reach the stage. Wearing a headband in *the colors of the Iranian flag*, the symbol of Ahmadinejad's campaign, Leili Aghahi, 17, waved at the president [emphasis added]. (Erdbrink, p. A4)

Not unlike McCain's rebuking tweet, the Ahmadinejad strategists' decision to rally at a central mosque and employ the nationalistic symbolism of the large crowds waving the flag of the Islamic Republic is clearly a tactic of political theater. But how this event is represented in media discourse through comparisons with the Mousavi rally and supporters can be seen as invoking the tension between traditionalism and modernism, that is, discourse which has extensively shaped Western understandings of Iran and other Muslim countries (Rajaee, 2007; Vahdat, 2002). The description of Mousavi supporters in the same *Washington Post* article illustrates this tension:

> Supporters of Ahmadinejad's main challenger, former prime minister Mir Hossein Mousavi, had to be *more inventive* to find a place for their rally. Over the weekend, a government organization refused permission for his campaign to use Tehran's 120,000-seat Azadi Stadium for a rally originally planned for Sunday. But in less than 24 hours, *using text messages and Facebook postings*, thousands of Mousavi backers gathered along Vali-e Asr Avenue, Tehran's 12-mile-long arterial road [emphasis added]. (Erdbrink, p. A4)

In this description, the comparative construction *more inventive* not only creates a potentially negative view of the Ahmadinejad supporters' use of traditional symbols of religion, politics, and culture, it also suggests an identification that indexes the notions of innovation and development inherent in many Western understandings of modernity. In addition, the rhetorical arrangement of the comparison could establish the traditionalism of the Ahmadinejad supporters, presented first as a kind of normative baseline of archetypical (if not stereotypical) Western representations of Muslims as theocrats—the 'mad mullahs' trope of religion and politics intertwined, as discussed above—which the Mousavi supporters, presented second in the report, then seem to eclipse, at least according to secular Western perspectives. This rhetorical arrangement of events in the *Washington Post* report could create a comprehension for readers that would indirectly structure their mental models about the election and, by extension, their beliefs about Iran (van Dijk, 1998).

   In the same excerpt, the references to activists' use of text messaging and, especially, Facebook, which, by 2009, had already become hugely popular in the U.S. and, in July of that year, would reach 250 million users worldwide, could be seen as working to further establish constructions of Mousavi and his supporters as linked, or perhaps more aligned, through their use of mobile technology, with the global north, that is, from where social media such as Facebook originate.[11] Within the fluid ideological constructions of U.S. legacy media discourse, references to technology such as these might be viewed as an example of what Szerszynsky and Urry (2006) have called *banal globalism*. Based on Billig's (1995) theory of *banal nationalism*, in which the ideological symbols of nationhood, often through metonymic imagery, are *enhabited* in contemporary daily life and thereby become part of social agents' *habitus* (Bourdieu, 1990), banal globalism extends the symbolic realm to the global. In this case, the use of a global form of social media and communication like Facebook could conceivably be seen as metonymy for a cosmopolitan citizenship and participation in a global community. If so, this construction might signal, on the protesters' part, an affinity with or desire to participate in global culture. Conversely, as I consider in later chapters, it might simply be the tactical application of technological tools for specific communicative purposes. Either way, and more importantly, the metonymic association, functioning cognitively like metaphor but at the level of association rather than substitution, could work to construct for readers the protesters' identities as more aligned with U.S. cultural and political hegemonies. That is, in this instance, the ideological indexing comes not from the protesters' practices, but in how those practices are made available in discourse to readers and the subject positions that discourse creates for the construction of the protesters' identities (Jaffe, 2009). When compared to the nationalism of the flag-waving Ahmadinejad supporters rallying *en masse* outside a central mosque, it is not hard to imagine which group—in a comparison abstracted in the media discourse as a symbolic way of being (Szerszynsky & Urry; van Dijk, 1998)—might appear more amenable to U.S. foreign policies and geopolitical aims for a post-9/11 readership contemplating the complications and potential ramifications of a nuclear standoff with Iran. Put another way, the protesters could be viewed as examples that many U.S. readers might make a larger set of conclusions about: if 'we' must choose to support one side, it is likely that someone using Facebook shares more of 'my' beliefs than someone waving a foreign flag outside a mosque. Although that interpretation risks oversimplification, I argue that it nevertheless demonstrates the ways in which this type of discourse, for both the subjects it works to create and the positions for those subjects to occupy in a coherent narrative or understanding of a news-mediated event, can help shape ideological perspectives and show how ideologies can constrain and shape discourse (van Dijk).

These identifications grew stronger and more frequent after the protests broke out and reports of protesters' use of social media as organizing and citizen journalism tools entered the election crisis news frame, examples of which can be seen in Table 3.7.

As can arguably be seen, adjectives such as *wired* and *tech-savvy*, when pre-positionally modifying the nouns *dissidents* and *protesters*, can work as labels that create group identities for the protesters while also delimiting their subjectivities. According to some established sets of beliefs, they might also suggest a sense of logical equivalence between the concepts of *technology* and *justified protest*. In this sense, labels such as these could work metaphorically to create a blended space in which the construction of the Iranian protesters' political subjectivities is networked with the use of technology. If so, this construction would grant technological forms typically associated with the global north the status of liberating forces of democracy, especially

Table 3.7 Constructions of the protesters as networked with technology and the West

Source	Date	Example
USA Today	June 17	Tech-savvy protesters can also reach **Twitter** using **proxy tools** readily supplied for free at proxy.org, notes Chris King, director of product marketing at Palo Alto Networks, a network security firm.
Washington Post	June 17	to avoid disrupting communications among **tech-savvy Iranian citizens** as they took to the streets to **protest** Friday's reelection of President Mahmoud Ahmadinejad
USA Today	June 19	"**Obama** may well feel a **kinship with the protesters**, who, like his own supporters, tend to be **young** and use the **latest communications tools** to get their messages out." (quoted speech of Fariborz Ghadar, a vice minister of the Iranian shah in the 1970s)
Wall Street Journal	June 25	. . . urges **Obama** to find new model of diplomacy that incorporates **wired dissidents**

when conjoined with references to the current U.S. president. Furthermore, in a global network society that prizes technology, if the pre-positional adjectives are considered evaluative, and thus judgment-indexing, they might also work metapragmatically to create the presupposition that being "wired" and "tech-savvy" are components of political savvy or success (Silverstein, 2003). Substantiating this interpretation is the indirect quotation from Ghadar (example 3 in Table 3.7) that links the opposition supporters to Obama and thereby also extends the Iranian election crisis news frame to include U.S. politics and creates a potential commonsense coherence between them.

The Twitter Micronarrative

Similar constructions of identity appear in the June 17 *Washington Post* article titled "Twitter Is a Player in Iran's Drama; State Dept. Asked Site to Keep Running." References to "tech-savvy Iranian citizens" form part of a report on the U.S. State Department's request to Twitter to delay routine maintenance that might limit or slow service during daylight hours in Iran's time zone. The article is careful not to overstate the influence of Twitter in the protests given the unknown number of Twitter users in Iran at the time and the fact that the tweets were largely written in English, not Persian.

But it does go on to say that Twitter, along with Flickr and YouTube, was being used to disseminate information and images outside of Iran to other activists, members of the diaspora, and a global public sphere, including reporters. This report, like a similar *Washington Post* article on June 21 and numerous others in the research corpus, helped further establish Twitter and other social media both in the election news frame and in conjunction with the protesters' identities. Overall, the keyword *Twitter* appears in the research corpus 244 times and frequently collocates with protesters' use of it and other forms of social media, as the sample of concordance in Table 3.8 shows.

As mentioned above, though there was a high volume of Twitter use during the election crisis, it is debatable whether Twitter had any measurable effect on the outcome of the protests. According to qualitative research done by the Web Ecology Project (2009), more than 2,000,000 tweets about the Iranian election were posted between June 7 and June 26, 2009.[12] But whether those tweets were directly related to the ongoing demonstrations or simply the protest *topos* as a "trending topic" on Twitter is unclear.[13] As Howard (2010) and others have argued, there was in fact a small number of Twitter users located in Iran at the time of the election. And for those tweets coming out of Iran, it is difficult to determine whether they were actually

Table 3.8   Sample concordance of Twitter in the news research corpus

keyword *Twitter*

"services like Facebook and	Twitter	—are being used to foment
using Internet sites like	Twitter	would be subject to retribution
to public forums like	Twitter	—offering them as so-called
Their signs, slogans and	Twitter	postings say nothing about
—are being thwarted by	Twitter	and the Internet. While
such as those tweets on	Twitter	.com, depends on the Internet
Web sites like Facebook and	Twitter,	which have become vital
Zahedan." Update / 6:21 P.M. A	Twitter	feed that seems to be associated
posted this message on	Twitter	late on Thursday: Sea of
:13 p.m. A blogger writing on	Twitter	reported one hour ago:
from England points out on	Twitter	that the same YouTube user
reliable information on	Twitter	writes that the rally in
slogans are passed round via	Twitter,	social networking sites
update from a blogger using	Twitter	says that another mass
reportedly using Facebook and	Twitter	to locate them; Mr. Ahmadinejad

posted by Iranians or activists who, as discussed in Chapter 2, had changed their geo-location settings to Tehran both to show solidarity with the pro-testers and to help foil Iranian government surveillance efforts. Still, some research has shown that for those Iranians with access to them, Twitter and other social media services did help disseminate information about the crisis and address a global audience. Based on her research, Snow (2010), for instance, has claimed:

> Twitter revealed public frustrations in real time, like a street-level focus group. Twitter comments reflected a population of Iranians who were pro-West, social media savvy, and global-media conscious. Tweets skewed overwhelmingly toward Ahmadinejad's main challenger, Mousavi, who was not just a real challenger, but also a symbolic repre-sentation of a new Iran. (p. 100)

In Snow's claim, the notion of Twitter as both a semiotic and symbolic resource is a potentially powerful one that coheres with my arguments above regarding the ideologically charged network of meaning established in the media discourse among Mousavi, the protesters, and the use of social media, as I show in Figure 3.3.[14]

Although this chart reflects my interpretations of the data, I argue that a shift does appear across the overall election news frame and from subframe to subframe in the positioning of protesters' identities, although a smaller one than in the discursive constructions of Mousavi's identity shown in

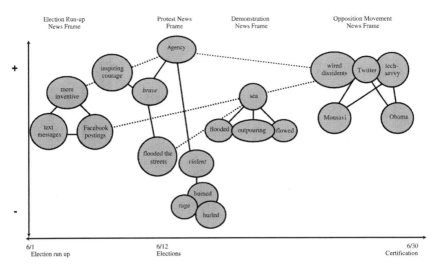

Figure 3.3   Conceptual blending networks of constructions of Iranian protesters in U.S. legacy media.

Figure 3.2 of the constructions of Mousavi's identity. Certainly, such shifts, whether strategic or not, are part of a discursive change that might also be mapped within a control paradigm of news discourse. Working, however, in a chaos paradigm, in which the news environment is marked by pluralities and unpredictabilities, the rapid and arguably angular shifts and coherences might be seen as reflecting the emergent and contingent ideologies of contemporary news discourse. That said, within the apparent dissensus there still appears some degree of consensus. After the election crisis broke out and the so-called Twitter Revolution micronarrative began to develop into its own news frame, there were reports, for instance, that compared protesters' use of Twitter and other social media to Cold War-era Radio Free Europe broadcasts and the *samizdat* grassroots publications circulated then covertly by Soviet-bloc dissidents. As interdiscursive links, these comparisons index pre-1989 ideological polarities in a way that, from certain hegemonic perspectives, might cause the Iranian opposition movement to seem to represent a polar struggle between traditionalism and modernity, as I summarize in Figure 3.4 below.

This discourse was, in turn, linked across various texts to references and comparisons to the 1989 student-led protests in Tiananmen Square. This connection would locate the 2009 Iranian opposition movement in a narrative of global youth democracy movements wherein the capitulation of the authoritarian Ahmadinejad government to protesters' accusations of election fraud would be another domino to fall in the triumphant march of democracy around the world. Although those wider discursive links are compelling and relevant, tracing them extends somewhat beyond the scope

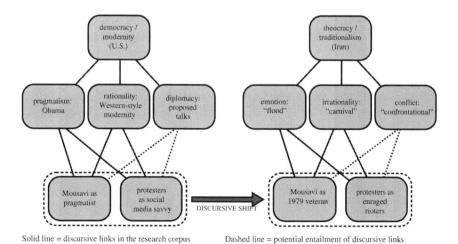

Figure 3.4 Summary of discursive shift in U.S. legacy media toward polarized ideological constructions.

of this study. Nevertheless, their seeming coherence helps underscore the process and strategies of the discourse formations I have analyzed above. In particular, these discursive shifts seem to show how the construction of ideologies in a decentered media environment appear, in one sense, to reflect the flux of meaning typical of both a chaotic news paradigm, as McNair (2006) has claimed, and the overall struggle for meaning in a vortex of globalized flows (Mittelman, 2004). In another sense, however, it could also be that, over time, there is a tendency for that flux to settle along existing coherences, or ideologies, both old and new. That is, in the chaotic battle with new media contenders to tell the news, legacy media outlets might resort to established, ideologically charged narratives as a means of maintaining their share of a fractured audience. While, at this point, somewhat speculative, that notion might nevertheless be important to understanding the contemporary processes by which, in a decentered new environment, ideologies come to be discursively constructed in the media.

PLURAL INTERPRETATIONS OF MODERNITY: CONCLUSIONS

In light of the arguments and analyses in this chapter, as well as claims made in Chapter 1, Snow's (2010) analysis above of Twitter's role in the protests, like the inclusion of the social media micronarrative in the overall news frame, seems to reflect in at least some of the current media scholarship a cyber-utopian viewpoint. As cyber-skeptics such as Morozov (2011) have charged, this perspective is undergirded with Western hegemonic perspectives about technology, democracy, and the role of the global north in the world. Morozov has labeled this triumphal cyber-utopianism the *Google Doctrine*, a geopolitical vision shaped by an "intense longing for a world where information technology is the liberator rather than the oppressor, a world where technology could be harvested to spread democracy around the globe rather than entrench existing autocracies" (p. 5). Like Snow's analyses, reports in the research corpus such as the June 18 *New York Times* article "Stark Images of the Turmoil in Iran, Uploaded to the World on the Internet" support Morozov's analysis of the pro-Western ideology inherent in cyber-utopian visions. In the report, activists' use of social media to upload accounts, images, and cellphone video captures of the demonstrations and clashes with police is cited as a successful tactical means of "circumvent[ing] the shroud of censorship their government was trying to place over the unfolding events" (Stelter & Stone, p. A14). While factually accurate, this description could be interpreted, as I argued above, as linking interdiscursively with Cold War discourses. In fact, in another June 18 *New York Times* article covering the Iranian crisis, the cellphone captures uploaded to YouTube are described as "samizdat video." It could be, then, that in a post–Cold War era bereft of the 'certainties' of polarized ideological worldviews, the notion of a collision between reactionary traditionalism and integrative modernism offers, in a vortex of discourses, illusions of coherence (Barber, 1995; Mittelman, 2004). Instead of Radio Free Europe broadcasts mythically soaring over communist walls to liberate the Eastern bloc, Western social media are skirting the repressive "shroud" of traditionalism to deliver democracy 140 characters at a time.

But celebratory visions of the supposedly liberatory functions of technology, either in legacy news reports or by Western policymakers enmeshed in a government–media nexus, crucially fail to imagine the unintended consequences of the new digital environment (Morozov, 2011). Morozov has contended that the U.S. State Department's request that Twitter delay its service maintenance, which was widely covered in the news and arguably legitimized, both for the legacy media and their readers, Twitter's role in the demonstrations, caused Iranian authorities "to respond with aggressive countermeasures that made using the Web to foster social and political change in Iran and other closed societies considerably harder" (pp. 25–26). Yet, this misrepresentation may be even more significant than the resulting surveillance of and cyber-attacks on Iranian activists. It may also point toward a continued trend in the West to fail to acknowledge a plurality of interpretations of modernity, especially in the Muslim world. In Iran, the struggle to come to terms with the *exclusive secularism* of modernity has shaped the major events of its recent history (Rajaee, 2007). As Vahdat (2002) has claimed, the Islamic Revolution of the 1970s was a "dialectical attempt to challenge the discourse of modernity" (p. xiii). And as I argued above, the subsequent shifts between moderatism and conservatism seen in the Khatami and Ahmadinejad presidencies suggest that struggle continues.

Yet, within that encounter with modernity, Iran has seemed to find in technology some purchase between East and West. Between their religion-inspired traditions and the colonial forces of exploitation stands the Internet, which can be used not only as a communication tool but as a means of spreading Islam (Varzi, 2006).[15] This *secondary production*, in which colonials are using, in technology, a colonizers' object differently than its original intended use, shows, according to Varzi, that "the fact that an Islamic country is on the internet (in what many believe to be a sign of 'secular' Western modernity) does not mean that the country is necessarily buying into Western notions of modernity" (p. 123). Surely, the protesters' use of Twitter and other social media to organize, coordinate activities, and disseminate information during a social movement to a global audience is not the same as spreading the word of God to the faithful. Still, U.S. legacy media's representation of this use of technology—which, as I have tried to show, may have actually been a misrepresentation on multiple levels—can plausibly be seen as extending the election crisis news frame to fit established sets of beliefs about modernity and faith, traditionalism and technology, and the spread of democracy around the world. Moreover, whereas previous controlling ideological news frames and media discourse allowed for a more facile construction of hegemonic narratives underpinned by dichotomous ideologies, the present entropic environment of global media and information flows means master narratives are more easily contested, challenged, and fractured by micronarratives pulsing across diverse and divergent networks. In this vortex, identity has become the organizing point of meaning. While this has helped break down hegemonic narratives, uncouple center-periphery mental models, fuel opposition groups, and open spaces for subaltern identities (Castells, 1997), it may also have meant, as I intend the above analyses to show, that still powerful hegemonic forces such as U.S. legacy media outlets can work within the fluidity of a chaotic news environment to create shifting, abstract constructions of agents and events that are more readily and subtly manipulated (McNair, 2006). This is not at all to say that subjects encoded in media discourse within a control paradigm were also not readily positioned and manipulated (Hall, 1977). Rather, as the contexts and conditions of production in which media discourses are produced and circulated have changed, so must the ways in which we try to understand the discursive construction of identities in the fluid ideological environment of a chaos news media paradigm (McNair).

NOTES

1. The ostensible reason given for this mild scoff is that the epithet had already been used to describe the April 2009 protests in Moldova, during which, it was reported, activists also used Twitter as an organizing tool. However, it is suggested that the label might also be an overstatement, at the very least, because a revolution had not occurred and did not appear imminent.

2. This is to say that ideology is socially constructed through language, or discourse, but does not necessarily reside in it. That is, *contra* some assumptions about the hermeneutics of CDA, the goal of analysis is not to unlock meaning, or in this case, ideology, but to try to indicate the process by which it is formed. If ideology is a set of organized assumptions or beliefs about the world, this suggests, as I develop below, the need for a cognitive dimension to the analysis of ideology in discourse.

3. My emphasis here is on relations of meaning, not the mappings of conceptual metaphor theory. I see this distinction as important because, perhaps not unlike the post-structuralist qualms about Saussure's langue and parole, a discourse-centered approach to language analysis is, in my view, more likely to accommodate, or be reconciled with, networked relations of meanings than mappings.

4. Source: Alliance for Audit Media. www.auditedmedia.com

5. Though not as widely circulated as the other newspapers in my corpus, I have included the *Christian Science Monitor* for the sake of balance, which, according to Adolphs (2006), is crucial to corpus construction. Due to current U.S. legacy media conglomeration, the top-circulating U.S. newspapers tend to occupy a similar range of viewpoints. Because of its strong journalistic reputation, the *Christian Science Monitor*, winner of seven Pulitzer Prizes, likely holds more cultural penetration than its circulation figures might indicate. Therefore, to diversify and balance the corpus, I felt it warranted inclusion

over newspapers with higher circulation figures but owned by one of the dominant media conglomerates.

6. Note: For the sake of consistency and comparison, I have used this same date range when constructing the Twitter, Flickr, and YouTube corpuses analyzed in Chapters 4 and 5.
7. For the electronic text analysis of my research corpus, I used the Simple Concordance Program (v.4.09), a concordance tool freely available for download from the Internet.
8. The *New York Times*' blog *The Lede*, like the blogs on many online newspapers, offers regularly updated news coverage alongside the news reports and articles that appear in the print editions.
9. Prior to the 2009 Iranian election, concerns about elections had been raised by the U.S. State Department, given the charges of voting irregularities that accompanied the first Ahmadinejad election in 2005.
10. The lexis *green* in the corpus data refers to the color largely adopted by Mousavi and opposition supporters and worn during demonstrations as a symbol of unity and, given that green is one of the traditional colors in Islam, of identity.
11. Source: www.web-strategist.com/blog/2009/01/11/a-collection-of-soical-network-stats-for-2009/
12. Source: www.webecologyproject.org/2009/06/iran-election-on-twitter/
13. On Twitter, "trending topics" are algorithmic measurements of the most popular, emerging topics of discussion at a particular time. Source: http://support.twitter.com
14. In Chapters 4 and 5, I discuss in detail the potentially symbolic aspect of protesters' use of Twitter and other social media.
15. See Chapter 2 for a discussion on the Iranian government's policies and funding of the widespread growth and development of information and communication technologies in Iran and the rise of a youthful, wired generation.

REFERENCES

Adolphs, S. (2006). *Introducing electronic text analysis*. London: Routledge.

Althusser, L. (1972). *Lenin and philosophy, and other essays*. New York: Monthly Review Press.

Arceneaux, N., & Schmitz Weiss, A. (2010). Seems stupid until you try it: Press coverage of Twitter, 2006–9. *New Media & Society*, 12(8), 1262–1279.

Axworthy, M. (2013). *Revolutionary Iran: A history of the Islamic republic*. New York: Oxford University Press.

Barber, B. (1995). *Jihad vs. McWorld*. New York: Random House.

Billig, M. (1995). *Banal nationalism*. London: SAGE.

Blommaert, J. (2008). *Notes on power. Working papers in language diversity*. Jyväskylä, Finland: University of Jyväskylä Press.

Boler, M. (Ed.). (2008). *Digital media and democracy: Tactics in hard times*. Cambridge, MA: MIT Press.

Bourdieu, P. (1990). *The logic of practice*. Stanford, CA: Stanford University Press.

Boykoff, J. (2006). Framing dissent: Mass-media coverage of the global justice movement. *New Political Science*, 28(2), 201–228.

Butler, J. (1990). *Gender trouble: Feminism and the subversion of identity*. New York: Routledge.

Castells, M. (1997). *The power of identity. The information age: Economy, society and culture, vol. 2*. Malden, MA: Blackwell.

Charteris-Black, J. (2005). *Politicians and rhetoric: The persuasive power of metaphor.* Basingstoke, UK: Palgrave Macmillan.

Chilton, P. (2004). *Analyzing political discourse: Theory and practice.* London: Routledge.

Chilton, P. (2005). Missing links in mainstream CDA: Modules, blends and the critical instinct. In R. Wodak & P. Chilton (Eds.), *A new agenda in (critical) discourse analysis: Theory, methodology and interdisciplinarity* (pp. 19–52). Philadelphia: John Benjamins.

Christians, C., Glasser, T., McQuail, D., Nordenstreng, K., & White, R. (2009). *Normative theories of the media: Journalism in democratic societies.* Urbana: University of Illinois Press.

Croft, W., & Cruse, D. A. (2004). *Cognitive linguistics.* Cambridge: Cambridge University Press.

Eggins, S. (2004). *An introduction to systemic functional linguistics.* New York: Continuum.

el-Nawawy, M. (2010). The 2009 Iranian presidential election in the coverage of CNN and Al-Jazeera English websites. In Y. Kamalipour (Ed.), *Media, power, and politics in the digital age: The 2009 presidential election uprising in Iran* (pp. 3–14). Lanham, MD: Rowman & Littlefield.

Entman, R. (2004). *Projections of power: Framing news, public opinion, and U.S. foreign policy.* Chicago: University of Chicago Press.

Erdbrink, T. (2009, June 8). A relative unknown leads challenge in Iran. *Washington Post,* p. A6.

Fairclough, N. (1992). *Discourse and social change.* Cambridge: Polity Press.

Fairclough, N. (1995). *Media discourse.* London: Edward Arnold.

Fairclough, N. (2001). *Language and power* (2nd ed.). Essex: Pearson Education Ltd.

Fairclough, N. (2003). *Analyzing discourse: Textual analysis for social research.* London: Routledge.

Fowler, R. (1979). *Language and control.* London: Routledge & Kegan Paul.

Fowler, R. (1991). *Language in the news: Discourse and ideology in the press.* London: Routledge.

Gheissari, A., & Nasr, V. (2006). *Democracy in Iran: History and the quest for liberty.* New York: Oxford University Press.

Gladwell, M. (2010, October 4). Small change: Why the revolution will not be tweeted. *The New Yorker.* Retrieved November 16, 2014 from www.newyorker.com/magazine/2010/10/04/small-change-3

Gladwell, M. (2011, February 2). Does Egypt need Twitter? *The New Yorker.* Retrieved November 25, 2014 from www.newyorker.com/news/news-desk/does-egypt-need-twitter

Goffman, E. (1974). *Frame analysis: An essay on the organization of experience.* Cambridge, MA: Harvard University Press.

Gramsci, A. (2003). *Selections from the prison notebooks of Antonio Gramsci* (Q. Hoare & G. Nowell-Smith, Trans.). New York: International.

Hall, S. (1977). Culture, the media, and the ideological effect. In J. Curran, M. Gurevitch, & J. Woollacott (Eds.), *Mass communication and society* (pp. 315–348). London: SAGE.

Hart, C. (2008). Critical discourse analysis and metaphor: Toward a theoretical framework. *Critical Discourse Studies, 5*(2), 91–106.

Hodge, R., & Kress, G. (1993). *Language as ideology.* New York: Routledge.

Howard, P. N. (2010). *The digital origins of dictatorship and democracy: Information technology and political Islam.* Oxford: Oxford University Press.

Jaffe, A. (Ed.). (2009). *Stance: Sociolinguistic perspectives.* Oxford: Oxford University Press.

Johnson, S., & Ensslin, A. (Eds.). (2007). *Language in the media*. London: Continuum.

Johnson-Cartee, K. (2005). *News narratives and news framing: Constructing political reality*. Lanham, MD: Rowman & Littlefield.

Johnstone, B. (2002). *Discourse analysis*. Malden, MA: Blackwell Publishing.

Keddie, N. (2003). *Modern Iran: Roots and results of revolution*. New Haven/London: Yale University Press.

Koller, V. (2004). *Metaphor and gender in business media discourse: A critical cognitive study*. Basingstoke, UK: Palgrave Macmillan.

Kövecses, Z. (2010). *Metaphor: A practical introduction*. New York: Oxford University Press.

Kristeva, J. (2002). "Nous Doux" or a (Hi)story of Intertextuality. *Romanic Review*, *93*(1–2), 7–13.

Kurzman, C. (2004). *The unthinkable revolution in Iran*. Cambridge, MA: Harvard University Press.

Lakoff, G., & Johnson, M. (1980). *Metaphors we live by*. Chicago: University of Chicago Press.

Lash, S. (2002). *The critique of information*. London: SAGE.

Li, J. (2009). Intertextuality and national identity: Discourse of national conflicts in daily newspapers in the United States and China. *Discourse & Society*, *20*, 85–121.

McNair, B. (2006). *Cultural chaos: Journalism, news and power in a globalised world*. London: Routledge.

Mills, S. (2004). *Discourse* (2nd ed.). London: Routledge.

Mittelman, J. (2004). *Wither globalization: The vortex of knowledge and ideology*. New York: Routledge.

Mody, B. (2010). *The geopolitics of representation in foreign news: Explaining Darfur*. Lanham, MD: Lexington Books.

Morozov, E. (2011). *The net delusion: The dark side of Internet freedom*. New York: Public Affairs.

Pêcheux, M. (1982). *Language, semantics, and ideology*. London: Macmillan.

Rajaee, F. (2007). *Islamism and modernism: The changing discourse in Iran*. Austin: University of Texas Press.

"Reading tea leaves in Tehran." (2009, June 18). *Christian Science Monitor*, p. 8.

Rich, F. (2011, February 5). Wallflowers at the revolution. *New York Times*. Retrieved November 25, 2014 from www.nytimes.com/2011/02/06/opinion/06rich.html?_r=0

Russell, A., & Echchaibi, N. (Eds.). (2009). *International blogging: Identity, politics, and networked publics*. New York: Peter Lang.

Saunders, G. (2007). *The braindead megaphone*. New York: Riverhead.

Scollon, R. (1998). *Mediated discourse as social action: A study of news discourse*. New York: Longman.

Semati, M. (Ed.). (2008). *Media, culture and society in Iran: Living with globalization and the Islamic state*. New York: Routledge.

Silberstein, S. (2004). *War of words: Language, politics and 9/11*. New York: Routledge.

Silverstein, M. (2003). Indexical order and the dialectics of sociolinguistic life. *Language and Communication*, *23*, 193–229.

Snow, N. (2010). What's that chirping I hear? From the CNN effect to the Twitter effect. In Y. Kamalipour (Ed.), *Media, power, and politics in the digital age: The 2009 presidential election uprising in Iran* (pp. 97–104). Lanham, MD: Rowman & Littlefield.

Stelter, B., & Stone, B. (2009, June 18). Stark images of turmoil in Iran, uploaded to the world on the Internet. *New York Times*, p. A14.

Sullivan, A. (2009, June 13). The revolution will be twittered. *The Atlantic*. Retrieved November 25, 2014 from www.theatlantic.com/daily-dish/archive/2009/06/the-revolution-will-be-twittered/200478/

Szerszynski, B., & Urry, J. (2006). Visually, mobility and the cosmopolitan: Inhabiting the world from afar. *British Journal of Sociology*, *57*(1), 113–131.

Talbot, M. (2007). *Media discourse: Representation and interaction*. Edinburgh: Edinburgh University Press.

Thompson, J. (1995). *The media and modernity*. Stanford, CA: Stanford University Press.

Vahdat, F. (2002). *God and juggernaut: Iran's intellectual encounter with modernity*. Syracuse, NY: Syracuse University Press.

van Dijk, T. (1998). *Ideology: A multidisciplinary approach*. Thousand Oaks, CA: SAGE.

Varzi, R. (2006). *Warring souls: Youth, media, and martyrdom in post-revolution Iran*. Durham, NC: Duke University Press.

Voloshinov, V. N. (1973). *Marxism and the philosophy of language* (L. Matejka & I. R. Titunik, Trans.). New York: Seminar Press.

Wallis, D. (2007). Michel Pêcheux's theory of language and ideology and method of automatic discourse analysis: A critical introduction. *Text & Talk*, *27*(2), 251–272.

Web Ecology Project. (2009, June 26). *The Iranian election on Twitter: The first eighteen days*. Retrieved November 25, 2014 from www.webecologyproject.org/2009/06/iran-election-on-twitter/

Wodak, R., & Meyer, M. (2009). *Methods of critical discourse analysis* (2nd ed.). London: SAGE.

Worth, R., & Fathi, N. (2009, June 12). Both sides claim victory in presidential election in Iran. Retrieved November 25, 2014 from www.nytimes.com/2009/06/13/world/middleeast/13iran.html?_r=1

Worth, R., & Fathi, N. (2009, June 14). Protests flare in Tehran as opposition disputes vote. Retrieved December 13, 2014 from www.nytimes.com/2009/06/14/world/middleeast/14iran.html

Worth, R., & Fathi, N. (2009, June 17). Rallying Iran: Time tempers a challenger forged in revolution. Retrieved November 25, 2014 from www.nytimes.com/2009/06/18/world/middleeast/18moussavi.html

Žižek, S. (Ed.). (1994). *Mapping ideology*. New York: Verso.

4 Borrowed Language
Reentextualizing Symbolic Resources and Discursively Constructing Stance

As during prior Iranian social movements, leaders of the 1978–79 Iranian Revolution utilized traditional networks of communication largely based in the mosques and bazaars to spread their messages and coordinate collective action (Keddie, 2003). Significantly different, however, were the tactical ways these networks were enhanced and extended by the then-innovative use of what Sreberny-Mohammadi and Mohammadi (1994) have dubbed *small media*: the photocopied leaflets and audiocassette tapes of revolutionary, anti-Shah messages from the Ayatollah Khomeini, the movement's exiled spiritual leader. This tactical use of small media was important, they have argued, because it helped create a political public sphere through which new networks of participation could be built upon longstanding cultural nodes of communication. Through these networks, revolutionary leaders and activists alike could disseminate oppositional discourse and mobilize the movement on a massive scale (Sreberny-Mohammadi & Mohammadi). As a result, the revolution's organization transformed from a hierarchical structure centered on a cadre of leaders into a *rhizome* formed around the counterpower of networked communications (Castells, 2009; Juris, 2008). As the mass demonstrations in Azadi Square of June 2009, punctuated by anti-Ahmadinejad cries of "Death to the Dictator," evoked the slogans and symbols of the revolution that had toppled the Shah Mohammad Reza 30 years before, the protesters' use of social media in 2009 to micro-coordinate collective action and report the events to a global audience suggests strong parallels with the use of small media in 1979. In fact, as Keddie (2003) has claimed, this similarity could already be seen during the Khatami-era student protests, when the use of the Internet and information and communication technologies (ICTs) "parallel[ed] previous uses of contemporary communications technology for oppositional purposes" (p. 311). These correspondences suggest, then, that activists' use of social media in 2009 cohered with both the discursive and organizational practices of past social movements and, more importantly for my arguments, the reentextualization of symbolic resources and repertoires from the master framework of protests in modern Iran (Jaffe, 2009; Poulson, 2005).[1] If so, and as I hope to show in the analyses that follow, this would challenge the 'Twitter Revolution' trumpeting by Andrew Sullivan and others who presuppose an unassailable link between neoliberalism and democracy (Dabashi, 2012). That is, those tweeting protestors might just as well have been borrowing creatively from their own symbolic resources as appropriating those of the so-called global north.

In this light, we might, ironically, see whatever parallels exist between 1979 and 2009 in how technology and the media—big or small, legacy or new—are bound up with Iran's ongoing struggle to free itself from Western influences and embrace a form of modernity compatible with its cultural values and experiences. Given the well-established roles that technology and media have played in cultural modernization, it is not hard to understand the strong push the Iranian government has shown in developing its national technology and information infrastructure—often at a pace that has outstripped its efforts for universal national literacy (Sreberny-Mohammadi & Mohammadi, 1994). Yet, given the Western cultural associations seen by some as bound up with technology, some conservative forces in Iran have tried to limit the negative cultural influence, or *westoxification*, that technological development is thought to incur by striving for a positivist modernity congruous with its local cultural and religious beliefs (Vahdat, 2002). In the way, therefore, that the populist use in 1979 of small media in an urban setting suggested a heterodox, 'Third World' model of revolution (Sreberny-Mohammadi & Mohammadi), the opposition movement's appropriation of social media and *translocal* symbolic resources in 2009 appears to reflect less the neoliberal logics of the marketplace than the participatory logics of the *commons*. By the commons I mean our collectively held and shared translocal resources, knowledge, and information as well as the rules and ethics according to which these resources are shared (Kluitenberg, 2010; Walljasper, 2010). By operating according to this logic, the activists, I argue, also seem to be further questioning and complicating the nexus of cultural tensions that have shaped much of Iran's recent political trajectory. Moreover, if periods of social conflict like the 2009 Iranian election crisis are symptomatic both of deep shifts in social logic and the rise of new ideas and social identities (Melucci, 1996; Poulson, 2005), the examination of activists' tactical cultural borrowings through critical discourse analytics may help us understand the ideologies underlying those shifts and the stances around which transnational imaginaries and globalized vernaculars of protest might have been—and might also be—discursively constructed (Appadurai, 1996; Meyerhoff & Niedzielski, 2003).

To explore these phenomena in this chapter, I first briefly extend the overview of historical, political, and cultural contexts presented in the previous chapters by discussing what Poulson (2005) has identified as the cycle of protests in Iran which has marked its struggle for sovereignty and modernity during the 20th century and of which the 2009 protests arguably appear to be a continuation. Second, for the analyses in this chapter I present a theoretical approach that links Poulson's theory of a master framework of

Iranian social movements to theoretical discussions in Chapter 2 on communication power and globalized social networks as well as those related to the sociocognitive discursive formation of ideologies discussed in Chapter 3. I expand those theoretical concepts to include the development of transnational imaginaries and *sociomental* bonds that can occur through shared activities of cognitive engagement, such as during social movements (Appadurai, 1996; Chayko, 2002, 2008), along with the protesters' use of English as a translocal language and symbolic resource (Lash, 2002; Pennycook, 2007). Finally, before analyzing a corpus of Twitter tweets and Flickr photos posted during the election protests by activists inside and outside Iran, I present an approach that, built upon the methods used in Chapter 3, also considers the *heteroglossia* and *polyvocality* of activists' discursive constructions of stance and the ways those indexical constructions appear to cohere symbolically, intertextually, and interdiscursively.

A QUEST FOR SOVEREIGNTY AND MODERNITY

In the way that the use of small media during both the 1979 Islamic Revolution and the 2009 presidential election protests suggests further parallels between these two social movements, it is also possible to see the 2009 demonstrations, along with the Green Movement that grew out of it, as a continuation of what Poulson (2005) has identified as an ongoing cycle of protests in Iran since the end of the Safavid Dynasty in 1736. As Poulson explains, much of the social protest of the post-Safavid era was focused toward state-making processes. This is particularly true of the 20th-century Iranian social movements, which were largely marked by the push for sovereignty at both the national and individual levels, with independence from Western influence being, as discussed in Chapter 2, a critical rallying cry of the 1978–79 revolution. As argued in Chapter 3, so too was Iran's struggle for a form of modernity that meshed with an Islamic religious framework in which reason is accepted "only if it is conditioned by revelation" (Rajaee, 2007, p. 239). Such an approach, then, in which power adjudicates between politics and culture, can be seen as fundamentally clashing with Eurocentric expressions of modernity that emphasize critical reason and place the individual at the center of modernity's project (Rajaee; Kamvara, 2008). The resulting tensions have generated in Iran, according to Poulson, a cultural narrative of national sovereignty and localized modernity that spans these cycles of protest, one which can also be taken up during new social movements as a means of legitimating collective action. For this reason, as well as those in the discussions of sociocultural and historical contexts presented above, it is plausible to consider the 2009 opposition movements as a continuation of that cycle. Moreover, understanding that cultural narrative as a master framework, that is, a sociocognitive construct, is important to establishing both a contextual link to the analyses presented in Chapter 3 and the context for those in this chapter, particularly in regard to how protesters used symbols and language to discursively construct the stances of their social movement and their identities within it (Poulson).

The push for sovereignty that Poulson (2005) identifies as the master framework of 20th-century Iranian social movements first appears in the Tobacco Movement of 1890–92, during which regional protests against the British monopoly of tobacco in Persia coalesced into a national protest against Western imperialism that ultimately pushed traditional leaders of government and social institutions to address their relationship with the West and the monarchy. Both of these relationships were further challenged during the Constitutional Revolution of 1906–09, with opposing sides divided according to their support for either a constitution or a traditional monarchical government. What both sides shared, however, was a common goal of gaining political and economic independence from Russian and British imperialism, a dialectic that drew the conflict to an end with the establishment of a constitutional monarchy and the creation of a national parliament (Axworthy, 2013). Though these broad political changes, along with the accompanying social transformations, seemed to proclaim Iran's self-realized entry into the modern era, they nevertheless failed to end Western influence. Following World War II, during which Iran was invaded by Soviet and British forces, Cold War tensions were played out in the power struggle between the local communist Tudeh Party and the Iranian National Front, a loose coalition of nationalist groups led by then–prime minister Mosaddeq trying to reassert constitutional elements of governance (Poulson). This ended, however, with the overthrow of Mosaddeq in the CIA-led 1953 *coup d'état* and the establishment of the U.S.-backed Shah Mohammad Reza's military regime. As a further instance of Western interference, the coup and the ensuing installment of the Shah created for many Iranians a fervent feeling of anti-imperialism that, coupled with religious beliefs, would vibrate though the 1963 Ayatollah Khomeini–led Qom protests against the Shah's social reforms and the increasing influence of the West—especially of the U.S.—in Iranian social, political, and economic affairs.

This cycle of struggle for sovereignty and a non-Westernized experience of modernity arguably reached its apotheosis in the anti-Shah demonstrations that ultimately grew into the tumultuous 1978–79 revolution (Kurzman, 2004; Poulson, 2005). According to Kamvara (2008), that revolution was fought over three main idealized identities: traditional concepts of Islam, Islamic reformism, and a secular modernism that sought a neutral, or non-Western, interpretation of modernity, a desire perhaps best expressed by the term *gharbzadegi*, commonly translated into English as *westoxification*. Popularized in the 1960s by prominent Iranian writer Jalal Al-e Ahmad, *westoxification* refers to the idea that, as a result of continual and perfidious imperialist influence and intervention in Iranian political and economic affairs, along with the concomitant adoption of Western-style culture, Iran's cultural identity had been lost and its economy rendered a passive market for the consumption of Western goods (Tazimi, 2012). Because, Al-e Ahmad argued, the only field not corrupted by Western influence was religion, it is perhaps unsurprising that *westoxification* became a pillar of the Iranian Islamic Revolution.

That revolution, however, did not settle Iran's ongoing internal struggle either to come to terms with modernity or its complex relationships with the West. According to Tazimi (2012), the 'double helix' of Iranian modernization, "with one strand representing western economic and military aspirations, and the other representing the backward political institutions" (p. 7), sparked a revolution in which the aim of catching up to the West was fueled by a desire to be unlike it. Even in the wake of the deep, widespread sociopolitical changes brought about by the revolution, there existed a continued desire for an Iranian brand of secular modernism (Kamvara, 2008). Chief among those calling for this vision of a modern Iran were the multitude of educated, urban Iranians who, in 1997, would help bring the reformist cleric Mohammad Khatami to power. The election of Khatami to the Iranian presidency initiated the reform movement that became known as the 2nd of Khorad Movement, in reference to the date of Khatami's election victory in the Iranian calendar (Poulson, 2005). As discussed in Chapter 2, this movement marked a shift toward establishing a more civil post-revolution society as well as more openness with the West, both politically, as marked by Khatami's proposed Dialogue of Civilizations, and culturally, as expressed in the desires of young, urban, educated, and wired Iranians to reestablish certain cosmopolitan aspects of past Iranian society (Varzi, 2006). Khatami's reforms, which included the rise of a critical press, allowed for new spaces of dissent that, together with the concurrent rise of the Iranian digital public spheres, helped create the conditions for the transclass youth-led protests of 1999, during which students called for greater civil rights and individual freedoms as well as the end of the *velayat-e faghih*, or rule by supreme leader (Rahimi, 2008; Yaghmaian, 2002). Iran's pursuit of modernity did not, however, mean a total rejection of tradition (Tazimi, 2012). And much in the way that conservative forces within the Khatami government would repress these protests and shut down most of the critical free press, conservative views in large sectors of Iranian society, under the legacy of *westoxification*, would continue to see Western culture as a deleterious influence. In 2005, the reformist Khatami was replaced by the conservative Ahmadinejad, who, since taking power, has scaled back or undone much of the cultural and economic liberalization instituted during the Khatami presidency.

What has remained, then, is an ongoing tension between conservative religious attitudes toward cultural aspects of modernity and a strong, widespread desire for technology without its cultural accoutrements. Vahdat (2002) has called this a *positivist modernity*, in which Western technology is used according to the doctrines of Eastern morality, a desire that is ironically perhaps not unlike the instrumentality in views espoused by Western technocrats and would-be "Google Doctrine" adherents (Morozov, 2011). Moreover, in the current standoff between Tehran and the West over the Iranian nuclear program, we can arguably see in that geopolitical power struggle the continuation of Iran's quest for sovereignty and freedom from external interference. This is why I argue that extending Poulson's cycle of protests to include the 2009 presidential election demonstrations establishes a crucial macrolevel context for the critical discourse analyses that follow.

Perhaps ironically, however, this dynamic in Iranian culture might also underlie demonstrators' use, as a form of small media, of Western-originating technology to address a global audience in English, the current global *lingua franca,* during the 2009 protests. That is, we may also see, as I aim to show in this and the following chapter, how the master framework of Iranian protest identified by Poulson could be extended to accommodate the features, theories, and symptoms of a global network society so that protesters' discursive practices and identifications might be understood as further expressions of sovereignty and a localized understanding of modernity (Mirsepassi, 2000). But before exploring that consideration, it is important to understand how the protesters adapted these tools and forms of mediation as both a counter-power and counterdiscourse to fit their communication aims, and how that use reflected an ongoing tension between the homogeneity of Eurocentric narratives of modernity and local experiences (Mirsepassi). To do this, I will first establish a theoretical framework that links social movement theory to those theories presented and operationalized in previous chapters, with the aim of limiting the so-called impressionism (Breeze, 2012) of how, through critical discourse analysis (CDA), I interpret the protesters' discursive practices and counterdiscourses and the manipulation of symbols within them.

RETICULATE SPACES AND THE LOGICS OF PARTICIPATION

While master frameworks, as both sociocultural narratives and sociocognitive discourse structures, can shape, inspire, and legitimize new social movements, the probability that a movement will occur typically depends first upon the existence of a political opportunity, some type of structural change or opening, such as an economic downturn or, in the case of Iran in 2009, an election crisis (Poulson, 2005). When such opportunities emerge, the state can be seen as vulnerable, temporarily creating for marginalized groups the potential for collective action and coalition formation, in particular for those groups already well organized (Parsa, 2000). As such, these opportunities, together with framing processes, are understood to be, in social movement theory, the primary mobilizing structures of collective social action (Poulson).

But social movements are more than outgrowths of political crises. They also point toward "a deep transformation in the logic and the processes that guide complex societies" (Melucci, 1996, p. 1). Consequently, in the way that social movements should not be reduced solely to their political dimensions, the framing processes that help mobilize them must not only be considered culturally and historically, as discussed above, but also ideologically. That is, if ideology, as I have argued, is a network of beliefs and symbolic frameworks by which social relationships are rationalized and legitimated according to a 'commonsense' cultural logic, it is therefore important to consider the organizing logic of master frameworks within social movements from an ideological perspective (Melucci). This is not, however, to conflate ideologies with either culture or frames. As Poulson has explained, if ideologies are the sets of beliefs used to justify or challenge a particular sociopolitical order, frames are the symbolic resources and cognitive cues by which collective action can be suggested or spurred in relation to those beliefs. This then means seeing social movement frames as strategically constructed, shared understandings of the world through which the processes of both self-identification and collective action in social movements can occur (Gillan, Pickerill, & Webster, 2008). It also means that, much in the way that ideologies can be reproduced discursively by agents' social practices, social actors can also manipulate symbolic forms and referents so that social movement frames cohere with their own interpretations of a political opportunity or crisis (Melucci; Poulson). As a result, from this dialogic framing process, not only can a context for social action be established and a movement's activities legitimized, but the interests of collective actors can also be coordinated according to ideological perspectives.

Social Movements and Communication Power

Crucial to this coordination and the overall mobilization of a social movement's symbolic resources are ICTs. As discussed in Chapter 2, in a globalized network society, ICTs can both facilitate the hegemonic practices and communication power of dominant forces and help weave together decentralized networks of opposition through coordination and the spread of counterdiscourses (Castells, 2009; Crack, 2008; Rahimi, 2008). As Gillian, Pickerill, and Webster (2008) have shown, the use of ICTs can also allow activists to exploit political opportunities by helping them reach a broader, even global, audience and thereby extend the reach of a social movement's frame. When the media—legacy or new, big or small—function as a platform for enacting local concerns on a global scale, transnational ICTs can both increase the opportunities for dominant ideological voices to be heard, as argued in Chapter 3, and allow for the creative social and pragmatic language functions of marginalized or opposition groups, as I intend to show in the analyses below (Johnson & Ensslin, 2007).

During social protests, the amplification through ICTs of an opposition movement's symbolic resources, such as its slogans and images, across local and global networks can raise the effects of communication acts to political moments (Sreberny-Mohammadi & Mohammadi, 1994). Not unlike the

Obama victory tweet of 2008, these discursive acts, whether of dominant or oppositional forces, can become ideological links between cognitive frameworks and social structures. Moreover, as 'small' media, social media forms utilize the infrastructural resources of institutional ICTs. But because their content is produced and distributed from multiple network nodes, social media can also function as tactical tools of popular mobilization for activists (Boler, 2008). According to Sreberny-Mohammadi and Mohammadi, the potential counterpower of small media in Iran rests in their embeddedness within existing cultural frameworks. In 1979, the informal ties established through mosque networks facilitated the successful broadcast of Khomeini's cassette tapes across telephone lines. Extending this notion to 2009, it was arguably the existence of a youthful society readily disposed to using Internet-based communications that suggested the tactical value of mobile social media during the protests and not their symbolic power as emblems of democracy, as some cyber-utopians and ideological pundits had supposed.

But technologies do not themselves bring about political transformations. They can increase social actors' capacities to coordinate protests and disseminate information, and, across global networks, cognitively extend political struggles beyond local contexts (Castells, 1997; Howard, 2010). But their effectiveness in social movements is dependent on numerous factors, including the strength of preexisting social networks and the specific ways in which activists use them to micro-coordinate collective action. Indeed, the effectiveness of Twitter and other social media during the protests, as discussed previously, has been debated. Fisher (2010) and Kamalipour (2010), for instance, have shown that Twitter facilitated both collective action in the streets of Tehran and, by sidestepping traditional gatekeepers and overcoming geographical limitations, the spread of information to a global audience that included Western news media unable to cover the protests themselves. Others, however, have claimed that Twitter's role was at best negligible and at worst an accelerator of chaotic online dissonance, a kind of 'cyberscreaming' that was of little reliable or verifiable signal intelligence (Acuff, 2010; Malek, 2010; Snow, 2010). In my view, the problem with both cyber-utopian and cyber-skeptic interpretations of social media's impact on the 2009 protests is that both are premised on the cultural logic of competition and the accumulation of power and thus impose neoliberal interpretations onto protesters' discursive practices (Fuchs, 2008; Russell & Echichaibi, 2009). This is not to say that protesters did not want a successful outcome for their movement or did not believe mobile social media would aid, in some way, their collective action. Rather, it is to contend that determining social media's impact on the protests solely according to the commonsense measure of a social movement's success—its impact on the state—discounts its potential mediating effects on discursive change and "the production of alternative values, discourses, and identities" during social movements (Juris, 2008, p. 291). For these reasons, I argue that both cyber-utopians and cyber-skeptics miss the potential symbolism of these discursive practices within the master framework of protests discussed above, and that previous analyses of social media usage during the 2009 Iranian protests, which have tended to fall into either camp, have therefore been insufficient. If, as Sreberny-Mohammadi and Mohammadi have argued, the use of Khomeini cassette tape broadcasts during the Islamic Revolution marked an alternative 'Third World' model of revolutionary process in which populist, urban, small media functioned as tools of popular mobilization, the use of social media during the 2009 protests to address a global audience may have been a transnational process equally characterized by a local set of beliefs, and thus an instance of vernacularized globalized language practices worth examining for the reasons I presented in Chapters 1 and 2. Furthermore, it is also worth our attention to examine this discourse beyond ideologies and the symbolic realm given how the use of social media during the protests reshaped, if temporarily and at various fractal edges, the *twittersphere* into a transnational political public sphere within the Internet's decentralized networked space of publics (Bohman, 2004; Russell & Echichaibi).

Forming Transnational Bonds

With both networks and social movements typically more rhizomatic rather than hierarchical (Juris, 2008), these reticulate public spheres tend to be heterogeneous, multiple, and—given access—inclusive (Fuchs, 2008).[2] As such, they can allow for the relatively fluid emergence of bottom-up organization and the temporary connecting of weak social ties that are hallmarks of social movements (Shirky, 2008). In the streets of Tehran, those ephemeral affiliations, galvanized by the symbols of a master framework of protest, would draw protesters together in what Durkheim called *effervescence,* or a shared spirit of energy and collective conscience (Brumberg, 2001). Online, with digital technologies extending temporary affiliations to a global scale (Juris), this collective energy could vibrate among the connections protesters made with the Iranian diaspora, global activists, and a global audience, producing what Howard (2010) has described as *network effervescence.* Admittedly, the energy in this rhizomatic organization may have produced, from a communication standpoint, a cacophony of simultaneous broadcasts that might indeed have seemed more like cyberscreaming than either microcoordination or public sphere debate (Malek, 2010; Shirky). But viewed at the collective level, the communication fueled by network effervescence could have helped form global *sociomental* bonds, or feelings of connectedness through shared cognitive engagements and social exchanges during activities like social movements (Chayko, 2002, 2008). That is, the multiplicity of interactions and relative ease of participation offered by online social networks could have facilitated the creation of a transnational collective conscience, albeit a situational, ephemeral, and fractal one (Fornäs et al., 2002). The cognitive destabilization such bonds would engender might, in turn, facilitate the possibilities of the multiple, imaginary worlds theorized by Appadurai (1996), in which the imagination as a social practice helps negotiate between local sites of agency, such as a social movement, and globally defined fields of possibility (Anderson, 2006; Brumberg). With imagination, then, as central to agency, we can begin to better see the symbolic effect of the Iranian activists' cyberprotest and use of social media and how the logics inherent in this understanding might offer critical alternative perspectives to neoliberal measurements. That is, as a sustainable alternative to capitalist logics of competition and the accumulation of power, we might instead measure the success of the 2009 protests according to the logic of participation that is itself part of a multiplicity of logics and heterogeneous worldviews in which transnational sociomental bonds are formed in the imagination and mediated across online social networks (Fuchs, 2008).

Global Englishes and Social Protest

A similar theoretical approach might also be useful in coming to terms with the Iranian activists' use of English during the protests. From an instrumental perspective, this phenomenon seems easy to understand: using English, a current global *lingua franca*, allowed Iranian activists to convey their messages across ICT-based social networks to an audience outside Iran and the Persian-speaking Iranian diaspora. But to limit our understanding of those practices at the level of utility is to deny both their potential symbolic resonance as well as the political implications of the use of English and the complex globalized networks in which that communication occurred. Before discussing those concerns, however, it is useful to briefly consider the history of English in Iran.

A significant linguistic presence in Iran for the last 50 years, English arrived in Iran primarily through British commerce and the close political relationship between Shah Mohammad Reza and the U.S. (Sharifan, 2010). Through the strong U.S. military and economic presence in Iran during the Shah's reign, along with his push for a Western model of modernization, English replaced French as the prestige European foreign language in Iran. English-language schools run by the British Council and the Iran-American Society offered—for those who could afford them—both local instruction and preparation for higher education abroad. But the 1979 Islamic Revolution complicated Iran's relationship with English. At perhaps the most reactionary extremes were attempts to ban English or cleanse it of its cultural baggage by replacing British- and American-produced English-language textbooks with Iranian editions featuring local content. Those perhaps striving for a more positivist form of modernity tried to relegate English to the status of an international link language used to export the Islamic Revolution to a non-Muslim world. Despite these efforts, as Sharifan has explained, "many Iranians still associate English with social prestige, as a tool which can not only open educational, social and professional opportunities, but also help in the construction of an educated, elite social identity . . . a 'modern-citizen' identity that distances them from less cosmopolitan identities" (pp. 140–1). For these reasons, English has managed to retain a vital presence in Iran, particularly among the social elite. Helping to maintain and expand this status has been the government's promotion of increased tourism and international trade to boost the economy after the Iran-Iraq war as well as the growth of the Iranian diaspora to English-speaking countries and the widespread use of the Internet (Sharifan).

As the case of English in Iran shows, the complex histories and cultural politics bound up in the spread of English around the world mean no use of English in a global setting should be understood as either neutral or utilitarian, as has been widely argued elsewhere (Canagarajah, 1999; Pennycook, 1994; Phillipson, 1992). Language, instead, is a site of struggle, and when English is viewed through the critical lens of globalization theory, as I have argued in Chapter 2 that it should be, it is possible to see how the global spread of English produces, in the form of *pluricentric* Englishes, both new forms of localization and, through *transcultural flows*, new forms of global identification (Pennycook, 2007). As Pennycook has argued, the notion of transcultural flows entails not just cultural movement, but uptake, appropriation, and creative refashioning. For that reason, within the global Englishes paradigm that I have adopted, the Iranian protesters' uses of English should be understood as examples of a *translocal* language. By translocal I mean how language both crosses localities linked by ICTs and media (legacy and new) and contributes to the hybridizing of exogenous cultures (Leppänen et al., 2009)—a language, as Pennycook has argued, "of fluidity and fixity, that moves across, while being embedded in, the materiality of locations and social relations" (p. 6). Furthermore, as the case of Iran also shows, English can function as not only a translocal vernacular, but also a prestige foreign language and international link language and therefore a source of symbolic capital and a gatekeeper to prestige positions in society (Canagarajah, 1999; Crystal, 2003). As a commodity, then, as well as a global *lingua franca* in a complex globalized market of linguistic and communicative resources, English possesses what Blommaert (2010) has described as a high value. This means that, in a globalized context of 'winners and losers,' the value of linguistic resources correlates with users' *voice* and *mobility*:

> people manage or fail to make sense across contexts; their linguistic and communicative resources are mobile or lack such semiotic mobility, and this problem is not just of difference, but of inequality. It is a problem exacerbated by the intensified processes of globalization. (Blommaert, pp. 3–4)

If so, for protesters who possess the high value linguistic resources needed to tweet in English to an unknown global audience, their capital is both social and cultural: their ability to communicate in English, a network standard

(Grewal, 2008), extended their networks of potential support and influence, while their knowledge of English, a language of global prestige, arguably increased their voice and mobility across those networks (Bourdieu, 1991).

While this translocal use of English in Iran must be understood within the context of globalization, we must not necessarily see English as globalized, but instead as vernacularized varieties and repertoires of English that exist and move across multiple scalar levels (Bhatt, 2008; Blommaert, 2003). This means, in my view, the protesters' use of English could also be understood as a form of borrowing from extant cultural resources, not unlike the reentextualization of symbolic resources from the master social movement framework. This notion of borrowing reflects my orientation toward cooperative logics and the notion of a commons as the wealth of shared resources, both cultural and natural, rather than competitive ones of privatization and accumulation (Hardt & Negri, 2009; Kluitenberg, 2010; Lessig, 2001; Walljasper, 2010). In a globalized commons of networked spaces and modes of knowledge, English, then, might be seen as a translocal resource through which knowledge and shared meanings, together with other semiotic and symbolic cultural resources, might grant collective actors both further power, or counterpower, and influence with groups who share in that knowledge's epistemic ideology (Kogan, 2005). This is not to discount notions of access required to participate in either the commons or globalized transnational public spheres in which English is a network standard (Grewal, 2008). Rather, I argue, and as I believe the analyses that follow show, that by borrowing English from a translocal commons, the Iranian protesters not only extended their communication power to reach a global audience, but also tactically employed this symbol of banal globalism as a kind of *terministic screen* that, through the present symbolic role of English in the world, works to direct global attention to particular phenomena (Burke, 1989; Szerszynski & Urry, 2006). That is, because linguistic choices index our perceptions of context, the tactical use of English as a symbolic and psychosocial rallying point (Edward, 2009) may have signaled, on the protesters' part, a particular stance toward how the local crisis born out of the election aftermath cohered with global frameworks of meaning. Therefore, it is possible that drawing attention to their movement through this symbolic action may have intensified their networked effervescence and the energized transnational imaginaries. However, that borrowing may also carry ideological implications that identify the protesters with globalized networks of power in ways that could be counter to their progressive objectives.

From a methodological standpoint, these considerations suggest employing, for descriptive purposes, the Bakhtinian concepts of *heteroglossia* and *polyvocality*. By heteroglossia, I mean the mixing, combining, and juxtaposing of communicative resources, such as style, genres, registers, and even languages, as reflections of the understanding of language as a site of struggle, or as Bakhtin (1986) claimed, "the coexistence of socio-ideological contradictions between the present and the past, between differing epochs of the past, between different socio-ideological groups in the present" (p. 291). The polyvocality inherent in this struggle not only challenges notions of discourse's self-contained meaning, but also replaces the notion of a single, hegemonic public sphere with a plural lattice of public spheres located at the interstices of different voices in society (Hauser, 1999). For interpretive purposes, I have built upon the sociocognitive approach to ideological analysis taken in Chapter 3 and the emphases on intertextual and interdiscursive relations to reflect both the local contexts and the materiality of that discourse, that is, the use of social media during a social movement. This includes considering the protesters' tactical use of social media during the opposition demonstrations both within the master framework of protests and the larger framework of globalized social movements (Boler, 2008). It also includes considering the indexicality of protesters' discursive practices through the analysis of stance. As Jaffe (2009) has argued, "the concept of stance is a uniquely productive way of conceptualizing the processes of indexicalization that are the links between individual performance and social meaning" (p. 4). I examine this process by using CDA to analyze both epistemic and affective stance with the goal of seeing how the Iranian protesters took up various positions in relation to particular subjectivities and social relationships, supported by the theory of *habitus* to consider how expressions of stance can convey one's position in a cultural field (Bourdieu, 1990; Jaffe). Also, as I argued in Chapter 3, the strong connection between style and metapragmatics to ideology (Silverstein, 2003; van Dijk, 1998) entails looking at both lexical and syntactical structures as well as the ways that protesters discursively signaled the events taking place, considerations that also allow me to expand the theoretical and methodological approaches to intertextuality and interdiscursivity taken up in the previous chapter.

CIRCULATION IS THE CONTENT: ANALYSIS

During the election crisis, two of the activists' discursive practices that appeared to strongly exhibit intertextuality and interdiscursivity were retweets (RTs) and the embedding of hyperlinks in posts. Similar to forwarding an email to a mailing list, *retweeting* another user's content to one's followers, together with hyperlinking, which I discuss below, is one of the most common functionalities and communicative practices employed by Twitter users. In my dataset of tweets tagged #IranElection, written in English and posted June 1–30, 2009, there were retweets in 72 of 238 total posts.[3,4] This rate of approximately one in three compares favorably with the results of the large-scale quantitative research conducted in 2009 by the Web Ecology Project. This study showed that during the first 18 days of the Iranian election crisis, one in four tweets about Iran were retweets of another user's content, as were approximately 40% of the tweets in the

140kit Iran Election dataset.[5] That both these rates are somewhat higher than the approximately one in five rate for general Twitter use (Sysomos, 2010) points toward the importance of retweeting during the protests.

This increase might be explained by the ways retweeting can amplify circulations of information and discourse across new networks. Given the exigencies of the crisis as well as the goals of the social movement that grew out of it, this functionality would clearly be valuable to social movement participants trying to disperse their message to a wider audience. What is more, in a horizontal or rhizomatic organizational pattern typical of social movements, each retweet has the potential to connect more of the movement's loose network ties (Howard, 2010) while also contributing to the formation of the movement's counterdiscourse (Castells, 2009). This sociability, in which decentralized discourses and communicative actions accumulate within the dynamics of network power (Grewal, 2008), could produce a form of counterpower employed by activists to oppose the power of sovereignty, a process suggested by both the offline and online struggles between activists and Iranian authorities. For these reasons, the discursive practice of retweeting might also be understood as a social movement tactic by which circulation not only amplifies discourses across networks, but increases both their use and exchange values by strengthening their network presence (Boler, 2008; Dean, 2008; Entman, 2004).

Recalling Blommaert's (2010) claim that in a globalized market of linguistic resources the so-called market winners and losers are determined according to voice and mobility, retweeting clearly has the potential to increase the uptake of circulations across networks. That it was through social media such as Twitter that, in the early days of the election crisis, news of the protests first reached Western legacy media outlets as well as networks of global activists suggests at least some support for that assertion, as the following example of a retweet by an activist in Canada appears to demonstrate.[6]

> RT from Iran: http://twitpic.com/7r4nw—http://twitpic.com/7r4pv—
> Iran / Tehran / protesters / Topkhone Sq #iranelection Jun 18, 2009

As a circulation of information both within the social movement and across translocal social networks, this post about the location and occurrence of a protest in Tehran, accompanied by links to photographs documenting that event and categorized by its hashtag, is amplified with each retweet across an extending lattice of public spheres (Hauser, 1999). The link between those spheres is suggested in the spatial deixis, which simultaneously indexes the situatedness of these utterances and the materiality of these practices (Leppänen et al., 2009). Indeed, the prefacing "from Iran" of the retweet situates the original utterance in a way that appears to validate the original circulation, an attribute that may afford it greater voice and mobility across networks. In that case, we might also see retweets such as this as a form of peer evaluation in a social movement that also functions as an epistemic community in which a network of knowledgeable actors coordinate and articulate a movement's aims (Dobusch & Quack, 2008; Kogan, 2005). In the following example, this notion of peer evaluation is intensified by the retweet count.

Iran / today / Krimkhan St / protest NOW #iranelection on Twitpic http://ree.tw/bzk (retweeted 131x http://ree.tw/bzl) Jun 17, 2009

Not only does the relatively high number of retweets seem to validate the original post's reentextualization in a globalized context, it could also position the retweeter as both a participant in a translocal social movement and a knowledgeable member of the epistemic community. In addition, the polyvocality of retweeting could also suggest a braiding of voices through which collective action is performed, as seen in this example:

usernameB: RT @usernameA: "perhaps a million protesting" http://bit.ly/QGk19 pic: http://twitpic.com/7gtbu #Iranelection #iran Jun 15, 2009

Here, by echoing user A's utterance as both a communicative act and a symbolic performance, user B becomes an imaginary co-participant in the street protest, and thereby empowered an activist.[7]

That credibility, however, like the discursive relation grown out of the intertextual link, may be less social than informationalized (Lash, 2002). In terms of both use and exchange value, that these tweets were written in English likely strengthened their mobility potential by allowing them to move among transnational flows of information across global networks in which English-language repertoires function as common communicative links.[8] In the understanding that communication is typically centered on the acquisition of cultural capital and symbolic gain (Bourdieu, 1991), the use of English might also have increased the message's value given the cultural capital commonly associated in many contexts, including Iran's, with knowledge of a high-status language, a value that appears to be validated, if not reproduced, with each retweet. Moreover, in globalized contexts in which information and communication technologies facilitate translocal connections mediated by language, English can be viewed as a possible mediating standard through which actors gain access to more participants and new networks and thus increase their network power. From the same standpoint, retweets could then be understood as a form of positive feedback that drives the adopting of this standard (Grewal, 2008). According to Grewal, in economies of scale, in which value is determined by demand and usage:

standards are more valuable when greater numbers of people use them because they offer a form of coordination that exhibits economies of scale; and second, that one effect of this coordination is, over time, to eliminate alternative standards that might have been freely chosen. (p. 26)

From a linguistic perspective, the notion of eliminating alternative standards might cohere with both the arguments of linguistic imperialism of the spread of languages such as English around the world and the notions of linguistic ecologies and the need for preserving linguistic rights (Phillipson, 1992; Phillipson & Skutnabb-Kangas, 1996). In that sense, the materiality of social media discourse and retweets as forms of positive feedback across global networks could be seen as reinforcing the adoption of both globalized social media and English as network standards. But underlying those arguments are emphases on English as a structurally determined, linguistically defined object (Blommaert, 2010). Instead, numerous studies have demonstrated both the pluralities of English used around the world and the creative, performative ways users employ English as a set of communicative resources and repertoires in diverse, localized contexts (Pennycook, 2007). If we extend these arguments to Grewal's notions of standards and network power, we might see how the counterpower of sociability is a form of structuration by which standards can become both pluralized and flexible and thereby limit structural coercion. This is not to deny the network power granted to languages such as English that dominate online discourse. Instead, it is to take up an alternative position that suggests how the tactical use of English during the opposition movement was a form of borrowing, or reentextualization, of communicative resources in a globalized context and then deployed as a symbolic resource within the social movement frame. In the follow example, as in the first example above and in numerous tweets in my dataset, the variety of English employed here appears to be vernacularized toward network standards of compression and discontinuity (Lash, 2002).

> RT @username: http://twitpic.com/7j6ox—Tehran / yesterday / crime #iranelection Jun 16, 2009

Here, within Twitter's 140-character limit constraints, the emphasis is on nouns at the expense of verbs and functional lexis, with the seemingly syntactical use of slashes linking spatiotemporal deixis with the noun *crime* in a way that, I argue, works to informationalize the discourse (Lash). Compressed messages flow more readily, and rapidly, across transnational information networks. But the lexical compression also compresses time and space as this discourse moves across scale levels. *Yesterday* and *Tehran* appear to function as time-space coordinates, with the tweet's date stamp further situating the message like a dateline for a news article. In this sense, the compression suggests an almost forthright simplicity and clarity. But as a byte in the torrent of real-time information flow, the specificity of those coordinates, I argue, speaks more of the medium than the message. With meaning in this severely compressed bit of information constrained primarily to what is suggested by word order, what appears to matter most is how the tweet, as a social action, verifies the act of witness, or participation, in a collective movement. If these time-space coordinates are nodes, *narrative* is usurped in the social movement frame by *network*. And with the attached image, by implicature, attesting to what these words seem to imply, the retweet works dialogically as a caption for the hyperlinked image, imbuing the utterance with an insinuated evidentiality to substantiate the claim of "crime."

Arguably, the vernacularization of English in the original tweet suggests a localized meaning and therefore lowers its mobility potential across transnational networks. At the same time, with the discourse informationalized, it is plausibly more easily commodified and thus made available for uptake from micro- to macroscale levels (Blommaert, 2010). As the process of retweeting facilitated the movement of discourse from a local to a global level, the shift in spatiotemporal reference created the possibility for new signification: at a local scale level, the utterance references a situated moment as a validation of its occurrence in real time; at a global scale level, the retweet shifts the utterance into a translocal, timeless flow of space and time (Castells, 1996). In that flow, the utterance's validity is potentially transformed semiotically from a subjective into a more general statement of fact and normative validation of epistemic stance. That is, for a local audience, the original tweet could have been used to inform activists of events and the dangers of participation—or even just to inform a wider local audience of what was happening. For a global audience, however, when the tweet becomes, through retweeting, rescaled as news, it arguably indexes an image of society, of mutual interest, if not dependency that, in turn, at a metapragmatic level evidences a particular epistemic stance or ideology (Blommaert; Jaffe, 2009; Silverstein, 2003).

At a global level, for an audience who can only bear witness to these events, the sense of normative validation entailed through the reentextualizing retweet comes from the promotion or 'upscaling' of the utterance to the discourse of news. In a statement of what is happening in the world, the retweet is employed like a journalist's quote of an eyewitness or participant that the retweeting user selects, among the countless utterances flowing across time-space, as newsworthy (Silberstein, 2004). If so, it may be tempting to see the seeming lack of evidentiality in the quotative "RT" as a neutral form of attribution in direct reported speech and the amplification as similar to that of agents' voices reported in legacy news media, magnified through publication and distribution, and then positioned within that discourse (Hall, 1977). Instead, the interpretative frame of validation, created through the intertextual link between retweet and tweet, could function dialogically, with the original tweeter 'selecting' users for retweeting his or her discourse. By constructing the tweet in the register of a journalist—the telegraphic text accompanying and captioning the documentary hyperlinked photograph—the user creates a recognizable voice that allows other users to judge it as valuable or authoritative and thereby more readily taken up in a wider network of discourse through the process of retweeting.

That is, within the logics of participation and the social movement frame, the practice of discursively constructing the tweet as an instance of citizen journalism enables the practice of retweeting as a form of *participatory interpellation* through which the audience's belief in the tweet's validity and reliability creates possibilities for both epistemic stance-taking and participation (Clift, 2006; Jaffe, 2009).

But doing so, I argue, also establishes an interdiscursive link through which the participatory epistemologies and ideologies of the social movement are brought into convergence, through the use of global networks, with those of communicative capitalism. According to Dean (2008), in the current contexts of communicative capitalism, the commodification of discourse has uncoupled communicative action from political principles such that:

> the use value of a message [has become] less important than its exchange value, its contribution to a larger pool, flow, or circulation of content. A contribution need not be understood; it need only be repeated, reproduced, forwarded. Circulation is the content, the condition for acceptance or rejection for a contribution. (p. 108)

For agents, Dean has suggested, this detachment both fetishizes communication and shifts communication from message or content distribution to one of contribution. In the following examples, we can see similar features to those discussed above. But if viewed as informationalized commodities, the expressions of stance, as considered above, appear to be less epistemic than affective.

> @username in Baharestan we saw militia with axe choping ppl like meat—blood everywhere—like butcher—Allah Akbar—#Iranelection RT RT RT 06/24/2009

> Iran / today / hafttir Sq / protest NOW #iranelection on Twitpic http://ree.tw/bzm (retweeted 123x http://ree.tw/bzn) Jun 17, 2009

> RT Iran: Very brutal death of a brave man http://twitpic.com/7nv7z—all I can do is to pray and CRY

For a local audience receiving these updates in real time, the potential increase in use value of these tweets (then amplified as retweets) is fairly clear. But rescaled to a global level, their exchange value seems to come from their affective qualities. In the first example, the sense of urgency implied stylistically in the repeated retweet request, much like a repeated exclamation point, suggests the user's impassioned emotional state, reflected in the visceral eyewitness description and religious invocation, all of which index an affective stance (Jaffe, 2009). As an intensifier, retweeting then might signify not only an amplification of discourses across wider social networks, but also an intensified emotional force. This interpretation might be supported by the retweet count in the second example as well as the style of the third, in which the intensifier *very* works to amplify the affect in the emotion-laden phrases *brutal death* and *brave men*. Arguably punctuating this expression of pathos is the invocation of faith and religion in "all I can do is pray," a somewhat fatalistic assertion that strongly indexes an epistemic stance but, when punctuated by the verb *cry* intensified with all caps, shifts the stance back to affect. As examples of the activists' Twitter-based discourse, these contributions might be seen, as discussed above, as a means of engendering networked effervescence through which participants could become linked, if only ephemerally, in sociomental bonds across transnational imaginaries. However, it seems just as likely to be an example of what Žižek (2007) has called *interpassivity*, or a form of communication for reaction, not response, or a way of connecting without really connecting. As examples of networked interpassivity, each retweet might be read as a reaction, an evaluation that does not take up or extend the proposition put forth in the original utterance but merely amplifies its affect. If so, as these data seem to suggest and as Dean has also argued, an Internet-based transnational public sphere might not be a locus of imaginary belonging but "an empty signifier of global unity . . . [in which] our networked communities produce our specific worlds as the global or global capital" (p. 117). That those worlds would be constructed in the fluid discourse of emergent sociability that is both materially situated and deterritorialized, I argue, reflects the ideological stances of those social agents whose discursive practices and performances shape that interaction and the construction of fluid ideologies (Johnson & Ensslin, 2007; McNair, 2006).

Hyperlinking and *Logos*

An additional means of circulating information and micro-coordinating social movement activities is the forwarding of hyperlinks. One of the most fundamental affordances of the web, hyperlinks are also common in Twitter, where users commonly circulate links as a means of filtering web content, as the examples above show. With Twitter usage in Iran at the time of the crisis highly concentrated in Tehran (Sysomos, 2009), the microblogging service could have readily offered young, urban protesters already disposed to using social media and ICTs an additional tactical resource as the exigencies of the election crisis, including the government-imposed communication blockades, intensified the need for information filtering. In my dataset, links appeared in approximately 95% of the tweets and targeted a range of site types, as shown in Table 4.1.

As the table suggests, activists tended to use hyperlinks conjunctively, connecting nodes of discourse and information as well as genres and modes of communication (Morgan, 2002). Furthermore, though the differences between hypertextuality and intertextuality have been debated (see, for instance, Riffaterre, 1994), it is easy to see how, like retweets, hyperlinks create manifest intertextual chains among texts given how links also

Table 4.1 Taxonomy of hyperlinks embedded in tweets in the Twitter research corpus

Hyperlink Target	n	Example
Legacy Media (e.g., BBC, the *Guardian*, CNN)	64	RT @username Iran Election Whistleblower Killed, From Guardian: http://bit.ly/3NC7x http://bit.ly/12kqL4 #iranelection
Uploaded videos (e.g., to YouTube, Qik)	54	@username Guy beaten to death video is up again http://bit.ly/12oZDT #iranelection Jun 14, 2009
Uploaded photos (e.g., to Twitpic, Flickr)	42	@username: Pictures from Tehran http://bit.ly/eTFuZ & http://bit.ly/132TNt #iranelection Jun 13, 2009
Social Movement Resources (e.g., proxy servers, first aid)	30	@username: List of fake & spam twitters: RT http://bit.ly/JcyIU good site to block spam misinfo #IranElection Jun 18, 2009
Other new media (e.g., Facebook, blogs, aggregators)	27	@username: #iran9 #iranelection http://blip.fm/~3yt0y just some music from the big Z @username Jun 16, 2009
Other protests	7	@username RT @username can u help us get the word out? Boston Protest: 20 June 2009 15:00–17:00 Copley Sq http://bit.ly/xukIX #iranelection 06/19/2009

suggest the presence of another text (Morgan). Accordingly, Myers (2010) has claimed that links might be viewed as synecdoche, with the URL referring to the whole of the hyperlinked text. According to Grice's cooperative principle, Meyer goes on to say, this part-whole relationship suggests that further information being offered is relevant to the post, and through implicature readers are drawn to another nodal point in a network of discourse that is meant to comment on the topic. In this sense, hyperlinks, like retweets, might function both as sources of support and credibility for a stance as well as a kind of metalanguage, or commentary on the text in which the link has been embedded (Johnson & Ensslin, 2007).

In that case, hyperlinks might be more than merely conjunctive. The resulting chain of polyvocal signification resulting from hyperlinking also suggests a constitutive intertextuality through which linked discourses might come to cohere. That is, the communicative practice of linking carries with it an associative 'logic' of the link that implies a coherence between the conjoined texts (Cali, 2000). If we accept this understanding of linking, then, as a rhetorical move, one that calls the reader into action, we might see how, as in example 1 in Figure 4.2, for instance, an opposition movement actor's linking to a Western legacy news media site could suggest to readers an assumed coherence between the ideologies encoded in those discourses (Fairclough, 2001). In that case, protesters' tweeted links should not only be seen as hybrid utterances or nodal points in a network of communication, or even coordinates in a real or imagined space. They could also be seen as extensions of power into cyberspace that can reflect a user's social and ideological associations (Crystal, 2001; Fornäs, 2002).

Clearly, those associations can range, even when, as in my dataset, the IranElection hashtag functions as a *metastance* that creates a framework for interpreting the linked text (Jaffe, 2009). Looking again at the examples in Table 4.1, the links, for instance, to proxy servers, lists of government sites of disinformation, or cellphone video captures of eyewitnesses/citizen journalists suggest an ideological stance somewhat apart from that suggested in links to legacy media or, as in example 5 from a member of the diaspora, to an Internet-based music recommendation site set to an inspirational song. But in each instance, the hyperlink, as a rhetorical move, becomes a resource for individual action by which users shape and assign their own subjectivities while creating subject positions for their audience.

What might complicate this move, though, is the use of shortened URLs. A by-product of hyperlinking within the character-limit constraints of microblogs, shortened URLs, as in the example below, still point toward the presence of another text and create an intertextual chain or claim in which understanding of texts are conditioned by those that precede them.

> RT proxy list for Iran: http://bit.ly/KFBtQ and in Persian http://is.gd/136wy—#IranElection Jun 16, 2009

In this example, the implicature creates the expectation that this retweeted hyperlink provides readers with resources for finding proxy servers to help circumvent the government's communication blockades. But the URL's seeming 'illegibility,' that is, the lack of a readable domain name as a cue to the content being linked to, flouts the maxim of quantity and obfuscates the 'putting it that way' of what has been implied. In this sense, this practice of hyperlinking might be less conjunctive than additive while also informationalizing the hyperlinked texts into forms of symbolic exchange (Lash, 2002).

This might also mean that the practice of hyperlinking is not only intertextual, but interdiscursive, linking genres and modes of signification (Fairclough, 2003). As Kress (2003) has argued, genres, as forms of social action, are encoded with power and thus can be imbued ideologically. As frameworks of experience, they might therefore also function as metastances that, as with hashtags, shape the interpretation of meaning in a way that implies ideology. For instance, in example 1 the user has not only linked to the British legacy newspaper the *Guardian*, implying a sense of positional coherence between the texts, but has also borrowed the compressed style and initial capital letters of newspaper headlines in a way that might also suggest, through reentextualization, a form of alignment (Jaffe, 2009). A different form of stance-taking might be seen in the use of variation or marked forms as style (Kiesling, 2009). In example 2, the use of the preposition *up* to denote *uploaded* or *functioning* (as in 'the server is back up') seems to index the positive symbolic value of technology jargon. In example 6, the shortening and lack of capital letters in "can u help us get the word out" indexes, it would seem, the informality and spoken qualities of genres like text messaging and online chat (Crystal, 2001). That is to say, the use of links may be a form of political action that both bridges network nodes and links genres of texts in ways that could also support the formation of counterhegemonic discourse. But because the conjunctive functionality of hyperlinks points as much to the links between nodes as to the gaps between them (Morgan, 2002), the result of high-frequency hyperlinking, as in the activists' microblogging discourse, might also produce a type of fragmentation that challenges the notions of connectivity and belonging rather than inspires the formation of sociomental bonds and networked effervescence.

Irony and Iconicity: Reentextualized Images

This paradox of networked connectivity and fragmentation might also be seen in the protesters' discursive practice of carrying, as placards, photographs taken by protesters and uploaded to and circulated through social media services such as Flickr, as seen in Figure 4.1. As discussed in Chapters and these communicative actions became symbolic practices that represented both the government's violent repressions and the activists' agency despite state-imposed censorship and communication blockades.

Figure 4.1   Local reentextualization of activists' photographs. © Hamed Saber.

In this image, the amplification of this discourse seems clear: the reentextualization of the documentary photographs, first, in the context of the protest in Iran and then at a secondary level of *mediality* (Johnson & Ensslin, 2007) on the Flickr social media platform, intensifies the circulation of the messages contained in them and therefore the possibility of their reaching a wider audience. But it also creates, within a multimodal text, complex levels of signification. In the image in Figure 4.1, the iconicity of the street sign appears to locate the spatial coordinates of the protest at that instant for both a local and a global audience, even when, in the latter case, the Persian script may be indecipherable. Meanwhile, the placard of black-and-white documentary images, presumably taken by activists and circulated through social media, appears to testify to the government forces' violent repression of the protests. This functions as a secondary form of signage, coincidentally held up by a Green Movement supporter, as suggested by the bandana knotted around the protester's wrist, in parallel with the street sign, whose color might be seen as reflecting that of the Iranian conservative party. Whether or not those layers of potential signification are received in a globalized context, they nevertheless suggest a compressed micronarrative that, through this process of symbolically borrowing images, is arguably more likely to move among global information and media flows (Lash, 2002).

In fact, we can see how the practice of reentexualization as a discursive tactic within the social movement framework became, I argue, an *order of normativity* (Blommaert, 2005) within the global movement that grew up around and cohered with the election crisis protests in Iran. An instance of this can be seen in Figure 4.2 in the Flickr uploads of Iranian photographs reentextualized as evidence and symbolic resources during solidarity demonstrations held in San Francisco.[9]

The reentextualized photographs create an intertextual affiliation between the Iran protests and those led in solidarity by global activists in an interdiscursive link between the visual images as documentation of the government forces' brutality. As an instantiation of global new media flows, they also appear to act as slogans, the typical contents of demonstrators' placard. In this case, however, the slogans are vernacularized through reentexualization and thus made more readily accessible transnationally across media platforms and cultures. Further evidence of how this can be seen is in Figures 4.3 and 4.4, in which the same documentary photograph is reentextualized, respectively, by a protester in Iran and an activist in San Francisco.

As these images suggest, the circulation of photographs such as these across communication networks seems both to amplify its message across those networks and, through intertextual and interdiscursive links, strengthen its symbolic power as both evidence of the events occurring in Iran and the protesters' agency—if not also the networked effervescence these circulations appear to inspire.

Figure 4.2   Reentextualization of documentary photographs in San Francisco. © Steve Rhodes.

That collective spirit of unity across social movement frames toward globally defined fields of possibility can be facilitated by the affordances of social media such as Twitter and Flickr, perhaps especially the latter given the iconicity and cross-cultural accessibility of visual images in postmodern societies. As the image in Figure 4.5 shows, the symbolic—and ironic—borrowing by global activists of the iconic 'Hope' images from the 2008 Obama campaign as a form of metalinguistic commentary on the Iranian election crisis also shows how discourses can cross social movement frames.

That image serendipitously with a local Gay Pride demonstration also suggests how this process of reentexualization can, as discussed above, be a form of indexical rescaling from a local to a global social movement. In the U.S., the 2008 Obama campaign drew heavily for support on a demographic—young, urban, educated, and wired—which, in Iran, had also largely supported the Iranian opposition candidate Mousavi and subsequently constituted the base of the anti-Ahmadinejad movement. Arguably, this means that the ironic "Nope" images also entailed the key slogans from Obama's campaign, hope and change. The latter slogan can be seen in Figure 4.6 on a supporter at a rally in Shiraz for the reformist candidate Mehdi Karoubi, who ran under the slogan "Change for Iran."

Figure 4.3 Police brutality photograph appearing in demonstrations in Tehran. © Hamed Saber.

Figure 4.4 Police brutality photograph appearing in demonstrations in San Francisco. © Steve Rhodes.

Figure 4.5 Linking political discourses and movement frames and networks.
© Karen Lynn.

Figure 4.6 Iranian protester with political slogan in Persian and English. © Pedram Viesi.

This use of English to express a slogan strongly echoing that used by the then recently victorious U.S. president in a historic election seems to be a rather clear deployment of global symbolic resources. This is not to say, however, that either the Iranian opposition movement actors or those global activists acting in solidarity with them were inherently Obama supporters. Instead, it is to suggest how the interdiscursive links created through this symbolic borrowing arguably increases the social movement discourse's voice and mobility across global networks. And as these discourses move across networks, it becomes more likely that borrowings and similarities can become nodes where discourses and frames can cohere. The use of English together with Persian in Figure 4.6 suggests a further layer of symbolic borrowing given Iran's complex relation with English, the West, and in particular the United States, as discussed above.[10] Placards written in English and held up for a global audience seem to strongly suggest the use of a network standard to increase the message's mobility. At the same time, the cultural capital required to produce a sign like this appears to be redeployed as a tactic of counterpower used to circumvent the government's banning of foreign journalists during the election aftermath.

In addition, the discursive practice of code-mixing can index stance while further pointing toward the formation within the global social movement framework of orders of normativity, as the image in Figure 4.7 of an activist in Washington, D.C. with signs in both Persian and English strongly suggests. The activist not only appears to be borrowing the practices of the Iranian protesters, but also repurposing them to speak back to the Iranian authorities who, as discussed in Chapter 2, had taken to surveilling both local activists' use of social media and Western media coverage of the election crisis as a means of leveraging both internal and regional support against the protesters.

For the Iranian protesters, these discursive practices might also point toward a tactical use of English as a means of *nominating* the election crisis struggle as not merely a local concern, but a global human rights issue (Melucci, 1996). As Melucci has argued:

> Contemporary movements strive to reappropriate the capacity to name through the elaboration of codes and languages designed to define reality, in the twofold sense of constituting it symbolically and of regaining it, thereby escaping from the predominant forms of representation. (p. 357)

At the same time, even if this form of intertextual linking across networks creates a participatory effect in which discourses and social actors' agency appears intensified, its symbolic value may be diluted in the current marketplace of networked communication capitalism due to weakened shared reference. It is this arena that communication, as Dean (2008) has argued, "has detached itself from political ideals of belonging and connection to function today as a primarily economic form. Differently put, communicative exchanges, rather than fundamental to democratic politics, are the

Figure 4.7   Activist in Washington, D.C. with placards in English and Persian. © Hannah Kim.

basic elements of capitalist production" (p. 105). Perhaps, then, what this means is that while activists may have increased the voice and mobility of their discourses by borrowing globalized forms of communication and symbolic purposes in the ways discussed in this chapter, those tactics may also have cost them much of the use value of those messages. That said, as the images above show, the symbolic exchange did appear to create further possibilities for the sociomental bonds that might work together toward a form of sociocognitive counterpower against hegemonic forces and toward common goals, even if ephemeral and imaginary.

BORROWING AS A TACTICAL STRATEGY: CONCLUSIONS

As I asserted at the start of this chapter, Iranian protesters' use of social media during the 2009 election protests bears a significant resemblance to the use of small media during the 1978–79 Iranian Revolution. This similarity points toward an extension of modern Iran's cycle of protests and the master social movement frame that has shaped it. Within that framework the use of social media, as part of the shift in social movements toward rhizomatic structures formed around communication, also suggests similarities in tactics. As Renzi (2008) has argued, tactical media are networked spaces in which counterdiscourses can be symbolically fashioned and refashioned, a view that coheres with those of de Certeau (1984), who saw tactics as spaces of the other and the disempowered who borrow the symbolic resources of the powerful. But does the practice of borrowing those resources and deploying them within the social movement frame entail importing—if not completely, then partially—the ideologies and stances imbued in those practices? That is, as de Certeau also claimed, if entailed in a strategy is the power to transform the uncertainties of history into readable spaces, the Iranian activists' practice of reentexualization, as I have tried to show above, appears to make their local struggle more readable to a global audience across transnational media and information flows. The discursive practices and orders of normativity evidenced in the data above seem to attest to the success, within the logics of participation, of those tactics.

At the same time, this process of borrowing as a means of extending their local struggle toward globally defined fields of possibility also seems to mean that, in those discontinuous networked spaces flattened by the informationalizing processes of global flows, their resonance, as well as the logics of participation upon which they appear to be based, become diluted through diminished shared references and their stance-taking constrained at the level of affect. If so, this could be due to the convergence of strategies and tactics that has resulted from our contemporary environment of interactive, multimodal, cross-platform mediascapes and global flows (Manovich, 2009), in which dominant forces mimic the tactics of the marginalized, such as remixes and reentextualizations, as part of their powerful strategies. Why not, then, also the reverse? That is, Iranian protesters' use of social media through the cultural logics of the Iranian social movement frame might also exemplify the appropriation of strategies as tactics, a concern I take up further in Chapter 5.

NOTES

1. By choosing here the term *reentextualization* rather than *recontextualization*, which in some literature is used synonymously, I intend not only to use the term preferred by Jaffe (2009), whose work on stance I have based my analyses upon, but also to emphasize the movement of texts across languages, modes, and genres over the movement of contexts, which is necessarily entailed in the former by the inherent situatedness of discourse.
2. See Chapter 2 for discussions of access and digital divides.
3. These publicly available data were collected using the free social media search tool Topsy (http://topsy.com).

4. The time frame for this dataset corresponds with those of the news data analyzed in Chapter 2 and the other social media texts analyzed in this and subsequent chapters.
5. Source: http://140kit.com. Retrieved March 9, 2011.
6. As discussed in Chapter 1, the locations of Twitter users became less clear as users in Iran tried to mask their Internet protocols (IPs) as a means of avoiding government surveillance. Meanwhile, many activists outside Iran temporarily changed their settings to show their location as Iran as both a sign of solidarity with the Iranian protesters and as a means of confounding Iranian surveillance attempts. For my analyses, this lack of verifiable location is, I argue, irrelevant because I am focusing on the bridging and extending of translocal networks, not specifically inside or outside Iran. That said, these facts do lend support for claims presented earlier in the chapter regarding the use value of protesters' tweets as signal intelligence.
7. I have anonymized usernames in my dataset to protect users' identities.
8. At the time of the protests, Twitter was not available in right-to-left languages such as Persian, which necessitated communication in a left-to-right language such as English. This fact supports the view that Twitter was of negligible value as a coordination and communication tool among the protesters given the rate of English-language knowledge, along with the then-penetration level of Twitter in Iran. That said, it also complicates claims that the only reason activists tweeted in English was to address a global audience.
9. In Flickr, users can label their uploaded photographs with titles, dates, and locations, as both of these were. However, Flickr also can be set to show Exchangeable image file format (Exif) metadata that tags images taken with digital cameras to include such information as the date, time, camera settings, and geo-location. When collecting my Flickr data, I used Exif metadata to ensure that the date fell within my chosen collection parameters and, whenever possible, relied on geo-location tags rather than user captions for my analyses.
10. The caption in Persian below the image in Figure 4.6 can be roughly translated as "Minutes after fans clash Mousavi and Ahmadinejad—June 20 M Street—Soil Shiraz."

REFERENCES

Acuff, J. (2010). Social networking media and the revolution that wasn't: A realistic assessment of the revolutionary situation in Iran. In Y. Kamalipour (Ed.), *Media, power, and politics in the digital age: The 2009 presidential election uprising in Iran* (pp. 221–234). Lanham, MD: Rowman & Littlefield.

Anderson, B. (2006). *Imagined communities: Reflections on the origins and spread of nationalism* (3rd ed.). London: Verso.

Appadurai, A. (1996). *Modernity at large: Cultural dimensions of globalization.* Minneapolis: University of Minnesota Press.

Axworthy, M. (2013). *Revolutionary Iran: A history of the Islamic republic.* New York: Oxford University Press.

Bakhtin, M. M. (1986). *Speech genres and other late essays* (V. W. McGee, Trans.; C. Emerson and M. Holquist, Eds.). Austin: University of Texas Press.

Bhatt, R. (2008). In other words: Language mixing, identity representations, and third space. *Journal of Sociolinguistics, 12*(2), 177–200.

Blommaert, J. (2003). Commentary: A sociolinguistics of globalization. *Journal of Sociolinguistics*, 7(4), 607–623.

Blommaert, J. (2005). *Discourse*. Cambridge: Cambridge University Press.

Blommaert, J. (2010). *The sociolinguistics of globalization*. Cambridge: Cambridge University Press.

Bohman, J. (2004). Expanding dialogue: The Internet, the public sphere and prospects for transnational democracy. In N. Crossley & J. Roberts (Eds.), *After Habermas: New perspectives on the public sphere* (pp. 131–156). Oxford: Blackwell Publishing.

Boler, M. (Ed.). (2008). *Digital media and democracy: Tactics in hard times*. Cambridge, MA: MIT Press.

Bourdieu, P. (1990). *The logic of practice*. Stanford, CA: Stanford University Press.

Bourdieu, P. (1991). *Language and symbolic power* (J. B. Thompson, Trans.). Cambridge, MA: Harvard University Press.

Breeze, R. (2012). Critical discourse analysis and its critics. *Pragmatics*, 21(4), 493–525.

Brumberg, D. (2001). *Reinventing Khomeini: The struggle for reform in Iran*. Chicago: University of Chicago Press.

Burke, K. (1989). *On symbols and society* (J. R. Gusfield, Ed.). Chicago: University of Chicago Press.

Cali, D. (2000). The logic of the link: The associative paradigm in communication criticism. *Critical Studies in Media Communication*, 17(4), 397–408.

Canagarajah, A. S. (1999). *Resisting linguistic imperialism in English teaching*. Oxford: Oxford University Press.

Castells, M. (1996). *The information age: Economy, society, and culture. The rise of the network society, vol. 1*. Cambridge, MA: Blackwell.

Castells, M. (1997). *The power of identity. The information age: Economy, society and culture, vol. 2*. Malden, MA: Blackwell.

Castells, M. (2009). *Communication power*. New York: Oxford University Press.

Chayko, M. (2002). *Connecting: How we form social bonds and communities in the Internet age*. Albany: SUNY Press.

Chayko, M. (2008). *Portable communities: The social dynamics of online and mobile connections*. Albany: SUNY Press.

Clift, R. (2006). Indexing stance: Reported speech as an interactional evidential. *Journal of Sociolinguistics*, 10(5), 569–595.

Crack, A. (2008). *Global communication and transnational public spheres*. New York: Palgrave.

Crystal, D. (2001). *Language and the Internet*. Cambridge: Cambridge University Press.

Crystal, D. (2003). *English as a global language*. Cambridge: Cambridge University Press.

Dabashi, H. (2012). *The Arab spring: The end of post colonialism*. London: Zed Books.

Dean, J. (2008). Communicative capitalism: Circulation and the foreclosure of politics. In M. Boler (Ed.), *Digital media and democracy: Tactics in hard times* (pp. 101–122). Cambridge, MA: MIT Press.

de Certeau, M. (1984). *The practice of everyday life*. Berkeley: University of California Press.

Dobusch, L., & Quack, S. (2008). *Epistemic communities and social movements: Transnational dynamics in the case of the creative commons*. Cologne: Max Plank Institute for the Study of Societies.

Edward, J. (2009). *Language and identity*. New York: Cambridge University Press.

Entman, R. (2004). *Projections of power: Framing news, public opinion, and U.S. foreign policy*. Chicago: University of Chicago Press.

Fairclough, N. (2001). *Language and power* (2nd ed.). Essex: Pearson Education Ltd.

Fairclough, N. (2003). *Analyzing discourse: Textual analysis for social research.* London: Routledge.

Fisher, A. (2010). Bullets with butterfly wings: Tweets, protest networks, and the Iranian election. In Y. Kamalipour (Ed.), *Media, power, and politics in the digital age: The 2009 presidential election uprising in Iran* (pp. 105–118). Lanham, MD: Rowman & Littlefield.

Fornäs, J. (2002). *Digital borderlands: Cultural studies of identity and interactivity on the Internet.* New York: Peter Lang.

Fuchs, C. (2008). *Internet and society: Social theory in the information age.* London: Routledge.

Gillan, K., Pickerill, J., & Webster, F. (2008). *Anti-war activism: New media and protest in the information age.* New York: Palgrave Macmillan.

Grewal, D. S. (2008). *Network power: The social dynamics of globalization.* New Haven, CT: Yale University Press.

Hall, S. (1977). Culture, the media, and the ideological effect. In J. Curran, M. Gurevitch, & J. Woollacott (Eds.), *Mass communication and society* (pp. 315–348). London: SAGE.

Hardt, M., & Negri, A. (2009). *Commonwealth.* Cambridge, MA: Harvard University Press.

Hauser, G. (1999). *Vernacular voices: The rhetorics of publics and public spheres.* Columbia: University of South Carolina Press.

Howard, P. N. (2010). *The digital origins of dictatorship and democracy: Information technology and political Islam.* Oxford: Oxford University Press.

Jaffe, A. (Ed.). (2009). *Stance: Sociolinguistic perspectives.* Oxford: Oxford University Press.

Johnson, S., & Ensslin, A. (Eds.). (2007). *Language in the media.* London: Continuum.

Juris, J. (2008). *Networking futures: The movements against corporate globalization.* Durham, NC: Duke University Press.

Kamalipour, Y. (Ed.) (2010). *Media, power, and politics in the digital age: The 2009 presidential election uprising in Iran.* Lanham, MD: Rowman & Littlefield.

Kamvara, M. (2008). *Iran's intellectual revolution.* New York: Cambridge University Press.

Keddie, N. (2003). *Modern Iran: Roots and results of revolution.* New Haven/London: Yale University Press.

Kiesling, S. (2009). Style as stance. In A. Jaffe (Ed.), *Stance: Sociolinguistic perspectives* (pp. 171–194). Oxford: Oxford University Press.

Kluitenberg, E. (2010). *Delusive spaces: Essays on culture, media, and technology.* Rotterdam: NAi Publishers.

Kogan, M. (2005). Modes of knowledge and patterns of power. *Higher Education,* 49(1–2), 9–30.

Kress, G. (2003). *Literacy in the new media age.* London: Routledge.

Kurzman, C. (2004). *The unthinkable revolution in Iran.* Cambridge, MA: Harvard University Press.

Lash, S. (2002). *The critique of information.* London: SAGE.

Leppänen, A., Pitkänen-Huhta, A., Piirainen-Marsh, A., Nikula, T., & Peuronen, S. (2009). Young people's translocal new media uses: A multiperspective analysis of language choice and heteroglossia. *Journal of Computer-Mediated Communication,* 14, 1080–1107.

Lessig, L. (2001). *The future of ideas: The fate of the commons in a connected world.* New York: Random House.

Malek, M. (2010). Cyber disobedience: Weapons of mass media destruction. In Y. Kamalipour (Ed.), *Media, power, and politics in the digital age: The 2009 presidential election uprising in Iran* (pp. 277–288). Lanham, MD: Rowman & Littlefield.

Manovich, L. (2009). The practice of everyday (media) life: From mass consumption to mass cultural production? *Critical Inquiry, 35*, 313–331.

McNair, B. (2006). *Cultural chaos: Journalism, news and power in a globalised world*. London: Routledge.

Melucci, A. (1996). *Challenging codes: Collective action in the information age*. Cambridge: Cambridge University Press.

Meyerhoff, M., & Niedzielski, N. (2003). The globalization of vernacular variation. *Journal of Sociolinguistics, 7*(4), 534–555.

Myers, G. (2010). *The discourse of blogs and wikis*. New York: Continuum.

Mirsepassi, A. (2000). *Intellectual discourse and the politics of modernization: Negotiating modernity in Iran*. Cambridge: Cambridge University Press.

Morgan, W. (2002). Heterotropes: Learning the rhetoric of hyperlinks. *Education, Communication & Information, 2*(2/3), 215–233.

Morozov, E. (2011). *The net delusion: The dark side of Internet freedom*. New York: Public Affairs.

Parsa, M. (2000). *States, ideologies, & social revolutions: A comparative analysis of Iran, Nicaragua and the Philippines*. New York: Cambridge University Press.

Pennycook, A. (1994). *The cultural politics of English as an international language*. London: Longman.

Pennycook, A. (2007). *Global Englishes and transcultural flows*. London: Routledge.

Phillipson, R. (1992). *Linguistic imperialism*. Oxford: Oxford University Press.

Phillipson, R., & Skutnabb-Kangas, T. (1996). English only worldwide or language ecology? *TESOL Quarterly, 30*(3), 429–452.

Poulson, S. (2005). *Social movements in twentieth-century Iran: Culture, ideology, and mobilizing frameworks*. Lanham, MD: Lexington Books.

Rahimi, B. (2008). The politics of the Internet in Iran. In M. Semati (Ed.), *Media, culture and society in Iran: Living with globalization and the Islamic state* (pp. 37–56). New York: Routledge.

Rajaee, F. (2007). *Islamism and modernism: The changing discourse in Iran*. Austin: University of Texas Press.

Renzi, A. (2008). The space of tactical media. In M. Boler (Ed.). *Digital media and democracy: Tactics in hard times* (pp. 71–100). Cambridge, MA: MIT Press.

Riffaterre, M. (1994). Intertextuality vs. hypertextuality. *New Literary History, 25*(4), 779–788.

Russell, A., & Echchaibi, N. (Eds.). (2009). *International blogging: Identity, politics, and networked publics*. New York: Peter Lang.

Sharifan, F. (2010). Glocalization of English in World Englishes: An emerging variety among Persian speakers of English. In M. Saxena & T. Omoniyi (Eds.), *Contending with globalization in world Englishes* (pp. 137–158). Tonawanda, NY: Multilingual Matters.

Shirky, C. (2008). *Here comes everybody: The power of organizing without organizations*. New York: Penguin.

Silberstein, S. (2004). *War of words: Language, politics and 9/11*. New York: Routledge.

Silverstein, M. (2003). Indexical order and the dialectics of sociolinguistic life. *Language and Communication, 23*, 193–229.

Snow, N. (2010). What's that chirping I hear? From the CNN effect to the Twitter effect. In Y. Kamalipour (Ed.), *Media, power, and politics in the digital age: The 2009 presidential election uprising in Iran* (pp. 97–104). Lanham, MD: Rowman & Littlefield.

Sreberny-Mohammadi, A., & Mohammadi, A. (1994). *Small media, big revolution: Communication, culture, and the Iranian Revolution*. Minneapolis: University of Minnesota Press.

Sysomos. (2009, June). *A look at Twitter in Iran*. Retrieved December 17, 2014 from http://blog.sysomos.com/2009/06/21/a-look-at-twitter-in-iran/

Sysomos. (2010, September). *Replies and retweets on Twitter*. Retrieved November 13, 2012 from www.sysomos.com/insidetwitter/engagement

Szerszynski, B., & Urry, J. (2006). Vusuality, mobility and the cosmopolitan: Inhabiting the world from afar. *British Journal of Sociology*, 57(1), 113–131.

Tazimi, G. (2012). *Revolution and reform in Russian and Iran: Modernization and politics in revolutionary states*. New York: I. B. Tauris.

Vahdat, F. (2002). *God and juggernaut: Iran's intellectual encounter with modernity*. Syracuse, NY: Syracuse University Press.

van Dijk, T. (1998). *Ideology: A multidisciplinary approach*. Thousand Oaks, CA: SAGE.

Varzi, R. (2006). *Warring souls: Youth, media, and martyrdom in post-revolution Iran*. Durham, NC: Duke University Press.

Walljasper, J. (2010). *All that we share: How to save the economy, the environment, the Internet, democracy, our communities, and everything else that belongs to us*. New York: The New Press.

Yaghmaian, B. (2002). *Social change in Iran: An eyewitness account of dissent, defiance, and new movements for rights*. Albany: State University of New York Press.

Žižek, S. (2007). *How to read Lacan*. New York: W. W. Norton & Co.

5 Collective Action and Networked Identifications

In the previous chapter I argued that the fields of reference from which protesters tactically borrowed symbolic and linguistic resources functioned as a strategy of counterdiscourse formation. Deployed both locally and globally, this strategy was also a means of strengthening their counterpower in a lopsided struggle against government forces. That process, despite years of Ahmadinejad's exclusionary policies and anti-Western rhetoric, seems to point toward a shift in the logic underlying Iranian society in which locally defined understandings of modernity might also resonate with the kinds of outwardly looking cultural reforms that marked the start of the Khatami era (Melucci, 1996). But if any 'dialogue of civilizations' emerged from the 2009 presidential election crisis, it was not one that transpired among international political and religious leaders—or even through legacy media. Instead, it largely occurred among global activists communicating through 'small' social media across networked transnational public spheres. As the evidence in the previous chapter suggests, this online engagement helped spark the networked effervescence that also inspired offline collective action, both globally in solidarity with Iranian activists and locally in the streets of Tehran, Shiraz, and other Iranian cities. As Afsaneh Moqadam (2010) has noted in his account of participating in the 2009 Iranian election protests:

> How many times, during the Khatami presidency, did the people indicate their willingness to follow their leaders into the streets? How many times were the people disappointed by their leaders' reluctance to risk their or anyone else's skin? The use of mass action is no longer a monopoly in the hands of the hard-liners. (p. 49)

Even without large-scale structural resources and hierarchical organization, protesters succeeded, through tactical forms of collective action, in communicating across weak network ties and organizing the largest demonstrations Iran had experienced since the 1978–79 revolution. Though these actions may not have inspired another revolution or even forced a new election, their symbolic and sociocognitive effects, as I argued above, seemed to resonate across social movement frames and translocal networks.

But the practice of micro-coordinating collective action and the circulation of discourse across scale levels might point toward more than new possibilities for collective agency, in both the streets of Tehran and transnational imaginaries. These practices might also signal shifts in the protesters' identities. As has been widely argued, the symptoms and syndromes of intensifying global connections that mark contemporary experience have significantly contributed to the forming of new, individualized subjectivities at the expense of old collective identities such as community and class (Giddens, 1991; Rustin, 2008). When mobilized within social movements and intensified by the exigencies of conflict, it is through this process, as Poulson (2005) has argued, that "actors manipulate symbols and language in order to create new ideas and new social identities" (p. 1). In recent social movements, the formation of new identities has typically been marked by a shift from individual to new collective identifications that should be understood not as essentialized or reified objects, but as the outcomes of interaction and collective action (Melucci, 1996). For that reason, examining this process, as well as the ways in which collective actors take up subject positions within the social movement frame, is essential to trying to understand how social movements can point toward deep shifts in a society's cultural logics. It is also relevant, I argue, to tracing the discursive changes that tend to emerge from social movements, as I have intended to do in this research.

For these reasons, I extend in this chapter the analyses and discussions of the previous one by looking at the various discursive strategies employed by activists, acting both locally in Iran and around the globe, to construct and perform their identities within the social movement frame. To do so, I first briefly present a theoretical framework in which I accommodate established understandings of the social construction of identity. I do this with respect to both the protests' historical contexts and the master social movement frame of modern Iran, as well as the considerations of globalization and communication power presented previously. Then, I examine activists' discursive strategies for constructing and performing their collective identities in ways that strengthened collective agency and extended the social movement frame. I also consider how those identifications are made within, and complicated by, the *place-identity nexus* (Dixon & Durrheim, 2000), which, as the data suggest, also significantly informed the election crisis struggle. I conclude by analyzing a YouTube video clip, "Where Is This Place?", which employs multimodal discourses to directly examine the place-identity nexus with respect to issues raised in Chapters 1 and 2 regarding how the protesters' actions, together with Western understandings of them, index a complex range of stances and overlapping ideologies.

MOBILITIES, CO-PRESENCE, AND DELOCALIZATION

In globalized contexts dialectically shaped by internal and external forces, identity has become a primary source of meaning and experience (Castells,

1996). With global flows *decentering* culture from the traditional deter-minisms of experience, identity has become a reflexive project in which we engage in the construction of self and realignment of habitus within local-ized global cultural fields (Appadurai, 1996; Featherstone, 1990; Giddens, 1991). Yet, this process, despite the intense pressures of commodified global values and lifestyles, is not exclusively homogenizing (Fine, 2007). Instead, it is argued, we retain the agency to see ourselves as connected to global concerns while situated in our local histories. And within the tensions of translocal cultural influences, our interpretations of these experiences can be divergent and multiple. For these reasons, identity is also now commonly considered to be neither stable nor singular, but multiple and hybrid—a process in the collective establishment of symbolic relationships of similari-ties and differences (Hopper, 2007; Jenkins, 2008). Within the processes of identifications, Castells (1997) has identified three general forms of identity construction that are important for my analyses: one, the *legitimizing identi-ties* built by dominant social forces as a means of maintaining and rational-izing their power; two, the *resistance identities* constructed by social actors in opposition to dominant social structures; and three, *project identities*, or the new identity constructions through which social actors redefine their social positions as part of a larger effort to transform society, as during social movements.

Underlying these theories are assumptions regarding the social con-struction of identity. With language at the core of our experience, our identities are understood to be formed in discourse, namely the dominant discourses of social structures and practices, a process by which agency can be controlled if not erased (Foucault, 1972, 1978). Yet, within these constraints, identity can be itself a discursive practice, one that we inhabit but also perform through the ways we repeat verbal and non-verbal signs or acts as a means of self-fashioning (Benwell & Stokoe, 2006; Butler, 1990). Capable, therefore, of both reproducing and destabilizing established discourses, we discursively construct our identities through a dynamic process of interaction and performance in which fluid, frag-mented, or hybrid identifications are made at the interstices of culture and communication (Bhabha, 2004; Featherstone, Lash, & Robertson, 1995). As argued in Chapter 2, these interstices typically bear the local-global tensions of a transnational network society (Castells, 1997; Goff-man, 1974), with language fundamental to that dialectical, translocal process. But when language is viewed not as an object but a set of linguis-tic resources, these tensions come to produce the *translocal vernaculars* that, in turn, constitute *translocal identifications*, or subjectivities that can both cross localities and be pulled in various directions (Brumberg, 2001; Ong, 1999).

Inherent in the discursive construction of translocal identifications is the belief that place is bound up with language in the constitution of identities. 'Where we are' has long been understood as strongly connected to 'who we are.' Place, though, is more than just a container for identities. Rather, like identity, it is something produced through interaction and collective co-construction. How we talk about 'where we are' comes to constitute our understandings of places and the various ways we occupy them. But in translocal contexts, the dynamic links in this *place-identity nexus* have become increasingly complex, and how this nexus is deployed in discourse is critical to the ways in which we accomplish social action (Dixon & Durrheim, 2000). In addition, the ways we understand, experience, and construct ourselves and the places we inhabit have been strongly influenced by the mobilities now afforded us by wireless technologies. That is, within the *space of flows* in networked societies, the increasing mobilization of social life has helped produce fluid, *delocalized* identities and experiences (Castells, 2009; Urry, 2007). With the old immobility of place delocalized, the boundaries between presence and absence have been blurred. For social actors, this means their agency can be extended through, on the one hand, the *co-presence* created by mobilized communication and, on the other, a *polychronicity* of experience (Caron & Caronia, 2007). A protester in Iran, for instance, could be participating in a street demonstration while tweeting or uploading cellphone video captures to circulate both to other local activists in Tehran or Shiraz and, simultaneously, to an unknown audience reading them in real time or reentextualized later in other activists' discourses. In social movements, therefore, the emphasis has shifted from individual to collective identifications as both a network of active relations and the cognitive process of jointly constructing a system for legitimating collective action (Melucci, 1996). And with cultural identity and the collective action underlying the processes of collective identification at the core of new social movements (Parsa, 2000; Poulson, 2005), analyzing the discursive construction of place and identifications in social movements is essential to trying to determine the impact of social movements on discursive change (Juris, 2008).

COLLECTIVE IDENTIFICATIONS AND DEICTIC SHIFTS: ANALYSIS

Given the context, the social movement goals, and the various deployments of symbolic resources within the social movement frame as discussed in the previous chapter, it is perhaps unsurprising that one of the most common forms of identification present in all three of my datasets are linguistic and visual representations of collective identity. As Melucci (1996) has argued, collective identity, as a cognitive process, refers to a network of active relationships between actors who interact, communicate, influence each other, and make decisions. This network of relationships becomes active in the transnational imaginary when, as in the following tweet from outside Iran, a user appears to perform his or her identity as a member—real or imagined—of the Iranian diaspora.

> @username For all my brothers and sisters in #Iran http://blip.fm/~3ua5k
> #Iranelection please please retweet this . . . please Jun 16, 2009

Here, the use of familial forms could cue not only cognitive associations of the diaspora, but also a symbolic extension of the social movement frame toward the cosmopolitan ethics of transnational logics (Ong, 1999). The amplifying *all,* entreating *please,* and dramatic use of ellipsis also produce a strong affective stance that works to create, through empathy, a collaborative or consensual subject-position for the audience (Jaffe, 2009). A similar process can be seen in the use of collective pronouns in the social movement discourse. Compared with first-person pronouns, plural personal pronouns tend to emphasize interaction with others and have been shown to signal more positive outlooks than first-person singular pronouns (Elson, Yeung, Roshan, Bohandy, & Nader, 2012). As has been widely argued (see Fairclough, 2001; Hall, 1996), the use of collective pronouns such as *we,* in dominant discourses, can be a means of clustering or eliding heterogeneous identities in ways that could support hegemonic encodings of cultural meanings or forms of structural domination. But in tactical counterdiscourses like those of the Iranian protesters, the use of collective lexical forms may function as an assertion of agency against control within the social movement frame. According to the large-scale quantitative content analysis by Elson and colleagues of Twitter tweets about the Iranian election during and after the 2009 protests, there was an elevated use of second- and third-person pronouns in the month that followed the election. This trend compared favorably with that of my Twitter dataset, in which there are 27 instances of *we* and 24 of the collective noun *people,* an example of the latter appearing in these tweets from inside Iran:

> @username People of Iran—THIS IS THE DAWN—This is the new begining—have hope and prepare—#Iranelection RT RT RT 06/21/2009

> RT Open Letter to the World from the People of Iran: http://tinyurl.com/nw95ev Please RT. #IranElection (via a user) Jun 16, 2009

> @username: http://twitpic.com/7h65h—Iran / Esfehan / fire / police & people #Iranelection Jun 15, 2009

In the first two examples, the collective noun *people,* though delimited by the prepositional phrase *of Iran,* creates a unified resistance identity that could work to support the movement's collective action. The third example is in the telegraphic style, punctuated by slashes, which, as argued in the previous chapter, suggests for a local audience the coordinates of collective action (or, in this case, violent conflict with the police) and, for a global audience, a caption for the hyperlinked image. Like the use of familial forms discussed above, the cognitive senses of unity in the social movement discourse formed by these uses of collective lexis might also legitimate particular actions within the movement. For the protesters, this may have included demanding a recount, even a new election, or the various forms of passive and active resistance.

Yet, as in dominant discourses, collective forms such as these in counterdiscourses can also elide differences within groups. If so, notions of individual agency and intentionality would be compromised, as would the performance of collective identities in transnational public spheres. In the following tweet from an activist supposedly tweeting outside Iran, the collective forms *we* and *people* (abbreviated) suggest, on the user's behalf, a complex instance of co-presence:

> @username We WANT A RE-VOTE NOT A RE-COUNT!! This will not stand. #Iranelection REMEMBER DO NOT TWEET NAMES FROM PPL IN Iran! http://blip.fm/~5ervw Jun 17, 2009

In the first part of the tweet, the inclusive *we* gathers the user into the demonstrating crowds in Iran speaking back to local forms of power, a clear instance of stance-taking supported by the emotive use of all caps and repeated exclamation points (Jaffe, 2009). In one sense, this action might simply be another example of how global activists echoed Iranian protesters' chants and slogans as a means of circulating their discourse and extending their movement's frame, with the tweet functioning as a kind of electronic bumper sticker in the transnational traffic of information and media flows. Seen this way, this type of discursive practice might support interpretations of Twitter's function during the 2009 protests as limited to temporary expressions or venting of emotions and therefore of little value as signal intelligence or movement coordination (Hashem & Najjar, 2010; Malek, 2010). But in the second part of the tweet, the use of "in Iran" adds a proximal-distant tension typical of globalized relations (Hopper, 2007). On the user's part, this tension evidences a reflexive awareness of an imagined audience as part of the dialectic interplay of internal and external forces in the identification process (Jenkins, 2008). Viewed as a movement in the place-identity nexus, it might also be an example of what Goffman (1974) called *keying*, or the action of shifting of frames as a means of redefining a situation. As Jaffe has argued, redefining experience through keying can allow for the layering or overlapping of frames through which a multiplicity of stances and identities can then be signaled. In the example above, the keying of a global frame overlays the discourse with the dialectic of local-global participation and co-presence through which the possibilities for agency can multiply. On the user's part, an imagined co-presence facilitated by the use of networked communication technologies might also add valence to the sociomental bonds the user appears to have formed with multiple audiences. In this overlap of frames, social movement actors can come to see and project themselves as powerful nodes between networks and within the social movement framework.

This evidence suggests, then, that tactics such as these appear to extend collective action or agency, even when individual identities are suppressed. This might understandably be the case within the social movement frame and the need to mobilize loosely affiliated actors around the election crisis. However, within overlapping frames and the dialogic experience of co-presence, such moves may also reflect a fragmentation of identity and heteroglossic struggle for meaning that complicates, if not dilutes, the resonance of these symbolic expressions. In the Flickr dataset, for instance, there are numerous images of global activists borrowing the symbolic resources of the Iranian protests, such as the Iranian flag, as a means of showing solidarity with the activists in Iran, as seen in Figure 5.1.

On the Berlin placard, the reentextualized Iranian flag, a symbol of Iranian nationalism, is laminated with use of German *Zusammen für Iran* ("Together for Iran"). In a similar image from the Flickr research corpus, the colors of the Iranian flag have been used to expressively amplify the slogan *Nous exigeons une election libre* ("We demand a free election) in an activist's placard in Paris.[1] In both examples, these appropriations of symbolic resources—flags, symbolic colors, languages—across contexts appear to create opportunities for wider discursive diffusion. As I argued in the previous chapter, the borrowing of the symbolic resources visible in Figure 5.1 works to amplify the Iranian protesters' discourse across new networks while also creating a sense of collective spirit, or networked effervescence,

Figure 5.1 Activists in Berlin demonstrating in solidarity with Iranian protesters. © Ronny Pohl.

between Iranian and global activists. In the process, it may also work to legitimize the Iranian protesters' struggle according to globally defined values. Yet, while the emphasis on unity in the Berlin placard appears to be orientated transnationally, the use, in the flag, of a symbol of *banal nationalism* (Billig, 1995) indexes the nation-state. Demands for free elections in the Paris placard suggest a universal right, emphasized by the collective *we*, but nevertheless seem to treat a political ideology as a global commonplace. Nevertheless, within the social movement frame, these discourses could concomitantly strengthen transnational sociomental bonds and reframe the election crisis as a global issue. If so, agents could feel further empowered locally to continue to struggle—or, for still passive observers, to join in—against the government forces, a possibility, I argue, that should be accounted for when measuring, as others have tried, the impact of social media during the protests. Or could it be, conversely, that by addressing a global audience across transnational networks, the protesters also create further opportunities for the movement's discourses, and their identities within them, to be more readily reshaped, or manipulated, according to others' ideological aims?

Networked Fields of Reference

It is also possible that this process of layering dilutes the resonance of symbolic resources across networks. The notion of 'togetherness' put forth by the Berlin placard (and the Flickr photo by which the slogan was further circulated) is seemingly agentless, as if the concept of unity, as a compressed bit of social movement discourse, triumphs the collective and collapses time-space relations. Similarly, in the Paris slogan, the collective *we* (*nous*, in French) functions as a node between proximal and distant networks. In one sense, this would seem to simply expand the collective identifications further across translocal networks. But redefining the antecedence in this way potentially strains the semantic binding between pronoun and referent and therefore complicates the identifications being made by these activists across networks. In other words, who does *we* specifically refer to in these examples, and which *we* is empowered to legitimately make such demands of a sovereign country? And as these symbolic resources, in this case of banal nationalism, are reentextualized into globalized contexts, it appears that their shared references can become weakened and thus constrained—if not further, then differently—in their effect.

Further evidence of this complexity can be seen in the image in Figure 5.2, in which members of the Iranian diaspora in Bern, Switzerland, are shown demonstrating in solidarity with the protesters in Iran.[2] The collective reflexive pronoun *our* in "Where are our friends?" on two signs appears to complicate, if not contradict, in one sense, the reflexive *their* of "Where is their vote?" and, in a slightly different sense, the use of the collective pronouns *we, you* (plural), and *our* in the slogan "To the people of Iran, We send

Figure 5.2   Collective pronouns in activists' placards. © Raphael Moser.

you our prayers and support." In this network of deictic references, the use of *we/our* and *you/their* sets up what seems to be a relatively straight-forward proximal-distant axis of relations with the activists in Switzerland at the *deictic center*, that is, the reference point according to which a deictic expression—in this case, a spatial one—should be understood, as represented in Figure 5.3.

But the reentextualization of the slogan "Where are our friends?" doubles the deictic reference for *our* and creates multiple, overlapping deictic centers. As a remix of the widely used slogan *Where is our vote?*, this use of *our* could reference the vote of hundreds of thousands of Iranian expatriates who voted outside Iran, including in Bern.[3] Yet, the phrase *people of Iran* suggests a cultural or ethnic identification as a member of the diaspora rather than a political one. Either way, this fluid field of reference reflects how deixis can crucially be reshaped as discourses and images move across networks and scale levels with the *space of flows* (Castells, 1996). It may also signal the complex ways deterritorialization can transform collective actors' loyalties, or at least how they are represented (Appadurai, 1996).

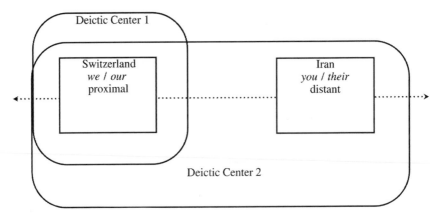

Figure 5.3   Shifting deictic centers in networked fields of reference.

Identifications in the place-identity nexus can also transform networks of reference bound up in symbols of *banal nationalism* (Billig, 1995). In Figure 5.1, the image of the Iranian flag overwritten with German strongly locates the activists both geographically and in the global imagination. But when moving across transnational networks, language, in this instance as a *mediatized* symbol of nationalism, can come to index global power through the cognitive associations bound up in commonplace understandings of the West's role in globalization. What is more, its layering on the Iranian flag above creates a co-presence that positions social actors in a multiplicity of roles (Caron & Caronia, 2007). As the image moves through social media across transnational network flows, activists' participation in a local demonstration becomes re-situated, through both rescaling and their own discursive practices, into a global framework of social movements. As discursive constructions of identity, these tactics appear to support the claims by Melucci (1996) and others that rather than structural determinants of identity, a shared deployment of symbolic resources appears to suggest a congruence in stance across local movements. Through amplification and uptake across global social media networks, this tactical employment of translocal symbolic resources might also point toward a discursive strategy among activists to bridge the local social movement frame with a globally aligned one. If so, these resources, taken together as part of a flow of images collected under the IranElection tag, evoke both further instances of networked effervescence as well as a shared horizon of concern—a global or cosmopolitan ethics that would transcend past constructions of identity (Chouliaraki, 2006). At the same time, as an intertextual chain of reciprocal references, they also delocalize activists so that they appear to float among contexts and potential fields of action in a way that, rather than redefining possibilities for agency and belonging (Caron & Caronia), might flatten or dilute the value of those expressions among global flows or constrain their meaning at the level of affect (Dean, 2012; Lash, 2002).

This *interobjectivity*, as Caron and Caronia (2007) have termed it, can also arguably be seen in the image in Figure 5.4 of activists demonstrating *en masse* in Tehran's Azadi Square. This scene, common in the Flickr dataset, clearly invokes iconic images of collective action and the populism of social movements. Yet, within historical contexts and across global flows, the *semiotics of the crowd* can also cue mental models of both democracy and the mass participation of the Islamic Revolution that produced the conservative elite against whom these protesters are demonstrating (Tambar, 2009). As a trope, then, within the social movement frame, this use of iconic crowd images could reflect some of the struggle for identity that has marked much of modern Iran's cycle of protests. This network of possible meanings is further complicated by the images of protesters photographing the crowd in a way that suggests a reflexive awareness of the material and political conditions of the protest and their individual participation within it (Mittelman, 2004). What results is a co-presence in which technical immediacy, through the use of the cellphone cameras, is put in the service of sociocultural immediacy to produce a multiplicity of identifications (Caron & Caronia, 2007). That is, by mediatizing the protests, agents' experiences become doubled in a way that could grant individuals the agency to reconfigure experience as documentary evidence, perhaps later for another audience (Chouliaraki,

Figure 5.4 Mass demonstration in Azadi Square, June 15, 2009.

2006; Talbot, 2007). In the photograph in Figure 5.5, an image documenting evidence of the government's violent repression of the protests becomes,
once circulated across networks, reentextualized as a symbolic resource
when employed, in this instance, as a placard in a San Francisco march in
solidarity with the Iranian protesters. But the image is further reconfigured
when subsequently remediated through the Flickr upload of the placard in
an image that, through framing, substitutes the activist's face with that of
the injured Iranian protester.

   If, as Jenkins (2008) has argued, the process of identification is based
on the systematic construction and signification of similarity and difference, this instance of remediation points toward a collapsed identification, or a collective co-presence at the node formed by the converging
discourses and contexts across time-space. And that these contexts are
linked is implied in both the uptake visible here and the mobility it entails
(Chouliaraki, 2006). What this appears to suggest, then, is the effectiveness of deploying communicative resources as forms of symbolic and social
capital to bridge social movement frames across global networks (Castells,
2009; Gumperz, 1982). Yet, according to Gumperz, it is when "communicative conventions and symbols of social identity differ [that] the social
reality itself becomes subject to question" (p. 3). If so, should we also see
as entailed in these attempts to bridge or even transform frame alignments
a belief that those social realities—a bloodied protester in Tehran and an

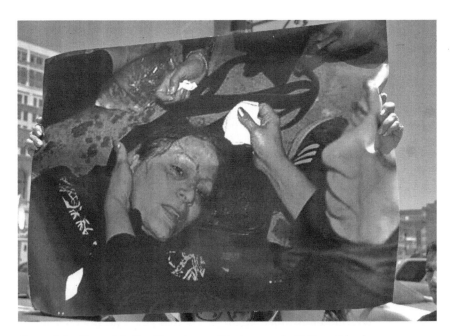

Figure 5.5   Placard in San Francisco solidarity march. © Steve Rhodes.

activist in San Francisco—could or should be similar? This is not to suggest that any act or process of symbolically identifying or empathizing with suffering or injustice is inherently an essentializing one; rather, that the discursive construction of similarities in these collective identifications, I argue, reflects an ideology oriented more toward the logics of collectivities and participation than that of individuals and competition, and our attempts to understand them through analysis should take that into account (Gumperz; Jenkins).

At the same time, we must accept that the logics of networks, and thus of informational capitalism, are integral to these processes of remediation, and in doing so, it is hard not to wonder whether the same economic and information systems that have weakened offline social solidarity also inherently undermine all genuine attempts at online solidarity predicated on those logics (Rustin, 2008). In this sense, within the social movement frame, the process of identification can itself become a potentially powerful form of stance-taking and counterdiscourse. In the following tweet, a user deploys both English and social media—in the form of both Twitter and, through the hyperlink to an uploaded cellphone video clip, YouTube—to legitimate a particular identity for Iranians.

> This is what real Iranians are: http://bit.ly/VhocZ #Iranelection

Substantiating that claim is a hyperlinked video clip of a street protest in Tehran that includes images of a large crowd marching peacefully, a police motorcycle burning in the street, and various protesters attending to an injured police officer, as seen in the excerpted frames in Figure 5.6.

In addition to offering validity and indexical meaning to the knowledge claim offered in the tweet, this hyperlinking between modalities and social media services gives activists a further means of creatively constructing their identities in discourse. In doing so through the tactical symbolic resources of a globalized vernacular and networked social media, they are empowered through both cultural and social capital to position their collective subjectivities at multiple scale levels: in the local context of the protests, the

Figure 5.6   Frames from June 2009 protest video uploaded to YouTube.

images of activists marching peacefully and altruistically aiding an injured police officer—particularly when defined as characteristic of "real Iranians"—also function as a powerful form of stance-taking on a global level. Yet, the process of remediation bound up in these identifications (and the counterdiscourse they help to construct) also suggests social actors' need for multiple forms of evidence to validate experience and/or knowledge. Such practices of rendering collective action as *techno-factual* suggests not only a reconfiguration of experience, but perhaps also an inversion of intimacy in a dialogic lifeworld (Chouliaraki, 2006). Put another way, these practices, I argue, point toward a need to ascribe value to experience according to contradictory logics or principles. As individuals reshape for local and global audiences their identifications as both participants and witnesses, activists and citizen journalists, they risk diluting the value of their symbolic and social capital and fragmenting their identities in the merging of the private and public spheres to which these actions seem to attest. As strategies for the formation of counterdiscourses and resistance identifications, these actions also suggest a dialectic of contradictory principles in which social movement actors' resources, like the constructions of ideologies in legacy media discourse presented in Chapter 3, are situated in a fluid discursive construction of potentially powerful forms of stance-taking and identification (Boehmer, 2006; Fornäs, 2002).

Where Is This Place? Discursive Reterritorialization

For collective identifications and collective actions to multiply and extend in scope within a social movement, there must be a social space free from repression or domination (Melucci, 1996). The process of multi-localization described above appears to be a viable way for activists to tactically deploy social media and global vernaculars in a strategy of reconfiguring boundaries and extending the social movement frame across global networks. Yet, those collective actions, themselves a form of stance-taking and counterdiscourse within Iran's master social movement frame, do not necessarily signal a lack of local struggle with the processes of deterritorialization inherent in globalized relations. Instead, the evidence I have collected suggests that tactical discursive constructions of place are highly valuable in the social movement discourse, and the creative process of reterritorializing place in discourse is an important act of symbolic resistance within the social movement frame.

One of the highest frequency keywords in the Twitter dataset, *Iran* appears 325 times in 238 total tweets at a rate of approximately 1.4, a frequency that compares relatively favorably with the rate of 1.8 in the 140kit dataset. This high frequency is understandable given not only the use of the IranElection hashtag, but also how, especially within the constraints of the microblogging genre, the word *Iran* could function effectively as a *topos* in the developing election crisis discourse. Yet, because it appears so much more frequently than, for instance, the collective pronoun *we*, it is hard to dismiss its potential significance in the discursive process of collective identification. In the following tweets, *Iran* appears as part of a set of coordinates in the developing post-election crisis.

> Iran / today / Krimkhan St / protest NOW #Iranelection on Twitpic http://ree.tw/bzk (retweeted 131x http://ree.tw/bzl) Jun 17, 2009

> Iran / today / hafttir Sq / protest NOW #Iranelection on Twitpic http://ree.tw/bzm (retweeted 123x http://ree.tw/bzn) Jun 17, 2009

For a local audience, this circulation of nodal coordinates in the ongoing demonstrations could have functioned as an act of micro-coordination to enlist participant support. It may also have been a warning to those seeking to avoid confrontations with government forces. For the user circulating these tweets, the specificity of the information and the supporting hyperlinked photograph create the role of engaged participant, while the emotive style of the all-capped deictic reference *now* suggests an affective stance that might, through its implied urgency, also function as a call to collective action that the retweets, as forms of peer evaluation, appear to support.

At a macrolevel, however, the rescaling process creates a shift in the field of reference so that what is being reported for an unknown global audience is not the specific event but the knowledge of the event that is then symbolically ratified by the retweets. The specificity, therefore, of these locations, together with the supporting hyperlinked images, might work to create a sense of authenticity—a clear, credible voice in the flows of 'cyberscreaming.' And as argued above, the telegraphic style functions as a mobile global vernacular readily amplified across networks. In this process of presenting experience as signal intelligence, the subjectivity constituted in this discourse shifts from witness and (perhaps) participant to citizen journalist, and the notion of place projected here operates less as a set of coordinates referring to a specific geographic location and more as a notion of place itself. For some, it might even signal a set of beliefs about that place: that Iran, now, is a place where protests, as manifestations of free expression and civic power, can and do occur. And with the slashes, reminiscent of those used in URLs, syntactically in the text, the deictic expression *now*, in the absence of a tensed verb, arguably shifts from an affective to an epistemic stance-marker. That is, as the notion of place seems to supplant, through discursive rescaling, reference to a place itself, temporal deixis, detached, in this case, from the moment's exigency, comes to reference *timeless time*, or what Castells (1996) has called the 'eternal/ephemeral' of network flows. As the space of flows dissolves time by disordering the sequence of events and making them simultaneous, society comes to occupy an eternal ephemerality in which *now* is always *now*, and place is time-bound.

Within the social movement frame, this reorganization of experience may invite further participation—real or imagined—across networks and thus extend collective agency. Liberated from the frictions of distance (Harvey, 1989), activists around the globe are free to participate or lend support, to protest in solidarity, share information about proxy servers, or link network nodes of signal intelligence, as the data in this and the previous chapter have shown. In this sense, by using social media and information and communication technologies (ICTs), social movements can work to occupy these spaces as acts of resistance and symbolic expression—as forms of counter-power (Castells, 2009). But if, as Manovich (2002) has argued, in the flow of transnational communication what matters is not the content but the sociability of communicative actions, is this participation, and the process of collective identifications it entails, only symbolic, no more than further instances of global interpassivity? If so, as a tactic of further engendering networked effervescence, the informationalizing of experience might mean that what matters is not where in Iran the protest is occurring but simply the fact that it is (Lash, 2006). In other words, the content of tweets such as these that might be most mobile across scale levels for a global audience is the construction of Iran as a place where protests can and do occur, where resistance and change are possible, regardless of whether this is actually the case. If so, the more this 'knowledge' is known and validated, the greater its circulation and amplification and the larger that space becomes within the transnational imaginary that audiences around the world are free to co-inhabit. Yet, the data presented in this chapter, as well as in the previous one, suggest that this kind of 'knowledge' is merely a public attestation of sociability that can only be, within a 'placeless' frame of collective action, ratified through quantification and commodification—by, for instance, 123 retweets from anonymous users or the techno-factual experience of mediatized co-presence, as seen in the evidence above. In that case, the informationalization of discourse in the social movement frame and the logics of participation appear similar to that of the logics of flexible capitalism.

Nevertheless, as a tactical tool of resistance, this process seems to allow social movement actors—at least within the space of transnational imaginaries—the creative agency to reconfigure or reterritorialize place and thereby transform experience and the resistance identities located within it. The metaphoric comparison in the following tweet, substantiated by the hyperlinked image, discursively reconfigures Iran as a space of resistance by creating a metaphorical equivalency between it and Palestine.

@username: http://twitpic.com/7fmo8—Iran is the same as Palestine #Iranelection Jun 15, 2009

This cognitive bridging could also align the Iranian protests with the interests of a wide range of contemporary global progressives for whom critical issues in Israel and Palestine are commonplaces in their social justice and activism discourses. It also works to discursively reconfigure Iran within global frameworks of reference networked to complex ideological stances on such issues as human rights and political sovereignty (Hopper, 2007; Mittelman, 2004). Projecting Iran symbolically, then, into transnational public spheres becomes more than a matter of expressing attachment or taking a stance; it also creates what Dixon and Durrheim (2000) have called a *grounds of identity*, which is both a sense of belonging to place and a rhetorical warrant through which social practices and relations can be legitimated. In this discursive construction of space, deployed as a symbolic resource, social actors can perform a variety of actions, from legitimating and justifying to excluding and blaming. As such, establishing a grounds of identity to legitimate claims of moral equivalency between Palestine and Iran would seem to signal a discursive strategy to reframe the election crisis as a human rights issue and thus a global concern. If so, this would be significant within Iran's master framework in that it links collective action to the secular ideals of social justice and human rights while also challenging isolationist policies and cultural attitudes of the Iranian conservative elite. In this sense, these types of discursive constructions of the place-identity nexus can function ideologically. As Dixon and Durrheim have claimed, "it is through language that places themselves are imaginatively constituted in ways that carry implications for 'who we are' or 'who we claim to be'" (p. 32). Yet, as the micronarratives of place and resistance come to circulate among the proliferation of global symbols, it is also possible that the resulting informationalizing of experience renders these narratives and the identifications within them as merely further instances of *banal globalism*, the unnoticed backdrop and symbols of the densely globalized network society (Szerszynski & Urry, 2006). I argue, then, that if in global public sphere discourse Palestine has come, in various ways for diverse groups, to function as a cue for legitimating a range of political stances and actions, suggesting Iran is its metaphorical (and perhaps moral) equivalent would align the protesters' social movement frame with an incongruous array of political frames. It would do so in a way that could denature the supposed emotive force of the intended comparison suggested by the hyperlinked photograph, in which street protesters, presumably in Tehran, throw rocks and bottles at heavily armed government forces. What this all may simply mean is that context, in the end, actually matters. Or, does it point toward a critical weakness of this type of identification—especially when rescaled across frames of reference—as a social movement tactic?

THIS PLACE IS IRAN: CONCLUSIONS

Within the place-identity nexus, then, the discursive construction of place is central to both the production of self and, when reconfigured in the space of flows, the processes by which identities can be dissolved (Dixon & Durrheim, 2000). But new identifications are central to transforming society (Castells, 1997). If so, the breakdown of old identities would seem to offer, at least within the social movement frame, opportunities for reconstructing resistance identities around shared principles into the project identities by which agents can redefine their positions in society and thereby work to transform it (Castells). The collective spirit of effervescence across global networks might seem to energize the possibilities for real change, but is that spirit resonant enough to endure its actual processes in local contexts? To that question, history suggests but one response. Those engaged in the struggle offer at least another. How some have approached their answer might be reflected in a final piece of evidence, the IranElection YouTube upload "Where is this place?". In the video, an unseen narrator recites a poem written in Persian as protesters shout from their rooftops into the Tehranian night "Allah-o Akbar!" ("God Is Great!"). In a culture where poetry and symbolic language are critical elements of millennia-old traditions, the use of poetry here as a symbolic resource is congruent with Iran's historical tradition of strategically deploying symbols, signs, and slogans during mass protests (Gheytanchi, 2010). As Gheytanchi has shown, protesters in 2009 frequently borrowed slogans from the 1979 Islamic Revolution, replacing the Shah with the Basij as their targets, and later used social media such as YouTube to spread slogans that had been chanted in the streets to a wider audience, including the Iranian diaspora, for whom cyberspace serves as a meeting point.

But more than just the tactical deployment of symbolic cultural resources reentextualized within the social movement frame as symbols of resistance, this use of emotive expression appears to function as counterdiscourse to the supposed dislocated, 'universal' perspective of 'objective' news (Chouliaraki, 2006). As the dark grainy images and muffled sound of the amateur video document the nighttime protests, the poem, performed like a voice-over, locates Iran not at nodal coordinates, but in a cultural field of values, ethics, and human concerns.[4] To define what appears to be the boundaries of this field, the speaker in the poem engages in a series of questions-and-answers that at once evokes the logic and systematicity of Socratic questioning and the emotive call-and-response of prayer:

> Where is this place?
> Where is this place where every door is closed?
> Where is this place where people are simply calling God?
> . . .
>
>   Where is this place where
>   so many innocent people are trapped?
>
> Where is this place where no one comes to our aid?
> Where is this place where only with our silence

we are sending our voices to the world

. . .

Where is this place where citizens
are called vagrants?

The poet's questions map a complex terrain defined by the tension between local and global networks of power and meaning. Protesters call out both to God and to a global audience while statist notions of citizenship contend with the transnational, cosmopolitan ethics of human rights. Yet, for all the dialectical complexity of the questions, the response is simple and unequivocal: "This place is Iran. / The homeland of you and me." As Melucci (1996) has argued, "contemporary movements strive to reappropriate the capacity to name through the elaboration of codes and languages designed to define reality, in the twofold sense of constituting it symbolically and of regaining it, thereby escaping from the predominant forms of representation" (p. 357). Though this is but one example of the various videos uploaded to YouTube under the IranElection hashtag, the suggestion here is that the process of reentextualizing symbolic resources within the tactical space opened up by new media presents the opportunity for agents to redefine reality. But does this practice presuppose or ignore the suspicion that technology can produce authenticity (Chouliaraki, 2006)? Where is Iran, this place, *real* as (re)defined here through layers of mediation? The use of poetry may evoke Iran's deep cultural traditions, but the voice-over reading might also reflect the discursive practices of legacy media, where inauthentic flows of images are crafted into a reality we have come to trust as authentic (Di Piero, 2009). If people are driven to seek out and create places compatible with who they are (Dixon & Durrheim, 2008), how authentic are the identifications—individual and collective, dialogical and multiple—made among these overlapping layers of signification? Is this the place where, within the competing logics of the commons and the market, the collective *we* breaks down, as in this rooftop poem recited to multiple unseen worlds, into *you* and *me*?

NOTES

1. The Paris image can be viewed at www.flickr.com/photos/9338327@N06/3664087662/in/photostream/
2. This location is based on the Flickr geo-tagging metadata for this upload.
3. Source: www.irantracker.org/analysis/2009-iranian-presidential-election-expatriate-and-foreign-voting-results. Retrieved April 28, 2013.
4. See Appendix B for the full transcript of the poem translated into English.

REFERENCES

Appadurai, A. (1996). *Modernity at large: Cultural dimensions of globalization.* Minneapolis: University of Minnesota Press.

Benwell, B., & Stokoe, E. (2006). *Discourse and identity*. Edinburgh: Edinburgh University Press.

Bhabha, H. K. (2004). *The location of culture*. London: Routledge.

Billig, M. (1995). *Banal nationalism*. London: SAGE.

Boehmer, E. (2006). Networks of resistance. In B. Ashcroft, G. Griffiths, & H. Tiffin (Eds.), *The post-colonial studies reader* (2nd ed.; pp. 113–115). New York: Routledge.

Brumberg, D. (2001). *Reinventing Khomeini: The struggle for reform in Iran*. Chicago: University of Chicago Press.

Butler, J. (1990). *Gender trouble: Feminism and the subversion of identity*. New York: Routledge.

Caron, A., & Caronia, L. (2007). *Moving cultures: Mobile communication and everyday life*. Montreal & Kingston: McGill-Queen's University Press.

Castells, M. (1996). *The information age: Economy, society, and culture. The rise of the network society, vol. 1*. Cambridge, MA: Blackwell.

Castells, M. (1997). *The power of identity. The information age: Economy, society and culture, vol. 2*. Malden, MA: Blackwell.

Castells, M. (2009). *Communication power*. New York: Oxford University Press.

Chouliaraki, L. (2006). *The spectatorship of suffering*. London: SAGE.

Dean, J. (2012, October 1). The limits of communication. *Guernica*. Retrieved April 13, 2013 from www.guernicamag.com.

Di Piero, W. S. (2009). *City dog*. Evanston, IL: Northwestern University Press.

Dixon, J., & Durrheim, K. (2000). Displacing place-identity: A discursive approach to locating self and other. *British Journal of Social Psychology, 39*, 27–44.

Elson, S. B., Yeung, D., Roshan, P., Bohandy, S. R., & Nader, A. (2012). *Using social media to gauge Iranian public opinion and mood after the 2009 election*. Santa Monica, CA: RAND Corp.

Fairclough, N. (2001). *Language and power* (2nd ed.). Essex: Pearson Education Ltd.

Featherstone, M. (1990). *Global culture: Nationalism, globalization, and modernity*. London: SAGE.

Featherstone, M., Lash, S., & Robertson, R. (Eds.). (1995). *Global modernities*. London: SAGE.

Fine, R. (2007). *Cosmopolitanism*. New York: Routledge.

Fornäs, J. (2002). *Digital borderlands: Cultural studies of identity and interactivity on the Internet*. New York: Peter Lang.

Foucault, M. (1972). *The archaeology of knowledge and the discourse on language*. New York: Pantheon Books. (Original work published in 1971.)

Foucault, M. (1978). *The history of sexuality* (Vol. 1). New York: Vintage.

Gheytanchi, E. (2010). Symbols, signs, and slogans of the demonstrations in Iran. In Y. Kamalipour (Ed.), *Media, power, and politics in the digital age: The 2009 presidential election uprising in Iran* (pp. 251–264). Lanham, MD: Rowman & Littlefield.

Giddens, A. (1991). *Modernity and self-identity: Self and society in the late modern age*. Stanford, CA: Stanford University Press.

Goffman, E. (1974). *Frame analysis: An essay on the organization of experience*. Cambridge, MA: Harvard University Press.

Gumperz, J. (Ed.). (1982). *Language and social identity*. Cambridge: Cambridge University Press.

Hall, S. (1996). The question of cultural identity. In S. Hall, D. Held, D. Hubert, & K. Thompson (Eds.), *Modernity: An introduction to modern societies* (pp. 595–634). Cambridge: Polity Press.

Harvey, D. (1989). *The condition of postmodernity*. Oxford: Blackwell.

Hashem, M., & Najjar, A. (2010). The role and impact of new information technology (NIT) applications in disseminating news about the recent Iran presidential elections and uprising. In Y. Kamalipour (Ed.), *Media, power, and politics in the digital age: The 2009 presidential election uprising in Iran* (pp. 125–142). Lanham, MD: Rowman & Littlefield.

Hopper, P. (2007). *Understanding cultural globalization*. Cambridge: Polity.

Jaffe, A. (Ed.). (2009). *Stance: Sociolinguistic perspectives*. Oxford: Oxford University Press.

Jenkins, R. (2008). *Social identity* (3rd ed.). London: Routledge.

Juris, J. (2008). *Networking futures: The movements against corporate globalization*. Durham, NC: Duke University Press.

Lash, S. (2002). *The critique of information*. London: SAGE.

Lash, S. (2006). Experience. *Theory, Culture & Society, 23*(2–3), 335–341.

Malek, M. (2010). Cyber disobedience: Weapons of mass media destruction. In Y. Kamalipour (Ed.), *Media, power, and politics in the digital age: The 2009 presidential election uprising in Iran* (pp. 277–288). Lanham, MD: Rowman & Littlefield.

Manovich, L. (2002). *The language of new media*. Cambridge, MA: MIT Press.

Melucci, A. (1996). *Challenging codes: Collective action in the information age*. Cambridge: Cambridge University Press.

Mittelman, J. (2004). *Wither globalization: The vortex of knowledge and ideology*. New York: Routledge.

Moqadam, A. (2010). *Death to the dictator!: A young man casts a vote in Iran's 2009 election and pays a devastating price*. New York: Sarah Crichton Books.

Ong, A. (1999). *Flexible citizenship: The cultural logics of transnationality*. Durham, NC: Duke University Press.

Parsa, M. (2000). *States, ideologies, & social revolutions: A comparative analysis of Iran, Nicaragua and the Philippines*. New York: Cambridge University Press.

Poulson, S. (2005). *Social movements in twentieth-century Iran: Culture, ideology, and mobilizing frameworks*. Lanham, MD: Lexington Books.

Rustin, M. (2008). New Labour and the theory of globalization. *Critical Social Policy, 28*(3), 273–282.

Szerszynski, B., & Urry, J. (2006). Visuality, mobility and the cosmopolitan: Inhabiting the world from afar. *British Journal of Sociology, 57*(1), 113–131.

Talbot, M. (2007). *Media discourse: Representation and interaction*. Edinburgh: Edinburgh University Press.

Tambar, K. (2009). Secular populism and the semiotics of the crowd in Turkey. *Public Culture, 21*(3), 517–537.

Urry, J. (2007). *Mobilities*. Malden, MA: Polity Press.

6   Effervescence or Resonance?
Closings

In the networked identifications of globalized social movements, it appears that entailed in the question *Where is this place?*, as the Iranian poet asks in the video clip, might also be the question *Where is where?* In one sense, this might reiterate long-standing questions within theories of globalization on how, through the syndromes and symptoms of our intensifying connections, our understandings of place have been transformed. Transformationalist theorizers of globalization have posited the obsolescence of nation-state boundaries and the deterritorialization of places and cultures. As globalization's universalizing logic spreads, places become disembedded from their local contexts, causing meanings—including those of who we are and what we believe—to become hollowed out and homogenized (Featherstone, 1990). Subsequent understandings of globalization, however, have tried to account for a range of experiences of global interconnectivity, including the power and counterpower potentials of all involved in globalization's processes and struggles, not just the elite. In a dialectic interpenetration of the distant and near, the global and local, locales are reterritorialized (Robertson, 1995), and our places within the mutually constitutive intricacies of the place-identity nexus become decentered and hybridized (Bhabha, 2004).

But if the multiplicities of these later theorizations, with their emphasis on difference, critically subvert the homogenizing essentialism of earlier ones, do they do so at the expense of crucially ignoring similarities (Featherstone & Lash, 1999)? Could a cultural logics of transnationalism, in which the tensions between local and deterritorialized experiences, enhanced through real and imagined mobilities, point toward a *flexible* sense of belonging, one that allows for a creative negotiation of our distinctions and similitudes (Appadurai, 1996; Ong, 1999)? As implied by our contemporary experiences of globalization, ripe with banality and devastation, repression and revolution, ephemeral sociomental bonds and seemingly insuperable divisions, it seems we do not yet know. And it remains likely that our newest theorizations will continue to fail to answer those questions. Yet, as I hope that my research has shown, in the space of flows and timeless time, asking *Where is where?* still matters. In the video poem "Where Is This Place?," the poet's susurrations, modulated as much to the protesters' rooftop chants of rebellion and prayer as, no doubt, the possible threat of Basij surveillance, suggest that this it does, and that entailed in that question is a need to also ask *who*, *how*, and *why*.

In this research I have considered the ways in which Iranian protesters constructed their identities in discourse and whether their localized use of social media, as acts of microresistance, granted them any legitimate measure of counterpower during the election crisis. In particular, I have argued that the networked identifications of both Iranian protesters and global activists acting in solidarity with them add to our understandings of the growing polychronicity and multilocalization of contemporary experience (Caron & Caronia, 2007). And bound up in our mobile co-presences, such discursive practices have further destabilized the socially constitutive process of locating ourselves—geographically, politically, and culturally—in discourse (Melucci, 1996). As discourses move across scales and networks, the deictic centers of our cultural fields of reference shift. Though these shifts appear to offer new possibilities for discursively constructing identifications, ideologies, and, therefore, new legitimizations for action and understanding, they are also subject to perhaps novel forms of manipulation as part of the ongoing battle in a network society for communication power, or the struggle to control the way we think (Castells, 2009; Juris, 2008; Kluitenberg, 2010). In the environment of a fluid ideological conjecture that defines our contemporary chaotic news paradigm, these shifts can make it easier to link identities and stances to seemingly contradictory, perhaps manipulative, discursive constructions (McNair, 2006). Meanwhile, in the flows of borrowed symbolic resources between local and global social movement frameworks, the rescaling of discourse across transnational networks can collapse the use and exchange values of activists' discourses into informationalized affect (Dean, 2012; Lash, 2002).

In these processes, a search for coherence can mean that mental models of novel events, such as the Iranian election crisis or perhaps even the ongoing Iranian nuclear threat, can readily be linked according to extant political valences with semantic, social memories (van Dijk, 1998). And the resulting links may, in turn, work to reshape ideologies. A new social movement borrows the symbolic resources of previous ones to help enact collective actions—and collective identifications—with new meaning. But the instability of shifting deictic centers allows old, polarizing ideologies to retain a certain ideological magnetism in shaping our meanings. Within the movement, when symbolic resources are reentextualized through social media and globalized vernaculars across transnational networks, the textures of a local frame alignment become flattened as global frameworks of meaning are bridged. The concomitant ease of circulating information across networks points toward social media's potential for counterpower in social movements. But if what validates these circulations is their amplification, the discourse of social media content—the 'news' posted by users—might be less meaningful than the social act of participation (Manovich, 2009).

Informationalized experience gains voice and mobility, and thus value in multiscalar flows. But is this value one that, like the compressed narratives of a retweet, syntactic only of affect, invoking only *interpassive* reaction, not response (Žižek, 1994)? Transnational identifications multiplied by co-presence help spark networked effervescence. A retweet of news coverage of the protests, as in these examples, might have encouraged activists, perhaps in different ways, both inside and outside Iran:

> RT @username: World is watching #Iranelection—GulfNews frontpage in Dubai today http://mypict.me/3OwW

> RT @username Entekhab News reported that Karroubi, Karbaschi and Moussavi are under home arrest. http://ping.fm/8Zvc7 #IranElection

Yet, as this effervescence diffused among network nodes, the deeper resonance of lasting sociomental bonds is uncertain. In Tehran, the barbed irony of the anti-Ahmadinejad slogan "Down with Potatoes!" becomes, at a global level, a legacy media joke. A slogan from the 2008 Obama campaign, *Hope*, is remixed as *Nope* into an act of protest in 2009 declaiming the legitimacy of the Ahmadinejad reelection. That this meme circulated in solidarity protests in Berlin and San Francisco (and doubtlessly elsewhere) attests to the flow of social movement discourses across transnational networks. Or does its circulation across networks into new contexts and movement frameworks flatten the complex signification of its reentextualized symbolic resources with social movement frameworks into little more than wry commentary, a small media irony? Meanwhile, the tactical practices of activists using social media to protest a contested election in Iran become part of ongoing ideological debates over the role of technology and the spread of democracy.

Perhaps, in the chaos of meaning, another important question remains, one also entailed in that poet's incantatory verse: how, within the contradictory logics of globalization, can the ways we enact our identities and ideologies in discourse continue to tell us where *where* is? As Blommaert (2010) has argued, globalization "is like every development of the system in which we live, something that produces opportunities as well as constraints, new possibilities as well as new problems, progress as well as regression" (p. 4). The commingling of these issues, I argue, can be seen in the translocal and deterritorialized sociolinguistic effects in the protester's poem, if not all the discursive practices I have examined, from its borrowed symbolic resources to its global vernaculars informationalized through network rescaling. Read against the shifting backdrop of a globalized place-identity nexus within transnational network societies, I argue that the poet's questions of *where*, together with how and why we consider where *where* is, point reflexively back at us—an *us* that, if we are to see these protesters' micronarratives as mattering, as I believe they do, appear to include both a resonant *we* and the effervescent, ephemeral sociomental bonds between *you* and *me*.

To try to understand how and why these micronarratives might matter, I have examined both legacy and new media discourses of a variety of stakeholders in the 2009 Iranian presidential election crisis. The discursive constructions of both the activists and U.S. legacy media, in their documentation and reportage of the post-election protest, intertextually draw on dominant narratives and images of Iran in the U.S. public imagination (Semati, 2008). The polychronic interaction afforded by mobile social media such as Twitter has helped shape online political discourse and microblogging as a field of social action (Caron & Caronia, 2007; Gillan, Pickerill, & Webster, 2008). Iranian protesters, together with members of the Iranian diaspora and global activists acting in solidarity with them, used social media to locate themselves and perform their identities online, identifications shaped by mobile technologies and global vernaculars of English (Caron & Caronia; Pennycook, 2007). Performed across nodes in global networks, the practices complicated then-common Western views of 'phatic' microblogging practices. More crucially, they also challenge U.S. legacy media outlets' discursive constructions of both the protesters and their use of social media while showing how activists' identities became caught up in Western ideological debates regarding modernity, technology, and the spread of democracy around the globe.

I have also tried to show the benefits of adopting theories of globalization in linguistic research frameworks. Though not without their contentions and ideological umbra, understandings of globalization can in particular help account for scale in web-based linguistic research, a crucial issue when qualitatively analyzing texts (Brooke, 2009; Zimbra, Chen, & Abassi, 2010). On the microlevel, activists' discursive tactics add to the narratives of vernacular globalization while calling into question the dominant narratives about Iran that appear to be encoded in U.S. legacy media discourse (Semati, 2008). And as the master framework of social movements in modern Iran seems to show, Iran's struggle to embrace a form of modernity compatible with its local cultural beliefs and understandings suggests a singular experience somewhat apart from that of others. Trying to understand Iranian protesters' discursive practices—both inside and outside of social movement frameworks—could also contribute to our understandings of the complex and often contradictory forces of globalization.

Network theories are also well suited to a sociocognitive approach to critical discourse analysis (CDA). On the one hand, notions of sociomental bonds and networked effervescence, especially when analyzing social movement discourse, help address the challenge of linking mind and society in a sociocognitive-orientated approach to CDA. Mobilities and social movement theories, on the other, offer useful ways of considering complex discursive constructions of self and stance in polychronic contexts and the place-identity nexus. By showing the potential for co-presence afforded by mobile technologies, we can see, for instance, how the resulting forms of collective action and meaning making move beyond established notions of web-based public spheres as simply alternative spaces for dissent. Still, when we adopt spaces for social activity, we assume the histories of those spaces. The novel, interstitial spaces of mobile, web-based social media can create opportunities to rescale collective action and dissent across global networks. But the social coordination, circulation of ideas, and transnational identifications—that is, the counterpower—that can result should be seen as bearing the influence, or ideologies, of the network. When activists adopt globalized social media for their practices, they adopt, at least in some form, the logics of globalizing networks. And because sociocultural capital is required to participate in these networked public spheres, they must be understood through relations of social power (Bohman, 2004; Hauser, 1999; Siapera, 2009). These understandings are also premised on the argument that both legacy and new media, as part of the *ideoscape* in Appadurai's (1996) five dimensions of cultural flows, allow for possible scripts of social practice and thereby a plurality of social worlds (Brumberg, 2001). With the imagination viewed as collective, protesters' discursive practices, although ultimately reflexive, nevertheless work to constitute the formation of transnational imaginaries and imagined communities (Appadurai; Anderson, 2006). But by examining these discursive practices through theories of global networks, I have tried to problematize Appadurai's failure to see, in the transnational imaginary, the same forms of unevenness and barriers to access that mark our everyday experiences of globalization (Ong, 1999).

In this sense, if we are to view, in any regard, a measure of success in the activists' tactical uses of social media and strategies of discourse formation, those uses can only be considered successful within an understanding of social power that recognizes who possessed the social and cultural capital needed to employ them in a social movement. Put differently, I contend that activists' transnational discursive practices show how social movement discourses can become amplified when they appropriate the standards of global networks, but those standards, for better or worse, also become inscribed as traces in those discourses. The rhetorical exigencies, for instance, of an activist's "NOW" in a tweet containing the coordinates of a protest in Tehran can become, when retweeted, the diluted 'ephemeral/eternal' *now* in the timeless time of networking logics (Castells, 1996). This, as Dean (2012) has argued (and I would agree), collapses crucial distinctions in these discourses between use and exchange value. They risk becoming technofactual, validating, at different scale levels, for a variety of participants, the seemingly contradictory experiences of transnational engagement and marking their identifications within the logics of the network. And so, by extension I would also argue the logics of participation and competition can become conflated in ways that may not always be compatible with a social movement's aims, even when they help inspire networked effervescence.

Though this sense of transnational collective spirit has been shown, here and elsewhere, to extend social actors' sense of solidarity and thereby encourage further participation (Tufekci & Wilson, 2012), these possibilities do not directly rebut the claim by Morozov (2011) and others that Twitter and other social media played no significant role in the 2009 protests. And neither should they challenge the critical ways Morozov has cautioned us against understanding the spread of technology as congruous with that of democracy, and vice versa. As I intended the analyses of U.S. legacy media to show, the 'Google Doctrine' discourses that Morozov has warned us against may in fact be little more than discursive ideological cover for an extant desire to frame events such as those in Iran in 2009 through the polarized ideological vision of the world as defined by the collision between reactionary traditionalism and integrative modernism (Barber, 1995). As Dabashi (2012) has argued, "the US/Iran neocon contingent has tried in vain to hijack the Green Movement, repeating ad the false mantra that there can be no democracy without neoliberalism" (p. 134). If so, this strategy may work to legitimize a particular set of political actions in response to the ongoing Iranian nuclear threat and, in arguably a contradictory way, may also help re-legitimize (at least, from U.S. perspectives) the protesters' identities according to those ideological beliefs. Yet, I have maintained that Morozov's arguably teleological focus on end conditions points toward larger failures within cyber-skeptical discourses to consider the effect of participation on the discursive construction of resistance identities or the enabling of political agency at a sociocognitive level (Castells, 1997). As Juris (2008) has suggested, what may really matter in social movements are the ways they create opportunities at microlevels for the constitution of new discourses and identities that could eventually contribute to macrolevel discursive change, if not social transformation.

As a form of symbolic exchange (Lash, 2002), protesters' micronarratives and mobile discursive practices, I have also argued, challenge the insufficient treatment of English as a mediating standard by Grewal (2008) and others in analyses of global networks. Activists' translocal discursive practices suggested, at least within social movement frameworks, that symbolic resources, globalized vernaculars, and networked genres might function more readily as network standards than either English as a linguistically defined object or any particular variety of English. That is, as Blommaert (2010) and others have argued, in considering the role of English in a globalized world, both as a commodified resource and a focus of instruction and study, we might be better off emphasizing vernacularized mobile resources and repertoires and the ways they move transnationally across scale levels in sociocultural, political, and historical contexts than particular varieties or, worse, standards.

In regards to methods, this approach might yield at least two potential benefits. First, in addressing the problem of doing qualitative research with online discourse, the implementation of network theories carries with it—or should—an understanding of the fractal nature of cyberspace (Brooke, 2009). That is, the Internet, and by extension the discursive practices that constitute its social dimensions, is composed of the same kinds of self-similar patterns, or fractals, that make up numerous natural and cultural phenomena. Because these patterns occur at different scale levels, we might say that the microlevel focus of qualitative, CDA-based research such as this, though still subject to the critical questionings of methodology I have discussed, can in fact point to macrolevel processes and phenomena in online discourse. If so, this would mean that the examination of online discourse could retain the importance of context inherent in qualitative approaches while pointing perhaps with more confidence toward larger-scale trends in the ways that quantitative studies aim to do, a need which, in the current era of Big Data, might be all the more pressing for researchers taking qualitative approaches. Second, as I have argued above, rescaling appears to distend and distort contexts in ways that complicate their roles in approaches to understanding discourse through CDA, for which considerations of context, as I have explained, are crucial. By including network theory together with understandings of globalization in my overall theoretical approach, I believe it has allowed me to consider the 'Englishness' of pro-testers' discursive practices in ways that both describe language as intrinsically linked to globalization but also offer an alternative way of discussing language other than according to difference.

In this sense, it might also be useful to import these similar considerations into college composition and English-language learning classroom settings. For instance, as Jarrat, Losh, and Puente (2006) have contended, working within the logics of a transnational framework might help students see that the flexibility of mobile sociolinguistic resources can offer them a crucially diversified range of repertoires needed to meet the complex communicative demands inside and outside of globalized classrooms. This flexibility might also help them recognize, as I have argued activists did through their tactical use of reentextualizations, how they can access a range of possible stances and subjectivities (Canagarajah, 1999) through their strategic use, tactical deployment, and symbolic borrowing of these communicative resources, and how that access might extend their potential for agency at multiple scale levels. It may also encourage the development of translocal multiliteracies. These would be based not only on the kinds of multimodalities exhibited by activists, but also on the understanding of how those texts move within and across local and global contexts. In the composition and language-learning classroom, this would mean emphasizing vernaculars, genres, and modes over standards and varieties as well as the critical thinking and linguistic awareness needed to negotiate diverse discursive environments (Cope & Kalantzis, 2000). Doing so might also crucially challenge the notion that, in the fractured cultural fields of globalized societies, a language like English can only function as a 'network standard' in standard varieties.

As a final consideration, I also suggest that beyond social movements we could learn from and apply in a variety of cultural fields and political arenas the creative ways that, as I have tried to show, Iranian activists negotiated the crucial tensions between not only 1979 and 2009, but also the logics of competition and participation that seem to presently mark our contemporary experiences of globalization. Operating within, I argue, competitive logics, commentators such as Frank Rich, who, as I discussed earlier, dismissed tweeting protesters as "wallflowers at a revolution," and Malcolm Gladwell, who claimed protesters' use of social media was the least important aspect of the 2009 demonstrations, may have missed the potentially powerful symbolism of these communicative and political acts. As Poulson (2005) has explained, during the Iranian cycle of protests, social movement actors have frequently drawn on local cultural and symbolic resources, such as *taquiya* and *bast*. *Taquiya* refers to the dissimulation of religious beliefs as a practical strategy for infiltrating an opposition organization or evading conflict. Perhaps, then, during the 2009 protests, Iranian activists' use of global social media might have been an instance of *taquiya*, in which reservations about adopting Western technological forms, especially those associated with the U.S., were temporarily set aside as a practical strategy for opposing government crackdowns. This alternative reading might further be likely given that addressing a global public sphere, that is, a secular construction based on rational-critical debate, is, as discussed above, generally at odds with Islamic beliefs (Siapera, 2009). *Bast* can refer to both the seeking of sanctuary during conflict or the occupying of symbolic spaces, as exemplified by the taking of the American embassy during the 1978–79 revolution. If occupying the embassy, a symbol of the U.S.-backed Shah's authoritarian regime, was an expression of counterpower, the use of social media originating from the U.S. might have been a symbolic act of resistance against the authoritarian, anti-West Ahmadinejad government. This is not to say that Iranian activists sought to 'occupy' U.S.-based social media. Nor is it to suggest, as the Google Doctrine adherents have, that using Twitter points toward a deep-seated desire for democracy. Rather, I suggest that activists' use of social media and vernacular linguistic repertoires should be seen as an example of a symbolic borrowing from existing cultural frameworks for creative acts of resistance and agency. Western ideological lenses, perhaps concepts such as *taquiya* and *bast* would challenge not only neoliberal rhetoric about technology fostering the spread of democracy, but also cyber-skeptic rejoinders, such as Morozov's (2011), which attack cyber-utopian ideologies without acknowledging their own. At the same time, it is hard to deny how, through the convergence of frameworks and cultural fields entailed in that practice of borrowing, the protesters' strategy may also mean that the logics of participation inherent in any social movement ultimately merge with those of the forces they oppose.

Regardless, by considering these possibilities, I argue we can better see how discursive practices create coordinates of social action that facilitate mobilities and complex identifications, imagined mobilities, and transnational lifeworlds. I also believe we are reminded of the importance of drawing on local cultural contexts in order to avoid reading the protests—from any ideological angle—through our own competitive logics, as appears to have been the case in the cyber-rhetoric debates that sprang up around the 2009 Iranian protests. Moreover, by considering above the use of highly mobile vernaculars of communication—in whatever mode—I do not make claims toward depoliticized notions of the utility of either English or Internet-based social media (Ives, 2006). Instead, my aim has been to question if we can also see that discursive formation as reflexive and participatory, rather than solely according to the logics of competition. Moreover, I have also sought to know whether doing so sheds additional light on the complex ways social movement actors can manipulate symbols, borrowed from extant cultural resources, according to their desires while performing their identities individually and collectively within translocally defined cultural fields. By analyzing various discourses within that dynamic tension, I believe we can continue to see and understand the meaningful and novel ways language comes to constitute who and where we are, as well as what we believe. And perhaps by doing so we might find new ways of working collectively to alleviate and transform our shared predicaments through the effervescence sparked by the contentions of those logics and the ongoing resonance of both our common and plural experiences.

REFERENCES

Anderson, B. (2006). *Imagined communities: Reflections on the origins and spread of nationalism* (3rd ed.). London: Verso.

Appadurai, A. (1996). *Modernity at large: Cultural dimensions of globalization.* Minneapolis: University of Minnesota Press.

Barber, B. (1995). *Jihad vs. McWorld.* New York: Random House.

Bhabha, H. K. (2004). *The location of culture.* London: Routledge.

Blommaert, J. (2010). *The sociolinguistics of globalization.* Cambridge: Cambridge University Press.

Bohman, J. (2004). Expanding dialogue: the Internet, the public sphere and prospects for transnational democracy. In N. Crossley & J. Roberts (Eds.), *After Habermas: New perspectives on the public sphere* (pp. 131–156). Oxford: Blackwell Publishing.

Brooke, C. G. (2009). *Lingua fracta: Toward a rhetoric of new media.* Cresskill, NJ: Hampton Press.

Brumberg, D. (2001). *Reinventing Khomeini: The struggle for reform in Iran.* Chicago: University of Chicago Press.

Canagarajah, A. S. (1999). *Resisting linguistic imperialism in English teaching.* Oxford: Oxford University Press.

Caron, A., & Caronia, L. (2007). *Moving cultures: Mobile communication and everyday life.* Montreal & Kingston: McGill-Queen's University Press.

Castells, M. (1996). *The information age: Economy, society, and culture. The rise of the network society, vol. 1.* Cambridge, MA: Blackwell.

Castells, M. (1997). *The power of identity. The information age: Economy, society and culture, vol. 2.* Malden, MA: Blackwell.

Castells, M. (2009). *Communication power.* New York: Oxford University Press.

Cope, B., & Kalantzis, M. (Eds.). (2000). *Multiliteracies: Literacy learning and the design of social futures.* London: Routledge.

Dabashi, H. (2012). *The Arab Spring: The end of post colonialism.* London: Zed Books.

Dean, J. (2012, October 1). The limits of communication. *Guernica*. Retrieved April 13, 2013 from www.guernicamag.com.

Featherstone, M. (1990). *Global culture: Nationalism, globalization, and modernity*. London: SAGE.

Featherstone, M., & Lash, S. (1999). *Spaces of culture: City, nation, world*. London: SAGE.

Gillan, K., Pickerill, J., & Webster, F. (2008). *Anti-war activism: New media and protest in the information age*. New York: Palgrave Macmillan.

Grewal, D. S. (2008). *Network power: The social dynamics of globalization*. New Haven, CT: Yale University Press.

Hauser, G. (1999). *Vernacular voices: The rhetorics of publics and public spheres*. Columbia: University of South Carolina Press.

Ives, P. (2006). 'Global English': Linguistic imperialism or practical lingua franca? *Studies in Language and Capitalism, 1*, 121–141.

Jarratt, S., Losh, E., & Puente, D. (2006). Transnational identities: Biliterate writers in a first-year humanities course. *Journal of Second Language Writing, 15*, 24–48.

Juris, J. (2008). *Networking futures: The movements against corporate globalization*. Durham, NC: Duke University Press.

Kluitenberg, E. (2010). *Delusive spaces: Essays on culture, media, and technology*. Rotterdam: NAi Publishers.

Lash, S. (2002). *The critique of information*. London: SAGE.

Manovich, L. (2009). The practice of everyday (media) life: From mass consumption to mass cultural production? *Critical Inquiry, 35*, 313–331.

McNair, B. (2006). *Cultural chaos: Journalism, news and power in a globalised world*. London: Routledge.

Melucci, A. (1996). *Challenging codes: Collective action in the information age*. Cambridge: Cambridge University Press.

Morozov, E. (2011). *The net delusion: The dark side of Internet freedom*. New York: PublicAffairs.

Ong, A. (1999). *Flexible citizenship: The cultural logics of transnationality*. Durham, NC: Duke University Press.

Pennycook, A. (2007). *Global Englishes and transcultural flows*. London: Routledge.

Poulson, S. (2005). *Social movements in twentieth-century Iran: Culture, ideology, and mobilizing frameworks*. Lanham, MD: Lexington Books.

Robertson, R. (1995). Glocalization: Time-space and homogeneity-heterogenity. In M. Featherstone, S. Lash, & R. Robertson (Eds.), *Global modernities* (pp. 25–44). London: SAGE.

Semati, M. (Ed.). (2008). *Media, culture and society in Iran: Living with globalization and the Islamic state*. New York: Routledge.

Siapera, E. (2009). Theorizing the Muslim blogosphere: Blogs, rationality, publicness, and individuality. In A. Russell & N. Echchaibi (Eds.), *International blogging: Identity, politics, and networked publics* (pp. 29–46). New York: Peter Lang.

Tufekci, Z., & Wilson, C. (2012). Social media and the decision to participate in political protest: Observations from Tahrir Square. *Journal of Communication, 62*(2), 363–379.

van Dijk, T. (1998). *Ideology: A multidisciplinary approach*. Thousand Oaks, CA: SAGE.

Zimbra, D., Chen, H., & Abassi, A. (2010). A cyber-archeology approach to social movement research: A framework and case study. *Journal of Computer-Mediated Communication, 16*, 48–70.

Žižek, S. (Ed.). (1994). *Mapping ideology*. New York: Verso.

Appendix A
Twitter Data

Dear Iranian People, Mousavi has not left you alone, he has been put under house arrest by Ministry of Intelligence #IranElection 4:37 PM Jun 13th, 2009 via web

Iran's Supreme Leader's official English website: http://english.khame nei.ir #Iranelection (via http://ff.im/485HP) http://ff.im/486qy

@username: Shiraz is burning—http://tinyurl.com/kprzae & http://tinyurl.com/llvk5g #Iranelection

@username: Photo: Tehran People's rally (Pro Ahmadinejad) today http://bit.ly/y95pG & http://tinyurl.com/kq9zho #Iranelection Jun 16, 2009

Iran / today / Krimkhan St / protest NOW #Iranelection on Twitpic http://ree.tw/bzk (retweeted 131x http://ree.tw/bzl) Jun 17, 2009

Iran / today / hafttir Sq / protest NOW #Iranelection on Twitpic http://ree.tw/bzm (retweeted 123x http://ree.tw/bzn) Jun 17, 2009

@username: ALL internet & mobile networks are cut. We ask everyone in Tehran to go onto their rooftops and shout ALAHO AKBAR in protest #IranElection Jun 13, 2009

@username: RT @username Pictures from today http://bit.ly/3wDOHT http://twitpic.com/7gtaq http://twitpic.com/7gt95 #Iranelection (via @username) Jun 15, 2009

@username: RT The Iranian Revolution Must Start Now http://bit.ly/vkVq5 #Iranelection Jun 20, 2009

Today's march Tehran The numbers! http://twitpic.com/7mi5l http://twitpic.com/7mi3f http://twitpic.com/7mi9j (via @username) #Iranelection

RT @username: Pictures from today http://bit.ly/3wDOHT http://twitpic.com/7gtaq http://twitpic.com/7gt95 #Iranelection Jun 15, 2009

@username: "perhaps a million protesting" http://bit.ly/QGk19 pic: http://twitpic.com/7gtbu #Iranelection #Iran Jun 15, 2009

Yesterday http://tinyurl.com/lbozp7 & http://tinyurl.com/lyut5k #Iran Election Stand in #Solidarity->http://tinyurl.com/nc2nnn Jun 19, 2009

RT @username Iran Election Whistleblower Killed, From Guardian: http://bit.ly/3NC7x http://bit.ly/12kqL4 #Iranelection

@username Tweeps; you're part of our revolution! keep these websites open http://bit.ly/12UQW0 & http://bit.ly/4y3eM #Iranelection Jun 14, 2009

RT from Iran: http://twitpic.com/7r4nw—http://twitpic.com/7r4pv— Iran / Tehran / protesters / Topkhone Sq #Iranelection Jun 18, 2009

@username: New YouTube #video—http://bit.ly/TvlLL & http://bit.ly/ ZOOGK #IranElection

@username: Pictures from Tehran http://bit.ly/eTFuZ & http://bit. ly/132TNt #Iranelection Jun 13, 2009

RT proxy list for Iran: http://bit.ly/KFBtQ and in Persian http://is.gd/ 136wy—#IranElection Jun 16, 2009

@username: WARNING: www.mirhoseyn.ir/ & www.mirhoseyn.com/ are fake, DONT join. #IranElection Jun 16, 2009

@username: People in Tehran shout: Down with dictator from their house roof http://bit.ly/gbVW1 #Iranelection Jun 14, 2009

@username: RT @mikl_em: "perhaps a million protesting" http://bit. ly/QGk19 pic: http://twitpic.com/7gtbu #Iranelection #Iran Jun 15, 2009

@username: "Check this video out—protest in Tehran http://bit.ly/cm GnX #Iranelection"

RT Iran: People are being shot on streets. http://ow.ly/eGU3 #Iranelec tion www.youtube.com/watch?v=9qo8_oBoTX4 Jun 18, 2009

information on using Tor to remain anonymous: www.torproject.org . . . Tor + Wordpress: http://is.gd/12g1P #Iranelection Jun 15, 2009

http://twitpic.com/7c7w5—she is . . . #Iranelection Jun 14, 2009

RT from Iran: Check this http://bit.ly/auv79 and http://bit.ly/3s9oY4 and http://bit.ly/PPZiD they killed people #Iranelection Jun 15, 2009

RT Iran—More vids from today's protests in Tehran http://is.gd/13IZ5 in front of IRIB building: http://is.gd/13IZQ #IranElection 6/16 Jun 17, 2009

@username: http://twitpic.com/7gkrq—attacked to university #Iranelec tion Jun 15, 2009

@username: Check this video out—Iran http://bit.ly/1860DA #Iranelec tion Jun 14, 2009

@username: http://twitpic.com/7h2nx—Iran / today / police & people #IranElection Jun 15, 2009

@username: http://twitpic.com/7gur5—Iran / today / Tehran #IranElection Jun 15, 2009

@username: Check this video out—crime http://bit.ly/1JsE9K #Iranelec tion Jun 18, 2009

RT @username: http://twitpic.com/7j6ox—Tehran / yesterday / crime #Iranelection Jun 16, 2009

@username: http://twitpic.com/7sv7j—She write: change for Iran #Iranelection Jun 19, 2009

@username: http://twitpic.com/7fmo8—Iran is the same as Palestine #Iranelection Jun 15, 2009

@username: http://twitpic.com/7c6jz—Iran / Tehran / fire & blood #Iranelection Jun 14, 2009

@username: Check this video out—university of Tehran http://bit.ly/noCoI #Iranelection Jun 15, 2009

Dispatch from Tehran: "The police are coming!" http://tr.im/oMZL #IranElection Jun 17, 2009

@username: http://bit.ly/jUY5K VOTE . . . my friends #IranElection Jun 16, 2009

@username: Check this video out—COME ON MOUSAVI http://bit.ly/12rrlX #Iranelection Jun 14, 2009

@username: http://edition.cnn.com/SPECIALS/2009/news/Iran.election/ check this page #Iranelection Jun 16, 2009

@username: http://twitpic.com/7gghp—attack to university of Tehran / crime #Iranelection Jun 15, 2009

@username: Check this video out—conflict in Shiraz http://bit.ly/rfRyU #IranElection Jun 15, 2009

RT Iran: www.facebook.com/pages/Mir-Hossein-Mousavi-/45061919 453?ref=mf—#Iranelection—PLS RT Jun 18, 2009

@username: http://twitpic.com/7fb1y—Police and security forces are beating people #Iranelection Jun 15, 2009

@username: Check this video out—Iran / last night / http://bit.ly/148qJe were is our vote? #IranElection Jun 14, 2009

RT Open Letter to the World from the People of Iran: http://tinyurl.com/nw95ev Please RT. #IranElection (via a user) Jun 16, 2009

@username: http://twitpic.com/7h65h—Iran / Esfehan / fire / police & people #Iranelection Jun 15, 2009

@username: Check this video out—they said: down with dictator http://bit.ly/1Anz7Q #Iranelection Jun 15, 2009

@username: Check this video out—one person dead in protest in Iran http://bit.ly/fXdoV #IranElection Jun 15, 2009

@username: Check this video out—Iran university/shiraz / tonight http://bit.ly/MV4Z7 #Iranelection Jun 14, 2009

@username: #IranElection Mousavi's letter to the Iranian people in English: http://ow.ly/dWZ8 Jun 13, 2009

@username: Check this video out—People wounded by police in Tehran http://bit.ly/45Gxtr #Iranelection Jun 17, 2009

@username: Guy beaten to death video is up again http://bit.ly/12oZDT #Iranelection Jun 14, 2009

@username: Check this video out—Mourning gathering in Tehran. http://bit.ly/LKRzP #Iranelection Jun 18, 2009

@username: Check this video out—shooting to people Azadi Sq http://bit.ly/mH2JE #Iranelection Jun 16, 2009

@username: http://twitpic.com/7mrcj—Iran / Karimkhan ST / protest NOW #Iranelection Jun 17, 2009

@username: http://twitpic.com/7p8zf—Tehran / karimkhan St / protest #Iranelection Jun 18, 2009

@username: http://twitpic.com/7qs4t—we are stay #Iranelection Jun 18, 2009

@username: Check this video out—crime crime crime_ Injured people http://bit.ly/5MEWb #Iranelection Jun 16, 2009

@username: http://twitpic.com/7k48l—attacked to people's home last night/north of Tehran #IranELECTION Jun 16, 2009

mousavi is posting direct here http://sites.google.com/site/mousavi1388/ tell everyone. #Iranelection

This is what real Iranians are: http://bit.ly/VhocZ #Iranelection

US rejects victory claim by Iran's Ahmadinejad http://bit.ly/o4mFo #Iranelection

Iranians in Belgium will gather in front of Iran embassy today www.Iranian.be/news/2009/06/003396.htm #Iranelection

Violence in Iran Tehran—http://bit.ly/ZIiym #IranElection

Pictures from Tehran http://bit.ly/eTFuZ & http://bit.ly/132TNt #Iran election

Wikipedia listed 13 June of Iran in its Coup d'état page! http://bit.ly/Sh9jm #Iranelection

"Etemad Melli" newspaper: Iran interior ministry announced Karubi in the 5th place in the election! http://twitpic.com/7d2ft #Iranelection

Isfahan University Dormitories were attacked last night. #Iranelection http://javanefarda.com/News.aspx?ID=585

Rt @username: Confirmed. Final exams of Sharif Univ posponed for two weeks

RT @username: World is watching #Iranelection—GulfNews frontpage in Dubai today http://mypict.me/3OwW

RT @username: 120 faculty of Sharif uni. have resigned. Protest infront of the uni. http://tinyurl.com/nqaxbc #Iranelection

at Valiasr, Karubi told he will stand till the end. link is in #persian #Iranelection http://bit.ly/66KTg

RT @username Entekhab News reported that Karroubi, Karbaschi and Moussavi are under home arrest. http://ping.fm/8Zvc7 #IranElection

Vote for Mirhussein Moussavi on CNN quick poll (http://cnn.com)

Follow #IranElection News on Twitter: http://ping.fm/Z3cil

Live coverage of Iran Presidential Elections by Guardian (http://ping.fm/Ri4Dd) #IranElection

#BBC coverage of Iran Election (http://ping.fm/AlghW) #IranElection

RT @TIME: The Man Who Could Beat Ahmadinejad: Mousavi Talks to TIME | http://tr.im/oj9J #IranElection

Iran votes in tight presidential election (http://ping.fm/R8GBQ) #Iran Election #BBC

Mowj online TV website has been blocked by government http://Iran.
mowj.ir/ #IranElection

Website of Iran's Interior Ministry is down: http://ping.fm/z52gj
#IranElection

RT @username Los Angeles Times: Iranians ready to decide presidency—
and maybe much more http://is.gd/ZWg1 #IranElection

Website of Interior Ministry now has a server side error due to heavy
visits: www.moi.ir #IranElection

RT @username: Mousavi's Tehran press conference audio recording
www.mediafire.com/?lz2zzd2jnww #IranElection

#CNN Coverage: Iranians head to polls in crucial vote (http://tinyurl.
com/msm2g8) #IranElection

RT @@username: Iranians in the US: now it's your turn to take this
dictator down! http://is.gd/ZSz7 #IranElection

BBC Persian special page for Iran Election (http://ping.fm/6E9gp)
#IranElection

RT @username: #IranElection Mousavi in Tehran press conference:
thank you for your vote, get ready to celebrate http://is.gd/103sw

RT @username: Thank you, Obama! Whoever wins election, U.S. wants
talks with Iran http://is.gd/10bMB #IranElection

@username: Allah—you are the creator of all and all must return to
you—Allah Akbar—#Iranelection Sea of Green

@username: This chilling tweet by "arrested" @@username could force
rethink of Twitter as dissident tool http://tr.im/q0IV #Iranelection
06/27/2009

@username thank you ppls 4 supporting Sea of Green—pls remember always our martyrs—Allah Akbar—Allah Akbar—Allah Akbar
#Iranelection 06/24/2009

@username we must go—dont know when we can get internet—they
take 1 of us, they will torture and get names—now we must move
fast—#Iranelection 06/24/2009

@username they pull away the dead into trucks—like factory—no human
can do this—we beg Allah for save us—#Iranelection 06/24/2009

@username in Baharestan we saw militia with axe choping ppl like
meat—blood everywhere—like butcher—Allah Akbar—#Iranelection
RT RT RT 06/24/2009

@username http://bit.ly/RbGhb—Article by Mohsen Makhmalbaf—
#Iranelection RT RT 06/22/2009

@username People of Iran—THIS IS THE DAWN—This is the new begin-
ning—have hope and prepare—#Iranelection RT RT RT 06/21/2009

@username mousavi is posting direct here http://sites.google.com/sit . . .
tell everyone. #Iranelection 06/14/2009

@username MOUSAVi—on his wesite—Wed Sea of Green is 100%
confirmed—no cancellation will be made #Iranelection RT RT RT

@username Karoubi—I demand release of all political prisoners immediately—#Iranelection

@username MirHossein Mousavi I am prepared For martyrdom, go on strike if I am arrested #IranElection 06/20/2009

@username MirHossein Mousavi BBC broadcasting details in Iran (Tell Everyone), http://sites.google.com/site/mousavi1388/bbc #IranElection 06/19/2009

@username MirHossein Mousavi New photos from today in Tehran http://flickr.com/mousavi1388 #IranElection

@username MirHossein Mousavi WARNING: www.mirhoseyn.ir/ & www.mirhoseyn.com/ are fake, DONT join. #IranElection 06/16/2009

@username MirHossein Mousavi Mousavi's message from Ghalam-News now on http://mousavi1388.wikispaces.com/Ghalamnews.org and http://ghalamnews.tumblr.com/ #IranElection 06/16/2009

@username MirHossein Mousavi @xarene http://mousavi1388.wiki spaces.com/Ghalamnews.org and http://ghalamnews.tumblr.com/ are now saying ghalamnews 06/16/2009

@username MirHossein Mousavi All Mousavi's news from Ghalam-News is now on google: http://sites.google.com/site/mousavi1388/ they cant block google #IranElection 06/16/2009

@username MirHossein Mousavi Mousavi & Karoubi will be on the way to the protest to ask people to remain calm http://is.gd/12m1a #IranElection 06/15/2009

@username MirHossein Mousavi Due to widespread filtering, please view this site for latest news from Mousavi (via GhalamNews): http://sites.google.com/site/mousavi1388/ 06/14/2009

@username MirHossein Mousavi Latest Mousavi Letter to Iranian People: www.flickr.com/photos/mousavi1388/3625088310/ #IranElecti on 06/14/2009

@username MirHossein Mousavi New YouTube vids. www.youtube. com/mousavi1388 & http://bit.ly/ZOOGK #IranElection 06/14/2009

@username MirHossein Mousavi Although several reports say that Mousavi is under house arrest, BBC confirms that Mousavi is NOT under house arrest: http://is.gd/11APp 06/14/2009

@username MirHossein Mousavi Latest YouTube vids. of protests in Mashhad tonight: http://bit.ly/4pJNYh #IranElection 06/13/2009

@username MirHossein Mousavi #IranElection Latest YouTube vid. from Shiraz (attack on Shiraz Univesity): http://bit.ly/J4qyd 06/13/ 2009

@username MirHossein Mousavi ALL internet & mobile networks are cut. We ask everyone in Tehran to go onto their rooftops and shout ALAHO AKBAR in protest #IranElection 06/13/2009

@username MirHossein Mousavi Use this to access Facebook from Iran: www.wwww.www.facebook.com/home.php 06/13/2009

@username MirHossein Mousavi #IranElection New YouTube vid. from Tehran: http://bit.ly/15kHdW 06/13/2009

@username MirHossein Mousavi Official: Obama Administration Skeptical of Iran's Election Results http://is.gd/10QAz #IranElection 06/13/2009

@username MirHossein Mousavi #IranElection Latest Mousavi letter to Iranian people (10 minutes ago): www.flickr.com/photos/mousavi 1388/3622281658/ 06/13/2009

@username MirHossein Mousavi #IranElection Latest YouTube vid from Tehran (riots in Vanak): www.youtube.com/mousavi1388 06/13/2009

@username MirHossein Mousavi http://is.gd/10LTN This Election Is Void. 06/13/2009

@username MirHossein Mousavi #IranElection Mousavi's supporters on streets of Tehran at 4pm local time (YouTube vid): http://bit.ly/QEyNr 06/13/2009

@username MirHossein Mousavi #IranElection Mousavi's Facebook page: http://bit.ly/15JH6O 06/13/2009

@username MirHossein Mousavi #IranElection Mousavi's press conference originally scheduled at 2pm Tehran time is postponed 06/13/2009

@username MirHossein Mousavi http://bit.ly/Pjt4v/ 06/13/2009

@username MirHossein Mousavi According to our 50,000 election representatives throughout Iran, Mousavi is the definite winner http://is.gd/10dz0 #IranElection 06/12/2009

@username MirHossein Mousavi Mousavi's Tehran press conference audi recording www.mediafire.com/?lz2zzd2jnww #IranElection 06/12/2009

@username MirHossein Mousavi#IranElection Mousavi in Tehran press conference: thank you for your vote, get ready to celebrate http://is.gd/103sw 06/12/2009

@username MirHossein Mousavi Mostafa Tajzadeh and Mohsen Aminzadeh (senior Mousavi campaign team members arrested) according to IRNA, http://bit.ly/JlYtq 06/12/2009

@username MirHossein Mousavi Mousavi will hold emergency press conference in 15 mins in Tehran http://havadaran.net/archive/00309.php #IranElection 06/12/2009

@username MirHossein Mousavi Huge turnout in Iran presidential poll, photos from today: www.flickr.com/mousavi1388 (SMS network still down). #IranElection 06/12/2009

@username MirHossein Mousavi @GreenMousavi #IranElection Iran's SMS system is take down! News from within Iran and also confirmed by GhalamNews http://is.gd/Z5d9 06/11/2009

@username MirHossein Mousavi #IranElection Overseas Iranians can find out where to vote here: http://bit.ly/3N4YcC 06/11/2009

@username MirHossein Mousavi http://is.gd/XD8i Mousavi boycotts TV debate due to unfair time allocation, 20 mins to Ahmadinejad, 1:41 to Mosuavi 06/10/2009

@username MirHossein Mousavi Ahmadinejad makes a quick exit from Sharif university after crowds shout "Ahmadi Bye Bye" and "Liar Liar" slogans: http://is.gd/XCmp 06/10/2009

@username MirHossein Mousavi Mousavi's internet TV channel blocked by AN's government less than 48 hours to election, see this to bypass filter: http://snurl.com/jttuv 06/10/2009

@username MirHossein Mousavi Election opponent accuses Ahmadinejad of lying in TV debate http://is.gd/Vot3 06/09/2009

@username MirHossein Mousavi Rafsanjani family to file lawsuit against Ahmadinejad http://bit.ly/10J5XP 06/09/2009

@username MirHossein Mousavi http://is.gd/Tiqs (PDF file) Mousavi's plans as shown in TV debate last night

@username MirHossein Mousavi We beg EVERYONE to ask their family & friends to VOTE on Friday. Please call your friends & family and ask them to vote 06/06/2009

@username Free Iran http://bit.ly/F3PqO Mohsen Sazegara Monday June 29, 2009 Iran Tehran Call for 3 day strike in Iran Neda gr88 Iran/election 06/30/2009

@username Free Iran NEDA Tehran ELECTION Iran gr88 Watch March in support of the Iranian people, Paris 28 june 2009 5000 thousand people http://bit.ly/zyFZo 06/30/2009

@username M. Zand RT @username: http://bit.ly/aDvDA #Iran June 28th 2009 #Iranelection 06/29/2009

@username M. Zand RT @username Mosque Ghoba June 28, 2009 Iran Protest video: http://bit.ly/qoCRq 06/29/2009

@username A Khatami just so everyone knows there was not a coup d'etat in Iran in 2009, it was all legal under the system of velayat faqih #Iranelection 06/09/2010

@username Iran RT @phloflo can u help us get the word out? Boston Protest: 20 June 2009 15:00–17:00 Copley Sq http://bit.ly/xukIX #Iranelection 06/19/2009

@username Iran (video)—18th June 2009–100000's protest against election fraud in Iran www.youtube.com/watch?v=bo65c1VEUXU #Iranelection 06/18/2009

@username Iran Peacefully demanding our freedom: Iranians silent protest 17 June 2009 http://bit.ly/OiWMp #Iranelection 06/17/2009

@usernameIran (video)—Millions of Mousavi supporters in Tehran; today- June 17, 2009 www.youtube.com/watch?v=VmhKQqRlsfo #Iranelection 06/17/2009

@username Iran "Iran Election protests in Paris- 14 June 2009" http://bit.ly/AoqCf 06/14/2009

@usernameIran 2009 Iranian election protests now on wikipedia: http://bit.ly/2L9TbU (not complete yet #Iranelection 06/14/2009

Calling but can't get through to Iran. Following news here http://Iran.twazzup.com/ and here http://memeorandum.com/ #Iranelection Jun 14, 2009

ystrday's rally: http://bit.ly/uNfft http://bit.ly/om5oD http://bit.ly/vcvFC http://bit.ly/w55ov http://bit.ly/YUFXC #Iranelection Jun 19, 2009

@username RT @username: Role of Mousavi in founding of Hezballah + Iran's intel service. http://bit.ly/2AVUH & http://bit.ly/DED6c #Iranelection

RT @username Pictures from Tehran http://bit.ly/eTFuZ & http://bit.ly/132TNt #Iranelection #Iranrevolution #Iranelection Jun 13, 2009

@username: RT @username: #Iranelection Paris Protests http://bit.ly/HuyGr, http://bit.ly/Xq3nU Jun 14, 2009

@username More vids from today's silent protest in Tehran http://bit.ly/LA907 http://bit.ly/yykP0 http://bit.ly/27lB18 #Iranelection #gr88 Jun 16, 2009

how to deal with tear gas: http://bit.ly/KfAGs #Iranelection Jun 16, 2009

@username: YouTube Blocked in Iran? Here's How to Circumvent an internet Proxy http://ping.fm/m3rkN #IranElection Jun 19, 2009

@username: whoa! Photo taken this afternoon of unofficial rally in Tehran. #Iranelection http://twitpic.com/7ki6e Jun 17, 2009

@username: Tehran, Twitter, And Human Connections http://tinyurl.com/kkq2b3 #Iranelection Jun 16, 2009

@username: #Iran timeline and how to find the latest on #IranElection from Breaking Tweets http://bit.ly/SYjQH (please RT) Jun 18, 2009

@username: http://blip.fm/~835r1 more music for u #Iran9 #Iranelection Jun 16, 2009

@username: RT @judyrey Updated fake #Iranelection tweeter list—http://twitspam.org/ Take a look Jun 17, 2009

@username: Iran protest images from around the web http://twurl.nl/ojigeo #Iran9 #Iranelection Jun 16, 2009

@username: Simple ways to help Iranian free speech: http://is.gd/13U0V #IranElection #gr88 Pls RT Jun 17, 2009

@username: BBC—Protest against Iran election results-please share-http://bit.ly/QKbxF #Iranelection PLZ RT Jun 17, 2009

@username: For all my brothers and sisters in #Iran9 http://blip.fm/~3ua5k #Iranelection please please retweet this . . . please Jun 16, 2009

@username: #Iran9 #Iranelection http://blip.fm/~3yt0y just some music from the big Z @username Jun 16, 2009

@username: We WANT A RE-VOTE NOT A RE-COUNT!! This will not stand. #Iranelection REMEMBER DO NOT TWEET NAMES FROM PPL IN Iran! http://blip.fm/~5ervw Jun 17, 2009

@username: list of hundreds of useful websites to inform yourself or find a way to help out #Iranelection http://bit.ly/Irannews Jun 18, 2009

@username: RT @username #IranElection Let Iran Know that the Global Community is Monitoring Their Every Move http://bit.ly/T03n8 Jun 19, 2009

@username: List of fake & spam twitters: RT http://bit.ly/JcyIU good site to block spam misinfo #IranElection Jun 18, 2009

@username: Protests Flare in Tehran as Opposition Disputes Vote http://bit.ly/EOFIu NYT #Iranelection Jun 14, 2009

so they say "Ahmadinejad 'nearing Iran election victory'" "http://bit.ly/5uhkZ either cheating going on or I have change country of birth!" @username Jun 13, 2009

Girl gets shot in Tehran http://bit.ly/LK5Zs #Iranelection

RT Iran: "Very brutal death of a brave man http://twitpic.com/7nv7z—all I can do is to pray and CRY"

Esfehan—Iran #Iranelection http://twitpic.com/7ki6e amazing

Calling but can't get through to Iran. Following news here http://Iran.twazzup.com/ and here http://memeorandum.com/ #Iranelection

wearing a green shirt "this is for the people of Iran," said Wyclef Jean @wyclef, with 300,000 followers. http://bit.ly/5D5PU

"Obama reluctant to criticise Iran" http://bit.ly/m16ar—"he's correct, otherwise demonstrators will be called US spies #Iranelection"

pictures of today—http://twitpic.com/7gtbu. #Iranelection (via @username)

Just saw this "Google translation tool aims to improve Iran info access" http://bit.ly/NjV49 #Iranelection

Ahmadinejad re-election sparks Iran clashes http://bit.ly/19RZ2x

first aid info in Persian: http://gr88.tumblr.com/ #Iranelection #gr88

RT @username: RT@BreakingNews: AP: latest pictures from Tehran www.flickr.com/photos/mousavi1388/

"The weapons have come out! http://bit.ly/1SrEWs #Iranelection" "Sky News has been running live tweets from inside Iran on it's home page since start of demonstrations" http://bit.ly/1hi2S #Iranelection

Iran to hold election recount' http://news.bbc.co.uk/1/hi/world/8102400.stm

NYC #IranElection rally @ Union Square www.youtube.com/watch?v=t15uhr0s3UU

sad sad story by a student http://bit.ly/2QjZS2 #Iranelection

RT from Iran. This is the picture of the man who killed 8 people on Monday http://tkp.gu.ma/ #IranElection #GR88

RT: Young Iranians girl after being shot at protest in Iran. http://tinyurl.com/kp3x7j #IranElection #gr88

RT: Iranians want peace, thousands of people rally for fair elections and peace in Iran PHOTOS: http://ow.ly/eGIj #Iranelection

@username: Execution in Iran, might be hard for some to watch www. ireport.com/docs/DOC-273840 #IranElection—this is not Iran

Demostration in silence in front of governmental TV station #Iranelection http://twitpic.com/7khkw

Bassij Open Fire on People at Azadi SQ/Tehran . . . #Iranelection http:// bit.ly/4yubyQ

RT @username http://bit.ly/TlTsQ #Iranelection—citizen journalism= evidence of thuggishness

Amnesty says up to 10 dead in Iran protests http://bit.ly/4qKT2 #Iranelection

Footage of 'Iran university attack' http://bit.ly/zsiPe #Iranelection like cockroaches

Mr Mousavi calls off the rally after being warned militias would be equiped with live rounds http://bit.ly/11gzES #Iranelection

Iranian who leaked election results may have been assassinated http:// bit.ly/11qpCk—needs to be confirmed

RT @jimsciuttoABC: #Iranelection here's out story from ABC incl cellphone video http://tinyurl.com/llvmh2

"RT @username: NEW footage of BASIJ in Tehran invading homes terrorizing ppl TONIGHT http://bit.ly/MKzXX #Iranelection #gr8"

Iranian opposition vows to keep pressure on regime with shows of strength http://bit.ly/fXReU #Iranelection

RT @username: BLOG: U of #Tehran dorms after last nights attacks! http://25khordad.wordpress.com/—scrollbar on left hand side

Mousavi ignores government order, calls for peaceful demonstrations http://bit.ly/19UTXq #Iranelection very brave man

RT @wired Activists use Twitter+web tools to launch online attacks on Tehran regime: http://bit.ly/19mf7h #Iranelection

RT @username: http://twitpic.com/7h41m pictures of killings in tehran today. #Iranelection (via @@username)—saddening

RT @username: another brave video from Iran http://bit.ly/15Oc6u #Iranelection—animals

mass arrests and campus raids as regime hits back http://bit.ly/IOJYC 500 opposition supporters arrested across country #Iranelection

RT @username: RT: Fear has gone in a land that has tasted freedom: http://bit.ly/CKJsz #IranElection GREAT ARTICLE!

Protests in other cities Isfahan, Shiraz, Rasht, Tabriz (from yesterday) http://bit.ly/12XDgY #Iranelection

U.S. Persian Gulf forces cautioned on encountering any Iranian military forces during potential unrest http://bit.ly/18EEnc #Iranelection

RT TIMES: http://tinyurl.com/mfbz8w More than 100,000 join defiant silent protest in Tehran #Iranelection #gr88

Iranian footballers wore green wristbands earlier today. They've been my heroes now they are angels to me http://bit.ly/wJUEj #Iranelection

RT @username RT @TimOBrienNYT: Mousavi reportedly arrested on way to Khamenei's house in Tehran: http://tinyurl.com/l3xblq

Breaking news 'Fatal Shooting At Tehran Protest Rally' http://bit.ly/RHPa

RT @username: Mousavi will hold emergency press conference in 15 mins in Tehran http://havadaran.net/archive/00309.php #IranElection

RT @username: Police and terrorist groups have attacked to some Mousavi campaigns and offices in Tehran. http://is.gd/ZQCX #IranElection #fb

RT @username: Mousavi's also leading in Malaysia 70% [Persian] http://is.gd/ZU1a #IranElection

RT @username: Mostafa Tajzadeh & Mohsen Aminzadeh (senior Mousavi campaign team members arrested) according to IRNA, http://bit.ly/JlYtq

RT @username: Breaking news about the wild attacks to Mousavi and his supporters in Shahre-Rey [Persian]: http://is.gd/ZBKR #IranElection

RT @username: Karroobi supporters are going to light candles in front of The Ministry of Interior: http://is.gd/ZG9q #Iranelection

@username Ahmadinejad: 14,011,664 (66%), Moussavi: 6,575,844 (33%) See here: http://tinyurl.com/n7oyde

@username@username 16 JUNE 2009—Doctors and nurses protesting in a major hospital http://bit.ly/IxAW4 #Iranelection #Iranelections 06/16/2009

@username RT @username can u help us get the word out? Boston Protest: 20 June 2009 15:00–17:00 Copley Sq http://bit.ly/xukIX #Iranelection 06/19/2009

Iran_news Payvand PDF report: Preliminary Analysis of the Voting Figures in Iran's 2009 Presidential Election from Chatham http://tinyurl.com/me9dyv 06/24/2009

Iran_news Payvand PDF file: Iran /death penalty—A state terror policy—April 2009 (fidh.org) http://bit.ly/124pqg 06/28/2009

aslanmedia Aslan Media Reza Aslan in TIME on how 2009 looks a lot like 1979: reading from @time http://bit.ly/4nRwvu 06/19/2009

Iranrevolution Iran Revolution Yesterday—Tehran June 22 2009 http://bit.ly/hWxdG 06/23/2009

Iranrevolution Iran Revolution CNN Video—Tehran June 24, 2009 (via Huffington Post) http://bit.ly/BuyRN 06/24/2009

Appendix B
"Where Is This Place?" Transcript

Transcript of "Where Is This Place?" June 19, 2009, Poems for the Rooftops of Iran uploaded YouTube at www.youtube.com/watch?v=pKUZuv6_bus

Friday the 19th of June 2009
Tomorrow, Saturday
Tomorrow is a day of destiny
Tonight the cries of Allah-o Akbar
are heard louder and louder than the nights before

Where is this place?
Where is this place where every door is closed?
Where is this place where people are simply calling God?
Where is this place where the sound
of Allah-o Akbar gets louder and louder?

I wait every night to see if the sounds
will get louder and whether the number increases
It shakes me
I wonder if God is shaken

Where is this place where
so many innocent people are trapped
Where is this place where no one comes to our aid?
Where is this place where only with our silence
we are sending our voices to the world
Where is this place where the young shed blood
and then people go and pray?
Standing on that same blood and pray. . .

Where is this place where citizens
are called vagrants?
Where is this place? You want me to tell you?
This place is Iran.
The homeland of you and me.
This place is Iran.

Index